Tribal Communities of India: Cultural Practices and Current Interventions

Tribal Communities of India: Cultural Practices and Current Interventions

Editors
Dr. Paramatap Pradhan
Dr. Shreekanta Kumar Barik

BLACK EAGLE BOOKS
Dublin, USA | Bhubaneswar, India

Black Eagle Books
USA address:
7464 Wisdom Lane
Dublin, OH 43016

India address:
E/312, Trident Galaxy, Kalinga Nagar,
Bhubaneswar-751003, Odisha, India

E-mail: info@blackeaglebooks.org
Website: www.blackeaglebooks.org

First International Edition Published by
Black Eagle Books, 2025

**TRIBAL COMMUNITIES OF INDIA:
CULTURAL PRACTICES AND CURRENT INTERVENTIONS**
Editors : Dr. Paramatap Pradhan, Dr. Shreekanta Kumar Barik

Cover & Interior Design: Ezy's Publication

ISBN- 978-1-64560-714-4 (Paperback)

Printed in the United States of America

CONTENTS

FORWARD

Prof. N. Nagaraju

Hon'ble Vice Chancellor
The English and Foreign Languages University
Hyderabad, Telangana, India

There are two reasons for writing this brief forward to this book on Tribal communities of India: Cultural practices and Current Interventions such an effort as this is timely and immediately relevant; secondly the editors, a member of one of the many culturally rich and vibrant indigenous/ tribal communities of Odisha, has been a colleague of mine since several years. The communities have been struggling since colonial times to keep their roots intact. Geographical divisions, linguistic challenges, climate change, natural disasters, migration and modernity, the challenges are too many; yet the communities are continuing with their lifestyles manfully, which commands respect specially in the current world of easy and affordable choices.

The book includes articles which describe the belief systems, spiritual practices, knowledge of the traditional medicine, myth and modes of performance, orality and features underpinning the community cohesion. Moreover, articles related to constitutional and legal safe guards, healthcare, education and other state- led initiatives and their effect on community lifestyles are included. Documentation, in varying degrees is being carried on the contemporary life these communities by conscious members like Paramatap Pradhan and Shreekanta Kumar Barik. More such efforts with increasing quality are the need of the hour, given the precarious nature of the communities in their inhabited areas. Any amount of encouragement could still fall short of the required efforts to conserve the cultures of these increasingly marginalized groups of people.

Best wishes are with all these diverse groups of people and with the editors.

PREFACE

India's cultural landscape is enriched by the presence of its tribal communities, which represents one of the most ancient and diverse segments of its population. These communities, deeply rooted in the country's ancient history, represent not only a significant portion of India's population but also a vital reservoir of indigenous knowledge, sustainable practices and cultural diversity. Often referred to as Adivasis, meaning "first dwellers" or "original inhabitants"- those who have lived on this land since time immemorial. They are the foundation of India's cultural diversity. Long before recorded history, before empires rose and fell, the Adivasis lived in close communion with nature, shaping unique cultures, languages and belief systems rooted in sustainability, spiritual connection and collective life. Their cosmologies, expressed through dance, music and myth, continue to embody worldviews based on balance, respect and harmony.

The present volume, Tribal Communities of India: Cultural Practices and Current Interventions is a curated effort to document, understand, and celebrate the living traditions of India's tribal societies. At a time when globalization and modernization continue to impact the cultural integrity of indigenous communities, this book seeks to provide a platform for showcasing their knowledge systems, rituals, art forms, spiritual beliefs, and ecological wisdom- many of which have been marginalized or undervalued in mainstream discourse. As Editors, our objective has been to bring together a multidisciplinary perspective that not only honors the traditional practices of these communities but also critically examines the ongoing efforts by government, non-government organizations, and the communities themselves to address socio economic challenges and ensure sustainable development.

This edited collection brings together contributions from scholars, researchers, and practitioners who have engaged closely with tribal communities across India. Through 20 case studies, and critical reflections, these chapters highlight a variety of indigenous practices- from healing systems, oral narratives, agricultural methods to festivals and crafts and medicines. For example, some studies examine the Ethnomedicinal plant use among tribal communities. The Banajara tribes of Bargarh district in Odisha and the Baiga tribe of Sonebhadra district in Uttarpradesh are closely connected to the nature and have inculcated ayurveda practices in curing various diseases. These tribe's knowledge of using the plant parts effectively plays a crucial role in traditional healthcare system where modern medicines fail to reach. Another study mentions the myth and history preserved in oral and dance drama tradition in and around Sunabeda hills, Nuapada, Odisha. The Chuktia Bhunjia triberesiding in this part of the country strongly believes in their clan. No one outside their clan can enter their cooking hut where their deities are lodged. The articles embedded in this editing volume also encompass such interesting tales about the tribe and their culture. One of the articles also seeks to explore that development can and must engage meaningfully with tribal culture- not as an obstacle to progress, but as an essential pillar of it. Through strategic investments in education, healthcare, infrastructure, livelihood generation and environmental conservation, Corporate Social responsibility (CSR) initiatives continue to envision long-term, inclusive growth. Apart from this article, this book also highlights about the constitutional and legal provisions to address the challenges faced by tribal communities in the rapid modernization era.

By presenting such a wide- ranging collection of case studies, this edited volume seeks to foreground the relevance of indigenous practices not only as cultural artifacts but as living systems of knowledge and meaning making. The contributors critically examine how these practices persist, transform or come under strain in the face of modernization, environmental change and socio-political pressures. Through these pages, we hope to shift the narrative from merely the indigenous practices followed by tribes to partnering with tribal communities in shaping their futures that honor their identities, strengthen their institutions and celebrate their cultural resilience.

We extend our deepest appreciation to all the contributors whose scholarly commitment and intellectual rigor have enriched this volume. Their insightful research, drawn from both field engagement and critical analysis, has helped illuminate the complexity, vitality and contemporary relevance of indigenous tribal practices in India. We are especially grateful for their sensitivity in working with tribal communities, and for their efforts to represent indigenous voices with respect, accuracy and care. This compilation would not have been possible without their valuable contributions, timely collaboration, and shared dedication to preserving and promoting the cultural heritage of India's tribal communities.

We also extend our sincere appreciation to the publisher, Shri Satya Pattanaik, Director BEB, Dublin,USA, for his unwavering support and commitment to this publication. His professional guidance, editorial assistance, and timely coordination have been instrumental in bringing this volume to fruition. We also convey our heartfelt gratitude to all individuals who have directly or indirectly walked beside us in bringing this book to life. Their well wishes and encouragement lifted our spirits and motivated us in this journey.

Dr. Paramatap Pradhan
Dr. Shreekanta Kumar Barik

Traditional Knowledge and Livestock Healthcare Practices among the Chuktia Bhunjia Tribe of Odisha, India

Dr. Bhubaneswar Sabar

Assistant Professor
Department of Anthropology & Tribal Studies
Maharaja Sriram Chandra Bhanja Deo University, Takatpur, Baripada, Odisha

Dr. Paramatap Pradhan

Assistant Professor, School of History,
Gangadhar Meher University, Sambalpur, Odisha
Email ID- param.3247@gmail.com

Abstract

This paper documents traditional knowledge of Chuktia Bhunjia tribe of Orissa pertaining to treatment of livestock diseases. It describes etiology of livestock diseases, symptoms, medications and treatment methods. The study conducted during 2022-23 among the Chuktia Bhunjia tribe living in Sunabeda wildlife sanctuary of Odisha using interview and observation method found that the Chuktia Bhunjia possess knowledge about curing thirteen livestock diseases. A total of 25 plant species are found to use as ethnoveterinary medicine. There are diversified explanations over the reliance of Chuktia Bhunjia over the ethnoveterinarians including that of poor communication to reach the modern veterinarians, easy availability of medicinal plants and eye witness that not only make their ethnoveterinary practice cost-effective but also fill the gap between demand and supply of animal healthcare. Nevertheless, forest policy and subsequent restriction of people by forest department to collect medicinal plants has affected their ethnoveterinary practice to certain extent. Thus, it is need of the hour to integrate the ethnoveterinary practice of tribals including Chuktia Bhunjia with modern veterinary knowledge.

KEY WORDS: Ethnoveterinary knowledge, Sunabeda wildlife sanctuary, livestock diseases, medicinal plants, cost-effectiveness, forest policy

INTRODUCTION

Archaeology provides us the evidence of domestication of animal especially cows, bullock, hen etc. by human being. It is reported that human being started to domesticate animals at the advent of neolithic period. Cows were used for milk; and buffalo and bullocks were used for agricultural purpose as today. The sacrifice of animals is also reported in prehistoric time to appease deities as today (Hough, 1934; Scanes, 2018). The tradition of using animals especially bullock and buffalo for agriculture still prevails in our society; although has been replaced by machines and technologies. In India especially livestock play crucial role in the livelihood of rural and tribal communities in term of contributing to agriculture, rituals and household income. Malvin Harris's *The Cultural Ecology of India's Sacred Cattle* (1966) well reflects the perception and spiritual relationship of people of India, especially those follow Hindu religion, with cow. The long interaction of the human being with livestock resources has developed a kind of livestock management practices among livestock owners. They have also learnt, with closed knit with the embedded ecological knowledge, to cure livestock diseases at community level which is popularly known as 'ethnoveterinary'.

This term "ethnoveterinary" was coined by McCorkle in 1986. It is dealt with indigenous knowledge, belief, skills, methods and practices relating to the health care of animal. It is defined as the community based local or indigenous knowledge and methods of caring livestock. This also includes social practices and the ways in which livestock are incorporated into farming systems. Ethno-veterinary medicine consists of local people's knowledge dealing with folk beliefs, skills and methods and practices pertaining to animal health care and production. This knowledge is based on close observation of animals and/or the oral transmission of experience from one generation to the next (Mathias-Mundy and McCorkle, 1989; Misra and Kumar, 2004). According to Mathias, Rangnekar and McCorkle (1999), ethnoveterinary not only includes treatments like herbal preparations, surgical interventions, indigenous vaccination but also includes people's ideas about disease causation, transmission including zoonosis, religious and cultural attitudes, beliefs and rituals, husbandry operations for overall good health, people's perception of relationship between environment and animal health care, and social organizations having know-how about animal health care. This practice includes folk etiology, symptoms and prophylaxes which they distinct based on what McCorkle (1989b) says 'clinical sign, epidemiological observation or supernatural explanation' (cited in Mithias-Mundy and McCorkle, 1995, p. 488) and local terminology, technology and the cultural and social systems pertaining to animals (ibid, 1995:497). It recognizes the cultural context of traditional practices of livestock management and marks the beginning of systematic exploration of local practices for the development of livestock population.

Past decades witness growing interests in interdisciplinary research on ethnoveterinary practices of both pastoralists and tribal communities among veterinary practitioners, livestock owners, field workers ethnobotanists and anthropologists. Owing livestock as important economic resource among rural folk in various parts of the globe, cattle's health has been a genuine concern to various societies. With the progress of ethnobotanical studies, the role of traditional knowledge in relation to veterinary medicine system has also acquired great attention (Jacob, Farah and Ekaya 2004; Torri 2013; Yineger *et al.*, 2007; Swamy and Reddi 2017). Evans-Pritchard's *The Nuer* (1940) provides us a worth reading ethnography on relationship between man and livestock especially cow and ethnoveterinary practices. Growing body of literature are found on ethnoveterinary practices of pastoralists and rural folk which show that the closed interactions of the people with the livestock allow people to understand the health of animal. They classify the animal diseases accordingly to the sign, symptoms and seasonality (Schwale and Kuojok 1981; Perry *et al.* 1984; Sollod *et al.*, 1984; Yinegar *et al.*, 2007; Torri, 2013; Aziem *et al.*, 2013; Aziz *et al.*, 2018).

In India, ancient literature such as the Vedas, and other written scriptures like Scand Puran (1000 BC), Devi Puran (2350 BC), Cherak and Shusruta (2500-600 BC) have long documented the treatment of animal disease by using medicinal plants. Attempts have been made in recent past to document the medicinal plants used in ethnoveterinary practices in India (Verma, 2014; Pragada and Rao, 2012; Bharati and Sharma, 2012; Usha, Rajasekaran and Shiva, 2015; Rautray *et al.*, 2015; Rehman *et al.*, 2022; Chaachouay *et al.*, 2022). Selvaraju *et al.*, (2011) noticed the frequent use of leaves in ethnoveterinary practices among Malayali tribe in Selum district of Tamil Nadu specially in treating fever, wound and dysentery. Mishra (2011) documented 24 plant species used in ethnoveterinary diagnosis among rural tribal of Ganjam district of Orissa who noticed that the life form of species used in medication are mostly of leaves followed by oil and rhizomes. The Gujjar of sub-Himalayan tract in India use 54 plant species in curing animal diseases (Gaur, Sharma and Painuli 2010). Santhivimalarani and Pavadai (2014) document 52 plant species used by tribes living in Kolli hill of Tamul Nadu, India to cure animal diseases. They report a total of 36 livestock diseases cured by these tribes in the form of drench, bolus and external application of medicine prepared out of these plant species. Meen *et al.*, (2020) too document 41 medicinal plants used among tribals living in Marwa region of Rajasthan to cure livestock diseases.

There are diversified explanations over frequent use of ethnoveterinary practices. Easy availability of medicinal plants, cultural acceptance, eye witnesses, and communication constraints are found as major factors enforcing them to rely ethnoveterinarians (Misra and Kumar, 2004; Sikarwar and Kumar, 2005; Jadeja *et al.*, 2006; Tiwari and Pandy, 2006; Nag, Galar and Katewa, 2007). Studies find that minimum side effect of ethnoveterinary medicine and its cost-effectiveness do influence people to depend on ethnoveterinary as it constantly provides cheaper options than comparable western drugs (Kiruba, Jeeva and Dhas 2006; Torri 2013; Lokhande, 2021; Oda et al., 2024). Besides, ethnoveterinary medicine is also believed to enhance the household income as most of the livestock owners notice proper growth of their poultry in particular (Torri 2013). In India, public veterinary health care reaches only 20 percent of livestock owners, leaving a big gap between the demand and the supply of health care services. Such lacuna along with the accessibility and capability push many rural folks to prefer to the traditional form of animal healthcare practices which fills the gap between demand and supply of health care services (Padma Kumar 1998; Torri 2013).

On above background, this paper attempts to document the ethnoveterinary practice of Chuktia Bhunjia tribe of Nuapada district of Orissa. It describes etiology of livestock diseases, symptoms, medications and treatment methods, besides, attempting to comprehend the factors causing to persistence reliance of ethnoveterinary practice among them.

Research Method
Area: Sunabeda Wildlife Sanctuary

The study was conducted among Chuktia Bhunjia tribe living in Sunabeda Wildlife Sanctuary (Map 1) during March 2022 to October 2022 at different time intervals. With a geographical location of 82º20" to 82º34" E. longitude to 20º24" to 24º44"N. latitude, the sanctuary is located at height of 2050 from sea level. It houses diversity of flora and fauna. It represents a pristine ecosystem of dry deciduous forest, river valley, hill and waterfalls. The total geographical area of the sanctuary is 600 Sq. Kms. The demarcated core and buffer zone of the sanctuary contain 243.60 sq. kms and 356.40 sq. kms respectively. There are 64 habitation villages housing about 20,000 human populations living in more than 5000 families (Govt. of Orissa. 2001). The majorities of the population are the scheduled tribes comprises of Gonds,

Bhunjia and Paharia, although the migrant non-tribal groups are reported to have been settled in some villages. The sanctuary is now a proposed tiger reserve.

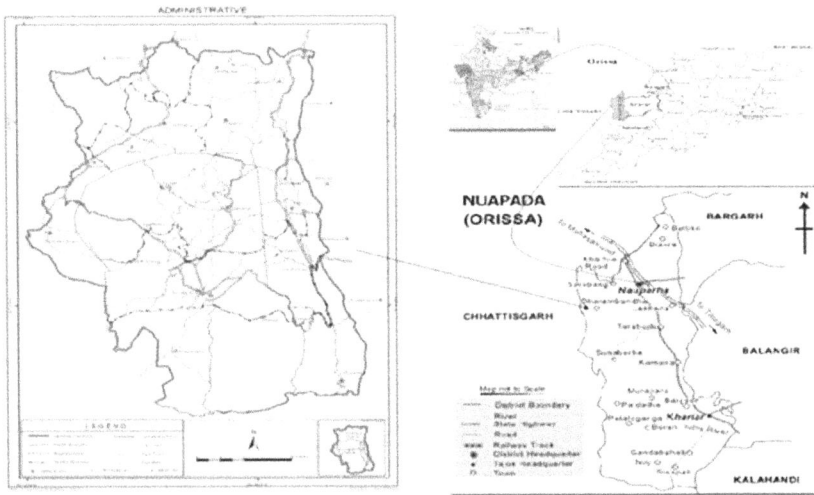

Map 1: Sunabeda Wildlife Sanctuary

People: The Chuktia Bhunjia

The Bhunjia is one of the tribal groups of in India and is distributed in the state of Odisha, Chhattisgarh and Maharashtra. They are divided into two broad social groups: Chinda Bhunjia and Chuktia Bhunjia (Russel and Hiralal, 1916; Dubey, 1961, 1963; Pattnaik *et al.* 1984; Mishra 2002). Each division has their own moiety (*got*): *Nitam* and *Markam*. Each moiety is subdivided into a number of clan (*Barga*) and each *Barga* has got a specific designation associated with a particular totemic object. Members of the same *Barag* consider them as descended form same ancestor who exist in the remote past. Two members from each *Barag* call them as *Dudhbhai*. Such relation is viewed from endogamy and worshipping the same ancestral deities. In Odisha they are largely found in Nuapada, Kalahandi and Nawarangpur district. The Chuktia Bhunjia are largely residing in Nuapada district and is identified as a particularly vulnerable tribal group (PVTG). They are largely concentrated on the Sunabeda Wildlife Sanctuary of the district located in western part of the district. Chinda Bhunjia is an acculturated section of Bhunjia and are found to reside in plain area. On the other hand, the Chuktia Bhunjia exclusively inhabit in the Sunabeda Wildlife Sanctuary along with other communities like *Gond, Paharia, Kultha* (an agricultural community), Kamar (Potter) and *dom* (scheduled caste). According to a base line survey by Ota, Mohanty and

Mohanty (2020) their total population is 3086 (1593 male and 1493 female from 938 household). They live in 35 villages/hamlets of SWS. With a sex ratio of 937, the literacy rate of Chuktia Bhunjia is estimated 24.54 (29.14 male literacy and 20.00 female literacy). They belong to Dravidian language speaking group (Russel and Hiralal 1916) who speak Bhunjia dialect (mixture of Oriya and Chhattisgarhi) for intra-group communication and local Oriya for inter-group communication. Although they were reported to practice hunting-gathering form of economy, inclusion of their habitat into the protected area forced them to become settled agriculturists. Still collection of minor forest produces (MFPs) constitutes an important source of their livelihood. They are animistic in nature and worship a number of natural phenomena. Majority of their festivals are associated with the agricultural practices and collection and consumption of various wild edibles. Goddesses *Sunadei* is the propitiate deity who is worshipped at every house of the Chuktia Bhunjia.

Data Collection

The data for this study were collected during March 2022 to October 2022 from different villages located in Sunabeda Wildlife Sanctuary. Data were collected through anthropological techniques of investigation viz. interview, observation and focus group discussions. Livestock owners were formally interviewed to document the livestock disease, identification of diseases, technique and medication of curing specific disease. The perception of livestock owners on the reliance of ethnoveterinarians were obtained through focus group discussion. The ethnoveterinarians and other specialist curing animal diseases particularly through mantra therapy were identified through snowball technique and were interviewed pertaining to their knowledge on medication. The medication and treatment process were also observed during fieldwork.

Livestock Possession by Chuktia Bhunjia

The Chuktia Bhunjia of the Sunabeda wildlife sanctuary, although, are not pastoral by occupation, they keep selected livestock with them. Almost every household keep cow (*gai*), bullock (*balad or baila*), buffalo (*pod-bhuis*), goat (*chhel*), sheep (*medhā* and poultry (*kukrā*). They use bullock and buffalo for ploughing agriculture land; and goat and sheep for consumption. They do not use un-castrated bullocks (*sandh*) for ploughing which they believe as chariot of Lord Shiva. They also sell goat and sheep occasionally to for monetary benefits, besides to sacrifice in certain rituals and festivals. The he goat (boka or bokda) is slaughtered for meat during marriage and other big festivals. No all household keep poultry for the reason being Goddess Sunadei is not offered hen. The offer only virgin she-goat (*pethi*), female sheep (*karhei*), un-castrated sheep (*garra*) to their deities during rituals and festivals. They do not sacrifice female goat (*Chhel/Chheri*) which they believe would affect breeding and make them to be cost-effective during rituals and festivals. They take utmost care of calves (*buchhra* for cow; *bagar* for buffalo) so they can be used in agriculture later. The un-castrated bullocks (*sandh*) are not used for ploughing which they believe as chariot of Lord Shiva. Their respects toward livestock are revealed from worshipping during *Nuakhai* (festival of eating new paddy), Dashra and *Diwali* (festival of light). In the day of Nuakhai first the saturated paddy is given to the cow and bullock. During Dasra and Diwali, they wash the feet and horn of bullock as well as paint the horns.

Livestock Diseases

The Chuktia Bhunjia of the study village perceive that livestock are also frequently affected by various diseases. Majority of livestock diseases are seasonal. The Chuktia Bhunjia attribute a number of factors that contribute to livestock diseases. Although many a times, they believe that change in weather result diseases in livestock; beliefs in supernatural cause is not ignored. They are of view that if a menstruating woman enters cow-shed without cleaning the body at morning, it not only annoys God Mirchuk but also lead to disease in livestock. Specific disease affects to specific livestock. For example, diseases such as *chapka* (foot-root), *sakfulla* (toungesil), *sorsia* (asthama), *hapar* are reported to affect only cow and bullocks. Goat and sheep suffer from enterotoxaemia type of diseases, blue tongue, and so on. Buffalos suffer from blue tongue, smallpox. Poultry suffer from *ragi* (smallpox) (Table 1).

The Chuktia Bhunjia name livestock diseases according to the body part of the livestock. These include mouth diseases (*mahagha*), foot root (*chapka*), throat disease (*galphula*) etc. They also notice some livestock diseases as short duration such as contagious ecthyma or mouth disease, foot root, cold, cough, sneezing etc. whereas enterotoxaemia, blue tongue, smallpox, ephemeral fever, pneumonia, etc. are considered to be longer duration diseases. The Chuktia Bhunjia identify specific disease through symptom of disease and vector of diseases which they said to have learnt through observation and lived experience living with livestock. Accordingly, they administer procedures and medication to control the diseases.

There are many criteria on which the Chuktia Bhunjias classify livestock diseases. Diseases are named according to the part of the body affected by diseases. These include mouth diseases (*mahagha*), foot root (*chapka*), throat disease (*galphula*) etc. Livestock are, however, affected by diseases of both short duration and long duration I never found any classification based on duration of diseases. Diseases like contagious ecthyma or mouth disease, foot rot, cold, cough, sneezing etc. are found for short time. In contrast, diseases of longer duration include enterotoxaemia, blue tongue, smallpox, ephemeral fever, pneumonia, etc.

Table 1: Livestock Diseases and Seasonality

Sl. No.	Livestock	Diseases affected (Local name)	Seasons
1	Bullock	Sorsia, Ekjhara, Chapka, Sakfula, Petfula	Rainy
2	Goat	Sakfula, Mahaghaa, Biari, Petfula	Rainy
3	Hen	Ragi, bird-flue	Winter
4	Cow	Sorsia, Chapka, petfula	Rainy and Winter

Source: Fieldwork, 2021-2022

Ethnoveterinary Practices and Animal Healthcare

The Chuktia Bhunjia encounter numbers of livestock diseases and administer local medicines accordingly (Table 2). The common diseases are diarrhea, mastitis and ephemeral fevers and are seasonal in nature. The people in all study villages expressed that they administer local method in curing livestock diseases particularly by using locally available medicinal plants. Only 03 ethnoveterinarians were informally interviewed who were found to, upon invited, cure livestock diseases in many villages. Yet, the household therapy to cure livestock disease is frequently reported among them particularly in the context of diarrhea, fevers, stomachache, moth disease and foot root. If they fail to cure, then only they rely on ethnoveterinarians or the government veterinary officer appointed in their locality. They completely rely on ethnoveterinarians to treat bone fracture and insect infection (*kir*a*).

It was reported from those who have experienced of administering plant-based medicine to treat livestock diseases that the procedure of medication does vary from diseases to diseases. The expressed that they prepare the medicine simply by crushing or making paste or decoction method. A specific decoction requires a mix of herbs although sometime single plant species is also used to treat a particular disease. All the medicine orally given to livestock are mixed with water which they believe easily dilute the medicine inside body. During fieldwork, 15 medicinal plants frequently used by the Chuktia Bhunjia were documented along with their procedures.

Table 2: Ethnoveterinary practices of Chuktia Bhunjia

Local name (Scientific Name)	Diseases cured (local name)	Part used	Medication
Ada (Allium sativum)	Cough/ Asthma (Sursiā)	Rhizome	Rhizome is crushed in a stone and mixed it with jaggary in a basket and orally given to the livestock for easy healing.
Badhal (Annona Squamosa)	Mouth disease (Mahaghā)	Leaves	The extracted leave juice is orally applied on wound part. Mixture of fermented cord water and salt is also applied on the wound.
Bhelwa (Cemararpus Anacardium)	Foot root (Chapka)	Fruits	The extracted pulp of Bhelwa fruit is applied over the foot and worm iron is smoothly heated over it. Mixture of salt, red chilli and butter milk is also orally applied on the affected part.
Bhuilim (Adrographic paniculata)	Diarrhoea	Fruits	Juice made of Bhuilim and Dalim fruits are orally given to the livestock to drink.
Dalim (Punica granatum).	Diarrhoea	Fruit' bark	The fruit's bark is finely chopped in a stone and orally given to the livestock to drink. This disease is usually affected to the calf and goat.
Dubjhar (Cynodondactylon)	Foot root	Whole	Finely chopped grass paste is properly mixed with same proportion of turmeric and is orally applied on the affected foot.
Hadsakra (Cissus quadrangularis)	Bone fracture	Stem	The method is almost similar as in the case of human bone fracture. Fractured bone is arranged by pulling back and forth and the hot paste made is orally applied over fractured part. Small piece of bamboos are tightly tied around the medicated part. A cloth is then tied over to so as to keep the medicine for longer. After fifteen day or so the tied cloth is removed.

Basanga (Justicia adhatoda)	Cough/ Asthma (Sursiā)	Leave	Usually leave is dried and later put on fire to make smoke so that the livestock inhale for a minute. So usually, it is applied in the closed cow-shed. It is believed to have inflammable character and therefore the crushed leaves are often mixed with a bucket of water along with other fodder and orally give to the livestock to drink.
Karanja (Pongamia pinnate)	Lice and flies	Oil and bark paste	The oil is orally applied over the livestock body. Finely grinded bark paste is also applied to kill the lice.
Mahul (Madhuca indica)	Smallpox (Ragi)	Flower	It only affects to poultry. This disease is believed to cause by supernatural. So, they cure it through ritualistic method. However, initially mahua liquor and turmeric (Curuma bonga) water is orally given to the poultry along with applying little liquor over the body. Ritually, the village priest collects a leave cup of raw rice from each household and goes to the forest with a chicken along with other elderly member of the village to bid the supernatural. He makes a chariot of Mandar (Hibisus rosasine) plant. Mandar flowers are kept over it. After doing puja there, the leave the chicken there and the rice is cooked and eaten there.
Oinla (Emblica offinalia)	Insect Infection (Kira)	Leaves	This disease is treated only on Sunday. The livestock is first laid down. The specialist then chants mantra by holding Oela in a hand. Once he starts chanting manta, insects fall down on the ground. It is done for three consecutive Sunday.

Pahargachha (Tephrosia purpurea)	Lice and flies	Bark	The bark juice is orally applied throughout the body. The oil made from Karanj seeds is also often applied.
Jada (Ricinus communis)	Castration	Stem	The bullock or goat is laid down and the testicles are stroked in two Shorea robusta stem. Finely grinded raw turmeric paste mixed with ricinus communis oil is then orally applied over it.
Kochila (Strychonos nux-vomica)	Foot root (Chapka)	Fruits	The grinded paste of Kochila fruit is gently applied in the wounded part. A cloth is then tied to avoid removal of medicine. By doing so medicine is easily absorbed in the affected part and remove the germ causing the diseases.
Tetel (Tarmarindus indica)	Stomach disorder/ Indigestion (Pet phula)/ fever	Fruits	9 black peppers are grinded with salt and the mixed with a bucket of water and given to the livestock along with bamboo leave. Sometimes Tetel (Tarmarindus indica) and red chillies are mixed in a bucket of water and is given to the livestock to drink.

Source: Fieldwork, 2021-2022

DISCUSSION AND CONCLUSION

Livestock is one of the important socio-economic resources for alleviation of poverty and raising the standard of living of the majority of population in rural areas. With the rising population and decline in per capita agricultural land available, it is predicted that the crop production alone will no longer be able to provide sufficient livelihood opportunities to the rural poor. Therefore, livestock offers immense potential for livelihood. In most of the Asian countries, livestock accounts for about 25 percent to the agricultural gross domestic products (Ranjhan 2007). Of course, Chuktia Bhunjia are not a pastoral community, but rearing of cow and bullock in each household become important livelihood engagement particularly in term of their contribution to agricultural sector. Their agriculture is combined with the human and animal power. Owing to the importance of livestock in the livelihood of rural poor and marginal farmers, government is constantly encouraging the Chuktia Bhunjia for animal husbandry mostly goatary and poultry in order to provide them regular cash income. Thus, the Chuktia Bhunjia of Sunabeda wildlife sanctuary always attempts to keep their livestock healthy by protecting their livestock from diseases. Livestock are reported often attacked by life threatening bacterial infection like pyogenes mastitis where there is less chance of survival. Yet with long interaction with livestock behaviour and ecological system, they have learnt that some plants such as that *neem (Azadirachta indica), Artemisia (Artemisia annua), Munga (Moringa oliefera)*, and *Menzati (Lawsonia intermis)* have antiviral, antiseptic and fungicidal properties and are constantly used to prevent such infection. The use of the leaves of *bakin (Melia azadarach)* and *karela (Momordica charantia)* is perceived to reinvigorate effect on the cattle and increase their resistance to parasites.

The indigenous knowledge-based ethnoveterinary practice of Chuktia Bhunjia does not constitute a practice alone but it has specific economic implications. Although no Chuktia Bhunjia were found to earn livelihood out of their ethnoveterinary practice but their reliance on traditional medicines to cure livestock disease make them economical and cost-effective due to its free availability in the forest. It is noticed that there is a veterinary office at Sunabeda to look after the health conditions of livestock to cure common livestock diseases such as lice infection, worms, wounds, diarrhoea, etc. But local people hardly access to this facility instead of relying on ethnoveterinarians largely for accessibility to plant medicines, eye witness, lived experiences and cost effectiveness. Certainly, the poor communication facility become obstacle for inhabitant of this wildlife sanctuary to reach to veterinary office for livestock cure; but the frequent complain over the irregular visit of Livestock Inspector (LI) to villages and monetary charge for their service compel them to be reliable to ethnoveterinarians. So, availability does not guarantee accessibility rather is governed by communication and people's acceptability. Further, the locally available medicinal plants and free service rendered by ethnoveterinarians always make their ethnoveterinary practice successful because it is difficult for them to afford modern medicines.

Interestingly, there are communalities in the healing of human and livestock diseases particularly in term of the use of medicinal plants. Not only certain plant species documented among them are used both in ethnomedicine and ethnoveterinary but also some ethnoveterinarians were found to cure human diseases. Most of the medicinal plants commonly used for the treatment of a number of conditions suffered by human beings are also used for similar conditions affecting animals. For example, *Asparagus racemosus* is used to increase milk secretions and *Punica gradatum* is used in the treatment of diarrhoea in both human beings and animals, however doses vary.

The traditional ethnoveterinary practice among the Chuktia Bhunjia is seem to have relevance for the Chuktia Bhunjia particularly owing the communication constraint and poverty, being able to bridge the gap between the demand and supply of animal healthcare. It continues to help them accessing the animal healthcare service freely and make their life cost-effective as the money need to be incurred is spent for other household materials. Since they are one of the particularly vulnerable tribal groups, they receive a number of benefits including animal husbandry. They are now found to keep livestock especially the poultry and goat for monetary benefit. But now a day owing to high treatment costs and inaccessibility of modern ethnoveterinary, the traditional ethnoveterinary have become a ray of hope for them to sustainably manage their livestock for better livelihood. Nevertheless, the proposed tiger project for Sunabeda wildlife sanctuary is obstructing the ethnoveterinarians and local people to exploit ethnoveterinary plants whereby to impacting on the livestock management. In this context, documentation, assessment, and promotion of ethnoveterinary practices does offer the possibility of a solution in reducing the increasing costs of meeting livestock health care needs. Net, integration of ethnoveterinary practice of tribe like the Chuktia Bhunjia with modern veterinary practice can best be a solution to offer sustainability of their ethnoveterinary practice.

References:

- Aziem, S., B. P. Chamola, S. Mahato and N. A. Pala. 2013. Utilization and traditional knowledge of ethnoveterinary medicinal plants in Tehri district of Garhwal Himalaya, India. *International Journal of Indigenous Medicinal Plants*, 46 (2): 1330-1337.
- Aziz, M. A., M. Adnan, A. H. Khan, M. Sufyan and S. N. Khan. 2018. Cross-cultural analysis of medicinal plants commonly used in ethnoveterinary practices at South Waziristan Agency and Bajaur Agency, Federally Administrated Tribal Areas (FATA), Pakistan. *Journal of Ethnopharmacology*, 210: 443-468.
- Bharati, A. K. and B.L. Sharma. 2012. Plants used as ethnoveterinary medicines in Sikkim Himalayas. *Ethnobotany Research and Applications*, 10: 339-356.
- Chaachouay, N., A. Azeroual, A. Douira and L. Zidane. 2022. Ethnoveterinary practices of medicinal plants among the Zemmour and

Zayane tribes, Middle Atlas, Morocco. *South African Journal of Botany*, 151: 826-840.

- Dubey, K. C. 1961   Possible origin of Bhunjia and other ethnic relationship: a new hypothesis', *The Eastern Anthropologist*, 4 (1): 49-58.
- Dubey, K. C. 1963. A study of Bhunjia settlement. *Vanyajati*, July: 132-135.
- Evans-Pritchard, E.E. 1940. *The Nuer: a description of the modes of livelihood and political institutions of a Nilotic people.* New York: Oxford university press.
- Gaur, R.D., J. Sharma and R. M. Painuli. 2010. Plants used in traditional healthcare of livestock by Gujjar community of Sub-Himalayan tracts, Uttarakhand, India. *Indian Journal of Natural Products and Resources*, 1 (2): 243-248.
- Govt. of Orissa. 2001. Boucher of Sunabeda Wildlife Sanctuary. Government of Orissa.
- Harris, M. (1966). The cultural ecology of India's sacred cattle. *Current Anthropology*, 7 (1): 51-66.
- Hough, W. (1934). The Domestication of animals. *The Scientific Monthly*, 39 (2): 144 150.
- Jacob, M. O., K. O. Farah and W. N. Ekaya. 2004. Indigenous knowledge: the basis of Maasai ethnoveterinary diagnostic skill. *Journal of human ecology*, 16(1): 43-48.
- Jadeja, B. A., N. K. Odedra, K. M. Solanki and N. M. Barayia. 2006. Indigenous animal health care practices in district Porbandar, Gujrat. *Indian Journal of Traditional Knowledge*, 5 (2): 253-258.
- Kiruba, S., S. Jeeva, and S. S. M. Dhas. 2006. Enumeration of ethnoveterinary plants of Cape Comorin, Tamil Nadu. *Indian Journal of Traditional Knowledge*, 5(4):576 578.
- Lokhande, K. S. (2021). Ethnoveterinary practices in Arjini/Mor taluka of Gondia District, Maharashtra, India. *International Journal of Sciences & Applied Research*, 8 (10): 01-12.
- Mathias-Mundy, E. and C.M. McCorkle. 1989. *Ethno-veterinary medicine: an annotated bibliography, bibliography in technology and social change.* Technology and Social Change Program Series No. 6, Iowa State University.
- Mathias-Mundy, E and C.M. McCorkle. 1995. Ethnoveterinary medicine and development- a review of the literature. In D. Michael Warren, *et al.* (eds) *Indigenous knowledge system: the cultural dimension of sustainable development* (pp. 488-498). London: Intermediate technology publisher.
- McCorkle, C.M. 1989. Veterinary anthropology. *Human Organisation*, 48

(2): 156-62.

- Meen, M. L., A. Dudi and D. Singh. 2020. Ethnoveterinary study of medicinal plants in a tribal society of Marwar region of Rajasthan, India. *Journal of Pharmacognosy and Phytochemistry*, 9 (4): 549-554.
- Mishra, D. 2011. Ethnoveterinary Practices and use of herbal medicines for treatment of skin diseases in cattle: A study in Polsara Block, Ganjam District, Orissa, India. *Veterinary World*, 4 (6): 250-253.
- Mishra, S.K. 2002. *Chuktia Bhunjia Sankriti O' Lokasahitya* (Oriya), Bhubaneswar: S.T.S.C. Research and Training Institute.
- Misra, K. K. and K. A. Kumar. 2004. Ethno-veterinary practice among the Konda Reddies of Eastern Godavari district of Andhra Pradesh. *Studies of Tribes and Tribal*, 2 (1): 37-44.
- Nag, A., P. Galab and S. S. Katewa. 2007. Indigenous animal health care practice from Udaipur district, Rajasthan. *Indian Journal of Traditional Knowledge,* 6 (4): 583-588.
- Oda, B. K., E. Lulekal1, B. Warkineh, Z. Asfaw, and A. Debella. 2024. Ethnoveterinary medicinal plants and their utilization by indigenous and local communities of Dugda District, Central Rift Valley, Ethiopia. *Journal of Ethnobiology and Ethnomedicine*, 20:32..
- Ota, A. B., B. N. Mohanty, and S. C. Mohanty. 2020. Particularly Vulnerable Tribal Groups of Odisha. Bhubaneswar, India: SC&STRTI.
- Padma Kumar, V. 1998. Farmer reliance on ethnoveterinary practices to cope with common cattle ailments. *Indigenous knowledge and development monitor*, 6 (2): 14-15.
- Pattanaik, N., P. K. Mohanty and T. Sahoo. 1984. Life in Sunabeda plateau: the anthropology of Bhunjia of Kalahandi, Orissa. Bhubaneswar: SC & ST Research and training institute.
- Perry, B. D., B. Mwanauma, H. F. Schels, E. Eicher and M. R. Zaman. 1984. A study of health and productivity of traditionally managed cattle in Zambia. *Preventive Medicine*, 2: 633-653.
- Pragada, P. M. and G. M. N. Rao. 2012. Ethnoveterinary medicine practices in tribal region of Andhra Pradesh, India. *Bangladesh Journal of Plant Taxonomy*, 19 (1): 7-16.
- Rautray, A. K., R. Sahoo, K. K. Sardar, R. C. Patra and A. Sahoo. 2015. Ethnoveterinary practices of small ruminants followed by rural folks in Southern Odisha. *Indian Journal of Traditional Knowledge*, 14 (2): 319-324.
- Rehman, S., Z. Iqbal, R. Qureshi, I.U. Rahman, S. Sakhi, I. Khan, et al; 2022. Ethnoveterinary Practices of Medicinal Plants Among Tribes of Tribal District of North Waziristan, Khyber Pakhtunkhwa, Pakistan. *Frontiers in*

Veterinary Sciences, 9. doi: 10.3389/fvets.2022.815294.

- Russel, R.V and R. B. Hiralal. 1916. Tribe and caster of the central province of India Vol. I. London: Mcmillan.
- Santhivimalarani, S. and P. Pavadai. 2014. Ethnoveterinary practices among tribes of Kolli hills in Tamil Nadu, India. *Journal of Medicinal and Aromatic Plant Sciences*, 36 (3&4): 75-81.
- Scanes, C. C. 2018. The neolithic revolution, animal domestication and early forms of animal agriculture. In C. G. Scanes & S. R. Toukhsati (eds.), *Animals and Human Society* (pp. 103-131). Cambridge: Academic Press.
- Schwale, C.W. and I. K. Kuojok. 1981. Practice and belief f the traditional Dinka healer in relation to provision of modern medical and veterinary service for the southern Sudan. *Human Organisation*, 40 (3): 231-238.
- Sikarwar, R.L.S. and V. Kumar. 2005. Ethnoveterinary knowledge and practices prevalent among the tribals of central Indian. *Journal of Natural Remedies*, 5 (2):147-152.
- Sollod, A. E., K. Wolfgang, J. A. Knight. 1984. Veterinary anthropology: interdisciplinary methods in pastoral system research. In Simpson J. R. and Evangelou P. (Eds) *Livestock development in sub-Saharan Africa: constraint, prospect policy* (pp. 285-302). Boulder: Westview Press.
- Swami, N. S. and T. V. V. S. Reddi. 2017. Ethnoveterinary medicine of tribes of Adilabad District, Andhra Pradesh. *Journal of Non-Timber Forest Products*, 24 (1): 55-58.
- Tiwari, L and Pande, P.C. 2006. Indigenous veterinary practices of Darmi valley of Pithoragarh district, Uttaranchal. *Indian Journal of Traditional Knowledge*, 5 (2): 201-206.
- Torri, M. C. (2013). Traditional veterinary in rural Tamil Nadu: Linking medicinal plants with local livelihoods and human health care. *Journal of Developing Societies*, 29 (1): 23-46.
- Usha, S, C. Rajasekaran and R. Siva. 2015. Ethnoveterinary medicine of the Shervaroy Hill of eastern ghats, India as alternative medicine for animals. *Journal of Traditional and Complementary Medicine*, 30: 1-8.
- Verma, R. K. 2014. An ethnobotanical study of plants used for treatment of livestock deseases in Tikamgarh district of Bundelkhand, Central India. *Asian Pacific Journal of Tropical Biomedicine*, 4 (supplementary 1): S460-S467.
- Yinegar, H., Kelbessa, E., Bekele, T., and Lulekal, E. (2007). Ethnoveterinary medicinal plants in Bale Mountains National Park, Ethiopia. *Journal of Ethnopharmacology*, 112 (1): 55-70.

Indigenous Forest Protection and Oral History: A Case Study from Western Part Odisha, India

Dr. Tirtharaj Bhoi

Professor, Department of History
Central University of Haryana, Haryana
Email: tirtharajbhoi@jammuuniversity.ac.in

Abstract

There is need of mass education and awareness on importance and benefits of forest at all levels. An active Forest Department needs to play vital role in forest protection and regeneration in the interest of the poor and marginalized. There needs to be laws in place in favor of forest and people. Within India, different tribal people exist in special eco-system with various levels of techno-economic development and for sustenance; the direct natural resources are utilized by them with their traditional knowledge and technique. Oral history is also the collective memory of human actions and experiences. The tribals preserved their oral tradition in connection with the forest protection in this area. The studies therefore try to cover a village Dhanrasi, which is the centre of indigenous forest protection in Himgiri block, Sundargarh district in western part of Odisha. It is focusing on in-depth study of actual condition pertaining in the village and the people's perceptions on a forest development related issues such as, traditional governance system of forest, status of present forest and PESA act, protection and rights over the forest, rights of other villages and future of the forest protection. Standard anthropological tools and technique has been used for data collection.

Key words: *Development, Governance, PESA. Physical environment, Protection.*

Introduction

The oral source is the inner voice of the voice less. This source is the right possibility to reconstruct the history of a community without history from the beginning. The Historiography of oral literature is produced from the collective thought of a community. The tribal oral history is written from their forest, mountains, sky, their belief system, trees folk song and dances etc. in recent year most of the historians accepted oral tradition as the sources of history study. In 1965, Jan Vasina first described about oral tradition in African society (Thompsom, 1978:20). Paul Thompsom devises three ways in which oral history can be put together are the single life story narrative, the collection of stories and argument and cross analysis (Thompsom, 1978:204-05). The first writing on tribal by colonial and missionaries attempt to "civilize wild tribe" was thus justified through these accounts and formed the basis of the interventions (Prasad, 2000:04). If we see the issues of governance, it identifies the power dependence involved in the relationships between institutions involved in collective action. The contribution of the governance perspective to theory is not at the level of causal analysis. Nor does it offer a new normative theory (Stoker, 1998:49-50). Its value is as an organizing framework. The value of the governance perspective rests in its capacity to provide a framework for understanding changing processes of governing. Theoretical work on governance reflects the interest of the social science community in a shifting pattern in styles of governing. The traditional use of 'governance' and its dictionary entry define it as a synonym for government. Yet in the growing work on governance there is a redirection in its use and import. Rather governance signifies 'a change in the meaning of government, referring to a new process of governing; or a changed condition of ordered rule; or the new method by which society is governed (Pradip, 1994:72).

On this level Kautilya's work is remarkably modern in the way it attempts to describe the impact of administrative governance mechanisms on the daily lives of the citizenry. He discovered the science of administration and used in the day to day practices (Shamasastry, 1960:10).

Adopted Methods:

An attempt is made to give an extensive evaluation of existing historical writings that deals with forest governance. It is focusing on in-depth study of actual condition pertaining in the village and the people's perceptions on a forest governance related issues such as, traditional governance system of forest, status of present forest and PESA act, protection and rights over the forest etc. Standard anthropological tools and technique has been used for data collection in the villages of Western part of Odisha.

Study Village:

The place where Dhanrasi village is located today was full of dense forest cover before two hundred years. Gradually people from Rayagada, Sambalpur, Chhatisgarh and some other places started coming here and settled here. It is said that, people had cut trees for making house and agricultural appliances and put fire to clear land for agriculture. The ash fell on the land after fire. Then they sowed paddy and Rasi (Til) in that land. Due to fertility of land and other climatic factors, there happened to be huge production of Dhan (Paddy) and Rasi (Til) and hence the name Dhanrasi. On this region the Geographers (Johnson, 2001) distinguish some fourteen physiographic regions in India and the area was covered one of four sub-regions in the "Plateaus and Basins" category. In ancient period part of the *dandakaranya* was governed by *Kusa* in his kingdom south kosala and the study area was under this domination (Sabhaparva,1962:591-92).

Common Migration:

The ancestors have come from different places at different intervals. It is believed that four families first came there from four different places such as *Netanagar, Kashidihi, Tinmina* and *Nachenmunda*. These families were from different caste groups such as *Kulta, Aghria, Bhoi and tribal Gonda and Bhuyan*. People still remember some of their names as *Pustam Sa, Debanand Dhudha, Jaya Keut, Phiru Goud* etc. Some of their descendants have shifted to Nuadihi and Chhattisgarh. The stream, plenty of forest resources like MFP, fruits and other forest food, land for agriculture with source of water were the major points of attraction for setting up habitation there in those days.

History of Land and Forest:

As far as village land is concerned, the land was very fertile in those days and people used to get good harvest from small patches of land without use of any sort of fertilizer or pesticide. Most of the land was *Guda* (sloping high land) type of land and hence people used to cultivate crops suiting the land geographical pattern. The major crops used to be minor millets like *Gurji*, small paddy, Til etc. Along with these, people used to depend on *Mahua*, *Tendu* and other forest products as part of their food habit. They used to go to Rayagada, a place far away to sell their surplus millets and small paddy in those days. Now the fertility of land has been significantly reduced. Some old persons in the village say, "Previously there were lots of snakes in the forests. They were the Laxmi (Goddess of wealth) for the village. When people started putting fire in the forest and cut trees, slowly the snakes disappeared.

Since then, the land fertility has been lost and production has become less." This village Dhanrasi was under control of king of Hemgir and later on converted to Zamindari system of governance. At that time, there used to be a Gautias called Chandan Singh. He used to collect tax from people. It was too exploitative that whenever Gauntias required some laborers people had to take their own food from home and work for Gauntia without wages. The persons who do not attend this call were being beaten up vehemently. Gauntia used to be the head of the village. The system was totally autocratic under king's and Gauntia's control. Gauntia was supposed to be the dictator for the village. King used to come to the forest to play poaching. People had to help the king's troupe in this act. This help or in other words "compulsion to go to forest for King's security as well as logistic providing and work" was termed as "Bethi" or "Bigadi". As per the order of the king, people had to act. Gauntia was provided better and fertile land near the village by the king. Civilians used to cultivate own Rayati land as well as encroach other non-agriculture land within village boundary. No one was allowed to enter in to *Gochar, Japti* (Reserve) or Khesra (Protected) forest areas for encroachment. Gauntia had ownership on all these resources on behalf of the king. Then in recent past, after elimination of Zamindari system, there was the revenue office and Tahsil court, where land related matters are being resolved. People who had huge patches had to lose some portion of it which was distributed among the poor in the village under Ceiling. Some people who still didn't have land, cleared forest patches to have their own patch of agriculture land.

Traditional Governance:

With the beginning of the Panchayati Raj system, in the beginning this village was coming under Garjanjore panchayat. In the year 1987, Dhanrasi was declared as a new ward and in the year 2002, the village got included in Kuchedega panchayat. This village has always followed a collective system of governance where, whenever any conflict or issue arose in the village, the matter was brought to the court of "Panchabhadra" i.e. the respected, older members of the village forming a bench. They used to resolve the matter. This governance system used to be unbiased and just for all. People used to swear in the name of "Bhagabat Gita" and God before the bench in this process. This was a very simple but just and accepted means of conflict resolution in the village. If someone was not satisfied with the proceedings of this bench, the matter was referred to respected elders from nearby five villages to decide over the matter. People used to respect and recognize their decision as final. This system of governance had its own legal recognition. In most serious matters, the case was supposed to be referred to the court. Most of the matters used to get resolved in the village itself.

Present Status of Forest:

The villagers are protecting forest in three parts or places. First their parents started protecting Gondadunguri, the nearby hill. Till date on the festival days, people go there and sow seeds of different trees. After few years, they started protecting *Gothani Patara* forest. Then, the youth group and other villagers got together and first collected *Gambhari* seed and started sowing at a place called *Talken* on the river bank of our village. The forest patches started growing well. Whenever there occurred any problem related to forest, all the villagers are called for a meeting and the matter is resolved there only. The village youth group and some aged persons were the pioneers in this process. To increase the support of villagers, they used to act plays on roadside (*Pathapranta Nataka*) spreading message of benefits of forest and need of conservation. Villagers have received enormous support from *PRAYAS* in the form of training, capacity building, and awareness. They provided seeds of Cashew, Radha Neem, Eucalyptus, Mango, Bela etc. to plant trees at a place called *Bhursitkuri* located towards West of the village. The total area under plantation and protection here is about 11 Acres. Women and children are the major participants in this seed sowing activity. There are some other small patches under protection namely *Barabudha patara, Dalkha patara, Bankheta patara* etc. respectively on south-east, west and south of the village.

The Protection System:

The villager used to have five to six times a year in the collective general village meeting on forest protection and related issues. Men, Women and Youth of the village participate in this meeting. Some people due to their otherwise personal engagements do not attend the meeting. This general body looks after the work of the Executive Committee on forest protection comprising eleven members. This also decides the members to represent in the executive committee. The Executive committee doesn't have a time limit but whenever General committee feels, they can bring in changes in the composition, rules and regulations of the executive committee. The role of the executive committee is to resolve the conflicts related to forest. When the matter remains unresolved, it is brought to the notice of the Village general meeting. The executive committee bears the responsibility of enforcing rules related to forest and whoever breaks the rules of forest protection is punished by this committee either in terms of collecting fine or begging excuse with a bond of non-repetition. There is wood, bamboo, *Madhu, Tendu leaf, Char, Mahua, Jhuna, Sal leaf* and *Siali* leaf etc available in nearby forests also which are not being protected by villagers. There is no restriction regarding collection of NTFPs from the protected patch of forest but People of neighboring villages have no rights over it. These people from neighboring villages also agreed to the villager's demand and respect their forest protection initiative. They initially had some disagreement over the matter with the neighboring village but soon the matter got resolved and it had no impact on the forest protection measures. Forest is full of resources and let us protects it, let us save it:

"Jungle karba sabhinka mangal,

Bhai buhen ek hema,

Ujuda jungle ke sajei dema."

(Forest will do good to all, O'brothers and sisters, let us together save the forest.)

Forest Protection and other Institutions:

The Villagers almost have no relation with outside agencies intervention on the issue of forest protection. Only when a serious situation arises i.e. when someone denies abiding by the village forest committee decision, the case is handed over to the forest department. Even they don't have much relation with forest department on this matter. Neither they are at loss nor in benefit from relationship with forest department. Forest department are pursuing them to form *Van Samrakshyan Samiti* (VSS) and make Forest Department a partner in the forest protection initiative. The people have relations with some other agencies like PRAYAS, a non-government organization for forest protection which provided them saplings for plantation in the barren land and trained them on plantation techniques and protection measures. No one has objected their forest protection initiatives till date.

Future of Forest Protection:

As far as future of forest is concerned, it is difficult to say, about the forest. One thing people have promised that they will continue forest protection. According to them, they don't know what the next generation would do with this forest, but, they will try to make them understand the importance of forest for existence of life. The rapid industrialization and mining processes are definitely a threat to today's forest. There is a need of mass education and awareness on importance and benefits of forest at all levels through local cultural media such as *Pala, Daskathia, Natak* etc to conserve forest. The role of Forest Protection committees has to be more effective. An active Forest Department needs to play vital role in forest protection and regeneration in the interest of the poor and marginalized. There needs to be laws in place in favor of forest and people. There has to be proper plan of afforestation every year on the waste land and forest management plans with people's participation. Both people and Forest Department can collectively make a lush and green forest possible. We the people of forest might not know cleanliness, good behavior etc but we love our forest.

When the rainy season arrives and there is no food left at house, we eat the dried forest food like Kendu, Chhatu, Kardi, Putu, Kurutu, and Char, Amba (Mango) by either boiling or frying it. These dried food and vegetables sustain our family throughout the rain. As we sing:

"Ame jangalia loka ho, jangala ama mulaka
Peta pain dana, roga ku oushadha, ei ama sukha dukha.
Phala mula sabu die ho Jhuna mahu sabu die,
Nija pua boli mane rakhithiba, na heba epari kie ho
Asa sapatha kariba ho jangala ku na katiba
Jangala katile barasa abhabe chatapata ame heba ho."

(We are the people of forest; forest is our kingdom. It provides food for stomach, medicine for illness, and shares our sorrows and happiness. It gives fruit and tuber, Jhuna and Mahu (Honey). Treat it as own son, no one else can be like that. Let us vow not to cut trees. If we destroy forest, in the absence of rain all will suffer.)

"Ahare chai kete sundara chai, eta aau kata nai
Ethanu tike chetare bhai
Jahata sarila Sarita galana, ethanu tike chetare bhai
Gacha ama bandhu sukha dukha sahi
Jete kati dele mana nai kare
Tathapi se nai die durei.
Gacha amara Ghara Duara sabu kame laguche
Jeri buti Ainla phala Harida Bahada miluche
Katuthile Tangari dhari hae kahe nai
Janam kala maa lekhe sabu achi sahi
Nijar lekhe taku tike dekha
Dekhu dekhu nai dia jalei "

(How beautiful and soothing this shade is, don't cut it. Now time has come to wake up. Whatever is lost is lost, now let us wake up. Trees are our friends always. They don't deny when we cut them. Never do they go away from us. It is used in house building and every work. Provides medicines like Ainla, Bahada, Harida etc. When we cut them using weapons it never protests. Like a mother it bears with us. Let us see it as our family member. Let us not get it burnt in front of our eyes)

"Dal khai ho…

Chalare tukel mane kurudu khai jima

Tora kurudu mora kurudu sika bhalai nema

Badkha dadat biha bele ghuduka bajai jima"

(Dalkhai ho ..., O young girls, let's go to the woods to eat Kurudu

Your Kurudu My kurudu, let's keep together, during the marriage of elder brother we will go to beat drums together"

"Ghubukudu Chang Chang, Paesa takar patare bhang"

(Ghubukudu Chang Chang, for one paisa we get a leaf full of Bhang)

Conclusion:

The Jungle Bachao campaign is continuing in the village and they intend to continue protecting and regenerating our forest. At least one more generation will care for and preserve the forest for the future. They are also teaching their children to preserve and protect the forest. There is a need to raise the consciousness of the community regarding forest protection by explaining the importance of forest in human lives. They will ultimately have to raise forest protection as an issue of importance in the *gram sabha* and involve the entire revenue village in this effort. The main threat to forest protection is posed by the surrounding villages where the forest has been completely destroyed and those villagers have no choice but to encroach on the forests of others. They are also worried about the forest department. They will not allow them to cut the forest, and if they persist despite warning, they will not hesitate to use violence.

References:

- Thompsom P, 1978, *The Voice of the Past Oral History*, OUP.
- Prasad A, 2000, "Tribal Society and History Writing in India" (ed) Sabyasachi Bhattacharya, *Approaches to History*, Primus Book, New Delhi.
- Stoker G, 1998, *Governance as Theory: Five Prepositions*, Blackwell.
- Pradip P, 1994, "*Sustainable Tribal Development,*" Golden Jubilee Issue on Sustainable Development, Indian Institute of Public Administration, New Delhi.
- Shamasastry, R, 1960, *Kautilya's Arthashastra*, Mysore.
- Sabhaparva, 1962, XIII,

Ethnomedicinal Plant use among the Banjara Tribe in Bargarh District, Western Odisha: A Preliminary Report

Ramesh Naik

Ph.D. Research Scholar, Sambalpur University, Jyoti Vihar, Burla
Email: rameshnaik10bgh@gmail.com

Abstract

The present paper is based on the Ethnomedicinal Plant use and the health status of the Banjara community in Bargarh district of Western Odisha. The Banjaras are the semi-nomadic tribe; they settle in the Bargarh District as well as in Odisha. This community has migrated from various regions such as Rajasthan, Maharashtra, Telangana, Andhra Pradesh, and Gujarat. The Banjara belongs to nomadic tribes enriching the ethnic heritage (Ethnomedicine) of Odisha. Although there are various medical facilities and medicines are available in locality however the Banjara communities practice their traditional medicines. The Banjaras are closely connected to their environment and exhibit unique practices related to sanitation, health, marriageable age, childbirth, prenatal and postnatal care, and the utilization of medical facilities. Ethnomedicinal plants play a crucial role in treating a variety of diseases, and many of these plants are also consumed as food. In curing different types of diseases and many of them are used as edible food plants. Bargarh has rich biodiversity consisting of a large number of plants, some of which are used for their medicinal value.

Keywords: Banjara, ethnomedicine, ethnic, nomadic, semi-nomadic

Introduction

Good health is essential for all people to work and grow. A healthy community is the foundation for building a strong economy. "Health is crucial for the moral, creative, physical, and spiritual growth of individuals," as stated by Charaka, the famous Ayurvedic physician. The World Health Organization (WHO) has greatly benefited humanity by fostering global collaboration in the field of health. It is important to focus on the health conditions and practices of tribal communities, especially in situations of poverty. There are two main reasons for this. First, most tribal people live in the forest and hill areas where modern healthcare is unavailable. Second, the rapid decline in the growth rate of the tribal population poses a threat to their survival. This calls for a closer look at their cultural habits and health practices.

Medicinal plants have become a global focus due to their significant impact on health in the worldwide. Herbal medicine has been important in maintaining healthcare for people around the world (Akerele, 1988). Medicinal plants are the foundation of traditional medicine, around 3.3 billion people in developing countries using them regularly (Dobriyal and Narayana, 1998). Despite the progress in modern medicine, around 80% of the world's population still relies on traditional medicine for basic healthcare, including in India (Upadhya, 2012).

Study Area

The Bargarh district is located in Western part of Odisha. Before 1992, it was part of Sambalpur district and became an independent district on April 1, 1993. The Bargarh district is located between latitudes 20°43′ and 21°41′ North and longitudes 82°39′ and 83°58′ East. Bargarh town, situated on the left bank of the Jira River. This district is surrounded by Chhattisgarh state to the north, Sambalpur District to the east, Balangir and Subarnapur to the south, and Nuapada District to the west. The district covers a total area of 5,837 km², of which 269.329 km² is forested. The town lies on the National Highway No. 6 and about 59 km west of Sambalpur. The area was originally known as "Baghar Kota," as evidenced by an inscription from the 11th century A.D (DSR 2019). The name "Bargarh" likely originated during the reign of Balaram Dev, the Chauhan Raja of Sambalpur, who established it as his first headquarters and built a large fort for its defense on the river bank of Jira (Sahu, N. K et al: 1980). Natural springs at Nrusinghanath, located at the foot of the Gandhamardhan Hills in the Padampur subdivision, form beautiful streams cascading down steep slopes. Agriculture is the primary livelihood for the tribal population, but they also rely heavily on forest resources for their livelihood and health needs. The district's unique physiography supports the tribal communities in preserving their cultural heritage and way of life.

As per the 2011 census, the percentage of the tribal population in Odisha is 22.85%. and the total Tribal population of Bargarh is 18.98%. There are 62 Tribal groups found in Odisha and 44 Tribal groups in Western Odisha such as Banjara, Gond, Binjhal, Kishan, Gouda, Saora, Bhuiya, Juang etc (ST-15, 2011). The Bargarh district is divided into 12 blocks and Tahasils. In each Tahasil of the district, the Banjara people have settled (Fig:1).

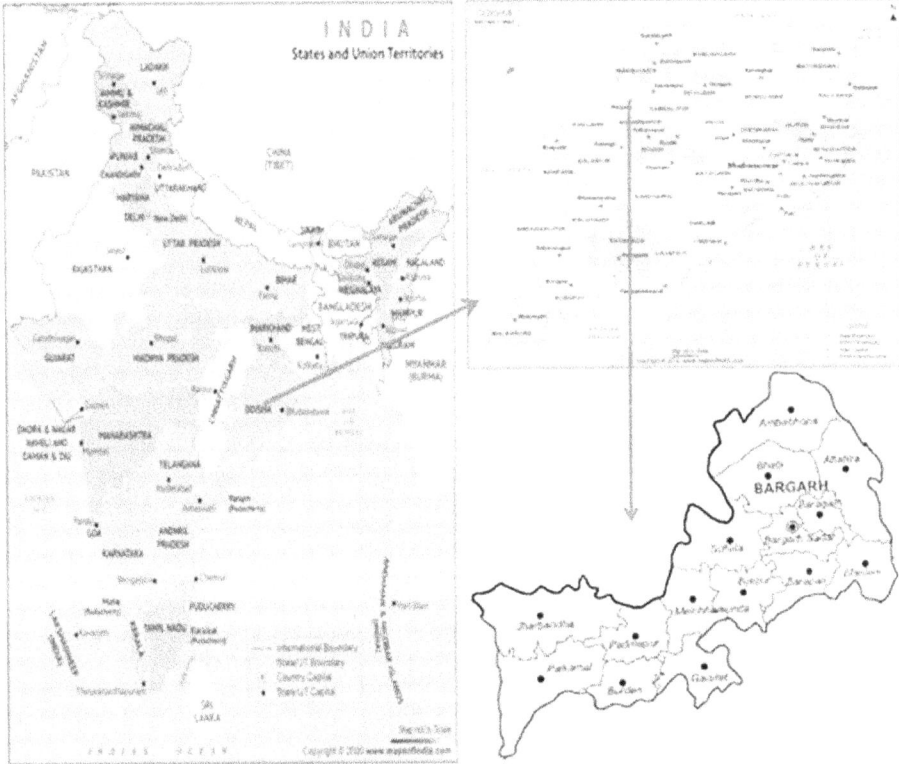

Fig: 1 Map of the Study Area

The Banjara Community

The Banjara community is widely distributed across India and is known by various names in different states. In Maharashtra, they are referred to as Banjara or Gor; in Karnataka, as Lamani; in Andhra Pradesh, as Lambada; in Punjab, as Bazighar; and in Uttar Pradesh, as Nayak, among others. The terms "Lambani" or "Lamani" are derived from the Sanskrit word *Lavana* (salt), highlighting their historical role as salt traders who transported this essential commodity across the country. In contemporary contexts, the term "Banjara" often refers to a nomadic community characterized by their unique cultural

Blocks
1. Ambabhona
2. Attabira
3. Bargarh
4. Barpali
5. Bhatli
6. Bheden
7. Bijepur,
8. Gaisilet
9. Jharbandh
10. Padampur
11. Paikmal
12. Sohela

practices, distinct attire adorned with specific ornaments, and a well-defined set of traditions and regulations (Badavath Ram Krishna, 2017).

The term "Banjara" comes from the Sanskrit word *Vana Chara*, meaning "wanderers of the jungle." The word Banjara is also derived from the word van, which means forest, and Jara, which means go that's why its means "go to the jungle" and they migrated from one place to another for their trade activities (Halbar, B. G., 1986). The people of Banjara who settle in Odisha, as well as in Western Odisha's districts like Bargarh, Sundargarh, Nawarangpur, Nuapada, Kalahandi, and Balangir. The community migrated from Rajasthan, Andhra Pradesh, Gujarat, Telangana, Maharashtra, Karnataka, Madhya Pradesh, Marwa etc. (M. Choudhary, 2018). They have a unique cultural tradition among all the tribal groups found in Odisha, and they speak Gor Bali language, and nowadays they speak contemporary languages based on their settlement, like Hindi, Odia, Telugu, Gujarati, Marathi, etc. The Banjara community, known for its rich cultural heritage and vibrant traditions, has long been an integral part of India's diverse social fabric. Traditionally they belong to trade activities like Turmeric, Salt, Spices on the Bullock Carts. But they also given important on collecting Ethnomedicine from the jungle and it's also influenced their socio-economic life (V. Upadhya, et.al, :2012).

Aims and Objectives

The aims and objectives are focused on understanding how this community uses traditional ethnomedicinal knowledge and practices for several health issues in the community.
1.   To investigate the traditional ethnomedicinal plant use by the tribe in Bargarh district.
2.   To study how its effect for the common health issues among the Banjara and non-Banjara community.
3.   To understand their ethnomedicinal practices among the tribes.
4.   To know the importance and preserving their traditional knowledge of ethnomedicine.
5.   To study how its effect on their socio-economic aspects of the community.

Methodology

During my research work, I visit and collected plants from various Tandas (Banjara settlement) of different villages. The study is focused on tribal villages like Khuntapali, Kalangapali, Dumerpali, Mahulpali, Kanekbira, Patharla, and others in Bijepur, Sohela, and Barpali Blocks. I visited these places in different seasons to observe the plants during their flowering and fruiting stages. During the fieldwork, the data is gathered through interviews with local experts (Suresan Naik, Lekru Naik, Todasang Naik, Jagadish Naik, Tapsi Naik, Srinath Naik), including traditional healers known as Vaidyas, elderly women (Hema Naik, Parbati Naik) and vendors of medicinal plants and observations during the preparation of herbal products. The collected information was meticulously documented. Besides, field trips are undertaken with some Vaidyas to study about availability of certain plants, and the findings were carefully recorded. The collected information is thoroughly examined and organized into a tabular format (Table 1).

Plants Collection

The present study revealed that most of the plants are found to have diverse local uses by the Banjara tribe in the region. Local traditional healers use different parts of plants, like roots, stems, bark, flowers, fruits, seeds, and gum, as medicine. These are usually prepared as pastes, decoctions, extracts, or seed oil. These herbs are easy to get with cheap rate and commonly seen in locality. The survey includes more than 60 types of medicinal plants used by the Banjara Tribe which are given below in details (Table 1). But some Plant are given with pictures (Fig: 2).

Preparation Medicine

Traditionally the community people have a deep understanding of local plants, minerals. These remedies are typically made using natural resources and involve a combination of plants, oils, roots, and sometimes animal products. Here are some formulas which is stated by a local Vaidya named Todasang Naik, that might be used by the community, though it's important to note that these vary widely based on the region and specific cultural practices.

1. Boil water and pour it over crushed or whole plant parts, then drink it once it cools.
2. Hard parts of plants like roots or bark are boiled for a longer time to get their medicine.
3. Grind herbs or plant parts and mix them with water or something else to make a paste.
4. Take a handful of fresh tulsi leaves, crush them, boil in water for 10-15 minutes, then strain.
5. Some plants are eaten directly by people, like musingapatar, Bela, Saga, Munga, etc.

Dosage:

Traditional healers are very much knowing the correct dosages based on their experience and knowledge of the plant's effects. It takes over dosages or misuse can be harmful. The dosages are based on the demand of a disease. It's all about depends upon the patients, disease, and Vaidyas.

Conclusion

The Banjara tribe's medicinal plant knowledge plays a crucial role in traditional healthcare, especially in rural and tribal areas where modern medicine is scarce. Their reliance on locally available herbs demonstrates an eco-friendly, sustainable approach to health and wellness. However, modernization and loss of biodiversity threaten this ancient wisdom. Documenting and integrating this traditional knowledge with modern science could help preserve their rich heritage and contribute to alternative medicine and ethnobotany.

The Banjara tribe, known for its nomadic heritage and deep connection with nature, has preserved a wealth of traditional knowledge about medicinal plants. Their use of herbal remedies has been passed down through generations, offering natural solutions for various ailments.

Table 1: Some Medicinal Plants

SL No	BOTANIICAL NAME	FAMILY	LOCAL NAME	PARTS USE	MEDICINAL USE
01	Abrus Precatorius Linn	Fabaceae	Gunj	Leaves	Fevers, coughs, colds
02	Achyranthus aspera Linn	Amaranthaceae	Apamarga	Leaves, Roots	Abdomen Pain
03	Azagdirachta indica linn	Meliaceae	Neem	Leaves, Seeds Bark	fever and worms
04	Butea monosperma	Fabaceae	Palash	Flower, Seeds	Diarrhoea
05	Clitoria ternetea Linn	Fabaceae	Aprajita	Roots, leaves	Fever, Cough

06	Dhatura metal Linn	Solanaceae	Kaladha-tura	Leaves, flower	Cough, asthma
07	Euphorbia hirta Linn	Euphorbiaceae	Dudhi	Leaves	Leucoderma, boits
08	Ficus religiosa Linn	Moraceae	Pipal	Bark, leaves, and fruit	Gynaecologi-cal disorder
09	Moringa oleif-era Lamk.	Moringaceae	Munga	Leaves, Bark, and Drumstick	asthma, cough
10	Ocimum sanc-tum	Labiateae	Tulsi	Leaves, Roots and Seed	Dry cough,
11	Phyllanthus niruri Linn	Euphorbiaceae	Aambla	Leaves, Bark, Roots, Seeds	Kidney stones, cold
12	Schleichera oleosa (lour.)	Sapindaceae	Kosum	Leaves, bark	colds, skin, fever
13	Syzygium cumini Skeels	Myrtaceae	Jamun	Leaves, Fruits	diabetes
14	Terminalia arjuna	Combretaceae	Arjun	Barks	Abdominal pain
15	Terminalia bel-lirica	Combretaceae	Baheda	Fruits	Bleeding
16	Vitex negundo Linn	Verbenaceae	Nirguni	Whole plants	Rheumatism
17	Tagetus petula	Asteraceae	Gendu	Leaves	Cuts and injuries
18	Allium sativum Linn	Liliaceae	Lasun	Roots	Antifungal, amoebiasis
19	Annona squa-mosa L.	Annonaceae	Sita phal	Leaves, Fruits	Treatment of dysentery
20	Withania som-nifera L.	Solanaceae	Ashwa-gandha	Roots, Leaves	Rheumatism

21	Acacia catechu	Mimosaceae	Khair	Bark	Cough, Skinn
22	Aegle Maeme-los	Rutaceae	Bel/ Bila	Fruirts, Pulk, Leaves	Diarrhea, Pimple, Acidity
23	Asparagus Racemosus	Liliaceae	Shatawari	Whole Plant	Epilepsy, Stomach
24	Caesalpinia pulcherrima L.	Caesalpiniaceae	Krishna chura	Leaves	Misoprostol
25	Citrus limonum L.	Ruteaceae	Neembu,	Seeds	Abortion
26	Mamordica charantia L.	Cucurbitaceae	Karela	Fruits	mid-term abortion
27	Thespesia populnea (L.)	Malvaceae	Bhendi	Seeds	Anti-implantation
28	Cicer arieticum L.	Papilionaceae	Chana	Leaves	Abortifacient
29	Carica papaya L.	Caricaceae	Amrutbhanda	Seeds	Abortifacient
30	Aloe-vera L. Burm.f.,	Liliaceae	Kuwari	Leaves	Skin, pimples
31	Cynodon dactylon (L.)	Poaceae	Harad	Leaves	Menstrual problem
32	Daucus carota L.	Apiaceae	Mula	Root	Piles
33	Ficus carica L.	Moraceae	Anjir/ Ghuler	Fruit	Asthma
34	Ficus religiosa L.	Moraceae	Pipal	Leaves, Seeds	Epilepsy
35	Mucona pruriens (L.) DC.	Fabaceae	Baikhujen	Seeds	Menstrual problem
36	Murraya koenngii (L.)	Rutaceae	Musin-giapatar	Leaves	Heart disease
37	Phyllanthus emblica L.	Euphorbiaceae	Ambla/ Ainla	Bark, Fruits	Leucoderma

38	Punica grana-tum L.	Punicaceae	Dalimb	Flower, Buds	Nasal polyp
39	Ziziphus jujube Lamk.	Rhamnaceae	Bor	Bark	gum swelling
40	Syzygium cumini (L)	Myrtaceae	Jamun	Leaves	Dental problem
41	Bombax ceiba L.	Bombacaceae	Simul/ Semel	Stem	Diarrhea
42	Dalbergia sissoo Roxb.	Fabaceae	Sisu	Leave	Cooling agent
43	Trigonella foenum-grae-cum L.	Fabaceae	Methi	Leaves, Seeds	Antidiabetic
44	Sida acuta Burm.f.	Malvaceae	Bajarmuli	Leaves	Ashtama, Cold
45	Momordica dioica	Cucurbitaceae	Konkodo	Roots	Diabetes
46	Amaranthus viridis	Amarantha-ceae	Kantaleu-tia	All parts	Scabies, Skin diseases
47	Bauhinia vahlii	Fabaceae	Kulersag	Seed	Headache
48	Butea mono-sperma	Fabaceae	Palasa/ Falsa	Flowers, roots	Leprosy, Skin
49	Basella alba	Bacillaceae	Poi	Roots	Irregular period
50	Curcuma longa	Zingiberaceae	Haldi	Rhizome	Jaundice.
51	Cocos nucifera e	Arecacea	Nadia	Oil	Hair growth
52	Chenopodium album	Chenopodia-ceae	Bathua saga	Leaves	Heart disease
53	Calotropis procera	Asclepiadaceae	Arakh	Juice	Skin disease.
54	Chloroxylon swietenia	Rutaceae	Bherua	Leaves	Fungal infection

55	Coriandrum sativum	Umbellifers	Dhania	Leaves	Headache
56	Cascabela thevetia	Apocynaceae	Champa	Fruit	Itches and abscess
57	Cassia fistula	Fabacee	Sunari	Leaves	Malaria, skin disease.
58	Justicia adhatoda	Acanthaceae	Basanga	Leaves	Cold fever, Cough
59	Achyranthes aspera	Amaranthaceae	Kukurdati	Stem	Tooth
60	Lagenaria siceraria	Cucurbitaceae	Lau	Pulp	Treat rheumatism
61	Mimosa pudica	Fabaceae	Lajakuli	Roots, leaves	Snake bite
62	Mentha piperata	Lamiaceae	Pudina	Leaves	Stomach pain
63	Madhuca indica	Sapotaceae	Mahul	Latex	Cracked feet.
64	Pongamia pinnata	Fabaceae	Karanja	Shoot, seeds	Skin disease
65	Psidium guajava	Myrtaceae	Pijuli/ Maya	Leaves	Loose motion.
66	Euphorbia neriifolia	Euphorbiaceae	Thua	Leaves, Latax	Piles, Cracks feet, Tumors
67	Ghrangea Mederaspatana	Asteraceae	Painjari	Leaves, Roots	Skinn, Joint Pain

Fig: 2 Some Important Plant

A

B

C

D

E

F

G

H

I

J

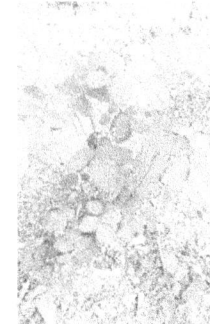

K

L

Fig: 2 (a) Ainla(b)Champa (c)Bhuler (d)Neem (e)Thua (f)Maya (g) Nirgun (h) Amrutbhanda(i)Pipal (j)Sisu (k)Poi (l)Mandar (m)Apamarga (n) Jada(o) Ghuler(p)Simuli (q) Painjari (r)Musingapatar (s) Siali (t)Kaladudhra (u) Palash(v) Palash(w)Nimbu (x)Tulsi

Reference

- Akerele, O. (1988). Medicinal plants and primary health care: an agenda for action. Fitoterapia. Vol. 59.
- Banjara, R., Sharma, K. R., & Pokharel, Y. R. (2023). *Phytochemical analysis,*

biological activities, and GC profiling of extracts of some medicinal plants growing in Nepal. Indian Journal of Natural Products and Resources, 13(4).

- Bhogaonkar, P., & Chavhan, V. (2013). *Traditional Banjara herbal medicine of Vidarbha, MS, India.* LAP LAMBERT Academic Publishing.

- Dobriyal, R. M. and Narayana, D.B.A. (1998). Ayurvedic herbal raw material. The Eastern Pharmacist. 31-35.

- Halbar, B. G. (1986), *Lamani Economy and Society in Change: Socio-cultural Aspects of Economic Change Among the Lamani of North Karnataka,* Mittal Publications.

- Jhankar, J., & Mohapatra, R. (2022). *Native medicinal plants in use to ameliorate different diseases by local tribal healers of Nuapada district of Western Odisha.* Journal of Pharmacognosy and Phytochemistry, 11(5), 55-61.

- Kanrar, P., Goswami, M., & Roy, S. (2023). *Health issues of the indigenous communities with special reference to the particularly vulnerable tribal groups (PVTGs) of Odisha: A review.* Papers on Anthropology, 32(1), 45-80.

- Lal, B. S. (2006). *Health status and health practices among the tribals: A case study in Andhra Pradesh.* Journal of Social Anthropology, *3*(2).

- Mohanty, P., Sahu, S. S., Sahoo, A. K., Parida, S., & Mahalik, G. (2020*). Ethnomedicinal survey of plants used by tribal in Nrushinghnath forest of Bargarh, Odisha, India.* International Journal of Botany Studies, 5(3).

- Padhan, P., Bindhani, B. K., & Nayak, J. K. (2021). *Perceptions and practices on malaria in a rural population of Koraput district, Odisha.* International Journal of Research in Medical Sciences, 9(5).

- Upadhya, V., Hegde, H.V., Bhat, S., Hurkadale, P.J., Kholkute, S.D., Hegde, G.R. (2012). Ethnomedicinal plants used to treat bone fracture from North-Central Western Ghats of India. Journal of Ethnopharmacology. Vol. 142.

- Sahoo, A. K. (2011). *Ethnomedicinal plants resource of Orissa (Vol. 1).* New India Publishing Agency.

- Sahu, A. R., Sahu, M., Mishra, S., & Ekka, N. J. (2021). *A preliminary report on ethnomedicinal uses of selected plants by Sahara tribal groups of Kangaon village of Bargarh district in western Odisha.* Journal of Medicinal Plants Studies, 9(3).

- Sahu, A. R., Sahu, M., & Mishra, S. (2020). *A preliminary report on the traditional use of selected plants of Fabaceae family at Bargarh district, Western Odisha.* International Journal of Herbal Medicine, 8(3).

- Sahu AR, Panigrahi SK, Nayak AK. (2013). *Survey of some important ethno-medicinal plants of Sohela Block, Western Odisha, India.* Life Sciences Leaflets, 11, 1-9.

- Sen, S. K., Pattanaik, M. R., & Behera, L. M. (2014). *Traditional use of herbal medicines against rheumatism by the tribals of Bargarh district, Odisha. Life Science Leaflets, 59-68.*

- Sen, S. K., & Behera, L. M. (2008). *Ethnomedicinal plants used by the tribals of Bargarh district to cure diarrhoea and dysentery.* Indian Journal of Traditional Knowledge, 7(3), 425-428.

- Sen, S. K., Pattanaik, M. R., & Behera, L. M. (2015). *Ethnomedicinal uses of plants related to delivery problem in Bargarh district of Western Odisha.* International Journal of Herbal Medicine, 2(5), 31-33.

- "ST-15: Scheduled tribe by mother tongue (for each tribe separately) (State/UT level), Odisha - 2011". Office of the Registrar General & Census Commissioner, India.

- Saxena, H. O., & Brahmam, M. (1994). The Flora of Orissa, Regional Research Laboratory (CSIR), Bhubaneswar, Orissa.

- Tugnawat, H., & Titov, A. (2020). *A study of medicinal plants used by the Banjara community inhibited in Neemuch District of Madhya Pradesh.* International Journal of Botany Studies, 5(5), 273-276.

- Wankhade, M. S., & Bokhad, M. N. (2021). *Investigation of ethnomedicinal plants used by Banjara tribe in Mantha Tahasil, District Jalana, Maharashtra.* International Journal for Modern Trends in Science and Technology, 7(10), 17-22.

Myth, Folk Drama 'Aala Udel' and Antiquities of Maraguda Valley

Dr. Fanindam Deo

Chairman, District Child Welfare Committee Nuapada (Odisha)
Email: fanindam@gmail.com

Abstract

This paper deals with the myth and history preserved in oral and dance drama tradition in and around Sunabeda hills, Nuapada, Odisha, relating to Raimado kingdom and its fall. In a preliterate society, oral tradition used to be a powerful media. Sunabeda being an adivasi dominated area, is very rich in oral tradition. Adivasi groups like Gond, Bhunjia and Paharia aiong with non-adivasi groups lived in close proximity; and though they remain socially distinctive, they influence one another and develop forms of mutual adjustment in their respective ways of life. On the occasion of Sunadei Jatra, an annual religious gathering to celebrate the blessings of deities Sunadei, Rupadei and Budharaja all adivasi groups and non-adivasis participate which reinforces a unique process of acculturation.

Keywords: *Myth, Folk Drama, Chaukhutia Bhunjia*

Introduction

Nuapada district is located in the western part of Odisha province, lying between 20^0 20′ N and 21^0 5′ North Latitude and 82^0 20′ E to 82 ^{0}40′ East Longitude. It is bounded in the north and west by Mahasamund district of Chhattisgarh and on the east and south by Bargarh, Bolangir and Kalahandi districts of Odisha. It is a small district, the length from north to south is about 150kms and its breadth from east to west is about 100 kms. Nearly twenty-two *adivasi* communities are identified in the district. The district with its abundant forest resources, plentiful fertile soil and water resources nurtured the societies of food gathers and hunters and settled agricultural societies side by side from early historical period. The natural terrain and conditions allowed numerous niches in which food-gathers and hunters have thrived from stone ages till today. The rock paintings of Jogimath-Risipitha and Ghatghumar remind us the creative expressions of the stone-age people. The river valleys of Jonk, Indra-Sunder and Udanti with favourable condition allowed some agricultural societies to settle down for cultivation. This helped in the development of prosperous villages, towns, forts and urban centres. Perhaps this attracted Saivaists, Budhhists and Jains to establish their centres in this area. Excavation and archaeological findings of Maraguda valley in Nuapada district have brought out a historical site which resembles the description of the Chinese pilgrim Yuang Chwang. The evidence of ruined forts, towns, temples and land grants, gold coins point towards the existence of an early state and urban centre. It is difficult to assign any specific reason for its disintegration since source materials are not yet scientifically examined. However, interestingly most of the ruins are found inside the deep forest and hill tops, in the area now inhabited by adivasis, Primitive Vulnerable Tribal Group (PVTG) and hunting –gathering communities. These places are still not properly connected by all-weather road and about ninety percent of the inhabitants are adivasis. The historical findings in the inaccessible pockets of Nuapada district prove contrary to the general view of scholars and settlement officers that Nuapada was the last area to see the light of improved Indian civilisation. Contrary to their opinion the findings in Maraguda- Sunabeda region prove the presence Saiva-Sakta, Budhist and Jain followers and urban settlements, forts in this area as early as 5th century C.E..Not that the *adivasis* had no capacity to build forts and towns; but only the *adivasi* mode of production could not sustain a kingdom and establish big forts and towns. By adivasi mode of production we mean *podu*, *Jhum* or shifting cultivation. Such mode of production could not generate adequate surplus to such forts and urban centres. Chandramani Patel, the Director, Maraguda Excavation Project and Superintendent of Odisha State Museum observed on the basis of the findings from Garhbhatta, Jumlagarh, Chheliagarh, Manikgarh of Sunabeda plateau and ruins of Maraguda valley on the river bank of Jonk that a planned urban centre was there in the hoary past. Further corroborating with ancient text he identified the ruined urban centre of Maraguda, Nuapada as the capital city of South Kosala Kingdom (Patel, 1995).

Folk belief

According to the folk belief (of Maraguda, Lodra, Tikrapada (now submerged under Patora Dam) and Kermeli villages, "seven hundred years ago Raimado (Maraguda) was a prosperous country with palaces, temples and forts. The kingdom was ruled by a just king named Bhikham. His kingdom extended up to the boarders of Mahoba kingdom (Budelkhand). The then Raja of Mahoba was Jaisal. The latter, on his hunting trips accidentally entered the territory of Bhikham and while roaming around he came to know that Bhikham had a daughter of exquisite beauty. Jaisal became curious to have a glimpse of her. He tried to enter the fort of Raja Bhikham. But the famous fort known as Manikgarh was so perfectly built and guarded by Bhikham's men that Jaisal's several attempts to scale the fort failed. The attempts and intension of Jaisal was reported to Bhikham by his spies. The latter entrusted his trusted commanders to have a watch on Jaisal. Jaisal while roaming around the formidable Manikgarh fort at last saw a *jalki* or swampy area near village Lodra which was unguarded by Bhikham's men. He decided to take the risk of crossing the *jalki*. Unfortunately, while crossing Jaisal's horse got stuck on the bog and could not come out. In that helpless state Jaisal was beheaded by Bhikham's men. The head was hanged on the lion gate of Manikgarh fort. A few days after the guardian deity of the fort appeared in a dream to Bhikham and expressed her anger over the cowardly way of killing a warrior and withdrew her support and protection to the fort.

The news of ruthless murder of Jaisal reached Mahoba. The two young sons of Jaisal Aala and Udel promised to avenge the treacherous killer of their father. With a formidable Mahoban army they proceeded against Bhikham. They encamped on the west of Manikgarh near Dharambandha. There they found it impossible to scale the fort from that direction. So, they shifted their camp to Tikrapada i.e north-west of Manikgarh fort where they found two obstacles, one a perennial stream called Girwar and second a river named Jonk. Finally, they made *lakhpole* or max bridge over the Girwar stream, crossed the stream and Mahoba army reached up to the gates of the fort. Bhikham was informed about the movements of Mahoban army. He entrusted his three commanders i.e Manik, head of the elephant force, Mukund, the head of cavalry, Sundar, the head of the artillery, to defend the fort successfully. Fierce battle took place; thousands of soldiers were killed near Tikrapada while defending the fort. At last, Aala and Udel entered the fort and beheaded Bikham and his family members. After avenging their father's death Aala and Udel collected the wealth of Raimado and went back. From that day Manikgarh fort and Raimado kingdom gradually collapsed. The name Raimado was changed to Maraguda, meaning where everybody was killed.

FIG-1: Practice of Local Folk Songs by Bhunjia Tribes

There are many more folk songs and myths preserved in the oral tradition of the locality. Each and every mound and ruins of the locality is known to the people, and carries a myth and feature in the local folk songs (Fig-1). To give one example, the Rani Gutki, prior to excavation was a heap of earth and not a single brick was visible from outside. But the people of the locality could tell that in the *Rani Gutki (Gutki means a small mount)* there was the Queen's palace earlier. When the excavation was done, a ruined building was unearthed which has been named as Rani Mahal by the Archaeologist and historians. Similarly, after the excavation of *Baipari Gutki* shown by the local people a ruined brick structure has been unearthed along with the precious stones. This indicates that in the past this building was meant for some business purposes.

Bhunjia

Nuapada district is considered as the home of Bhunjias as 75% of total Bhunjia population of Odisha resides in this district. Bhunjias also live in adjoining areas of Chhattisgarh State. According to R.V. Russell, "the term Bhunjia may perhaps signify one who lives on the soil, from *bhum*, the earth and jia, dependant on" (Russel, 1916). The local origin myth of Bhunjia says that the earliest name of Bhunjia was '*Matia*' (*Mat*-soil, *ia*-came from or origin-implying origin from earth) (Deo,1984). Though Bhunjias are the indigenous people of this area there is no reference to Bhunjia in Hindu literature and myths. British records for the first time show the Bhunjia as a distinct tribe. The Bhunjia belongs to the Dravidian group and speaks a dialect 'Bhunjia', a mixture of Chhattisgarhi and Koshali. Bhunjia tribe is a clan-based society. Clan is a closely integrated unit; all its members share the consciousness of a common mythical history which leads to clan solidarity. Earlier land was jointly owned by the members of the clan. In case of increase of population and shortage of cultivable land in a particular area, a section of the clan shifted to a new place of settlement but its members continued to maintain the previous relations. A member's relationship to the other member of his clan is unalterable. Bhunjias are broadly divided into two sub-sections i.e. Chinda Bhunjia and Chaukhutia Bhunjia. The former lives generally in the plains and have close contacts with other adivasis and non-adivasi neighbours whereas the latter prefers to live in the ecologically secluded areas; interior hills and forest. It is the mark of distance they maintain with non-chaukhutia that they don't allow the outsider to touch their cooking hut. R.V. Russell wrote, "If any man not of his caste touches the hut where a Chaukhutia cooks his food, it is abandoned and a fresh one built. At the time of the census, they threatened to kill the enumerator if he touched their huts to affix the census number. Pegs had therefore to be planted in the ground a little distance in front of the huts and marked with their number" (Russel, 1916). Migration was not permissible in Chaukhutia Bhunjia society till recently. Even now a days they do not allow. K.C. Dubey, while analyzing the myth and oral tradition of Chhattisgarh considers the Bhunjia as branch of Halbas of Bastar who fled from Bastar due to their quarrel with Dhakars (Dubey,1961). They came to Bindranawagarh, concealed their identity and introduced themselves as the Chindas. After sometime Gond came to this area and settled down. Chindas did not like the Gond intrusion and killed the Gond chief. The pregnant wife of the chief took shelter in Khariar (present Nuapada District). Here she gave birth to a boy who was named Kachna Dharwa. When Kachna grew up, he took revenge over his father's death. He burnt a number of Chindas to death in a cave, a few could escape and ran away, and they were called Bhunjia or 'the roasted one'.

In the 19th century the Bhunjia were *gaotia/thekedar* or the headmen of the village, and were responsible for revenue collection in their villages, and for that, they enjoyed some *bhogra* land or revenue free land of the village (Deo, 2009). However, later in the colonial period, they lost their land, position and influence to the non-tribals except in one village, Sunabeda. This village is situated on a plateau at the top of Sunabeda hills. Many Bhunjias preferred to withdrew to the deep forest in the interior and especially to Sunabeda plateau where Bhunjias were already living. Though there is no documentary evidence one may speculate as to what happened. When the administrative agents (Forest, Police and Revenue officers), visited their villages frequently on different occasions and plainsmen (businessmen, cultivators, moneylenders) settled permanently in adjoining area, the outsiders presented them with very serious difficulties in terms of their own ideas about keeping distance from outsiders. Therefore, the Bhunjias withdrew to inaccessible areas, where their own clansmen were already there, beyond the easy reach of the new forces in order to feel safer. This short run adjustment had cumulative implications. In case of Bhunjia, this short run adjustment and withdrawal resulted in the preservation of their unique culture and group solidarity. Some of the customs and traditions the Chaukhutia Bhunjias still preserve in the 21st century is a baffling. Many of them never use shoes not because they cannot afford but to show their profound respect to the mother Earth. The Chaukhutia Bhunjia women generally wear only white saree, use ornaments like necklaces made of beads and coil, glass and brass bangles, anklets and ear-rings made of either aluminium or silver but never use petticoat and blouse. They never use cot and sleep on the floor. They never take outside food. Bhunjias arrange pre-puberty marriage for girl children with an arrow popularly known as *kandbiha* or arrow marriage. They are reluctant to send their daughters to school after puberty. Their kitchen room, popularly known as *Lal Ghar* (Fig-2) (due to red mud wall & thatched roof) is the sacred hut of the Bhunjia tribe and they believe that their deities reside there. The kitchen house is built separately near their house. This is regarded so sacred that not only the outsiders but also the married daughters are not allowed to touch it. They burn down the kitchen shed and construct a new one if anyone outside their tribe enters into it. Thatched roof for dwelling house was common in Bhuanjia villages till recently. Now days they are using burnt earthen tiles instead of thatched roof. The Chaukhutia Bhunjia never eat food cooked by a man or woman who does not belong to their own community.

LAL GHAR [CHAKUTIABHUNJIYA'S KITCHEN]

FIG-2: Lal Ghar

Chuktia Bhunjia never allow outsiders to enter their clan and even their own married daughters are not allowed to return to the clan. They think themselves as 'chokh' or pure as they perform pre-puberty marriage of girls and don't allow other than their clan members to touch the cooking hut where their deities are lodged. The religious life of Bhunjia is very simple. They believe in many Gods and Goddesses (around 46 deities, 24 are from different *Tikr*i or region) who are worshipped in different months on different ritual occasions. Budharaja and Sunadei (Fig- 3&4) are the main God and Goddess of this tribe. Sunadei Jatra (Festival) is the main festival in which they worship Sunadei deity on the day following Vijaya Dasami.

SONADEVI TEMPLE , SUNABEDA   SUNADEVI TEMPLE IN SIDE VIEW

FIG-3&4: Sonadevi Temple and Inside View of Sonadevi Temple

The Chaukhutia Bhunjias have been declared as Primitive Vulnerable Tribal Groups (PVTG) of Odisha. They are found in Sunabeda plateau, Komna block of Nuapada district, Odisha sharing common border with Chhattisgarh State. It spreads over 1000 square kms. forming a considerable chunck of Nuapada district. The plateau varies between 300mts. to 955mts. River Jonk has its origin from this place. About 35 villages are scattered over the plateau. It is the home of Chaukhutia Bhunjia. The natural forest, perennial streams at the hill top attract attention. This place is known as Gauragarh. The climate is much cooler then it is in the plains. The area is natural shelter of wild animals. Therefore, out of 1000sq.kms. of total geographical area of Sunabeda 600 square kms was declared as Wild Life Sanctuary in the year 1983.

Bhunjia Version of Aala Udel Myth
Balibhikam was a just king ruling a kingdom *Gudarai*j with formidable forts and prosperous villages. He was a Bhunjia and enjoyed the blessings of the presiding deities Sunadi, Rupadi, Dwarasani and Budharaja.Balibhikam used to visit Sunabeda region, a part of his kingdom on hunting trips. No outsider ever dared to enter his territory. Once Raja Jaisal's (the ruler of

Mahoba) soldiers by mistake entered the Sunabeda jungle in their hunting trip. They were tracked down by Balibhikam's soldiers and were driven away with a warning not to enter again into Balibhikam's territory. The soldiers of Jaisal on their return praised the scenic natural beauty and importance of Sunabeda jungle and requested their ruler to conquer and include this region in the Mahoban empire. Jaisal agreed with the proposal and made elaborate preparation to attack Balibhikam's kingdom. The latter got the information of the intention and preparation of Jaisal through his spies. Therefore, he made elaborate defensive strategies. He connected the hills of Sunabeda with high and wide wall and road with ditch at the end. This was the strategy to allure the enemy to a trap and kill.

The fierce battle took place between two equally formidable kings but finally Bilibhikam's strategy succeeded. Jaisal's soldiers fell in the trap and faced *dhwansh* or demolition. The points of dhwansh are Kharaldhas, Beniadhas, Godhas, Gogdhas. Jaisal, sensing certain defeat fled the battlefield out of fear but unfortunately his horse got stuk on the bog, *jalki* or a swampy area near village Lodra. In that helpless state Jaisal was beheaded by Balibhikam. Jaisal's queen Deola gave birth to two posthumous sons at Mahoba and named them Aala and Udel. They were taken care by Mahil, brother of Jaisal. They were trained properly in *shastra* and *sastra*. On attaining adulthood Aala became the king and Udel became his deputy. One day Mahil narrated the circumstances leading to the assassination of Jaisal. Aala and Udel took oath to avenge their father's death.

Aala and Udel invited Balibhikam for a duel. The latter accepted the challenge. Before proceeding to the battle field he informed the queens that in case of his death on the battle field pigeon would fly back which he was caring. Balibhikam was killed and the pigeon flew back. On seeing the pigeon, the three queens became remorseful. The elder queens advised the third one Kamla Sati to leave the kingdom as she was pregnant to save the heir of their clan. She escaped to Garhbhata and then to Sandohel hill where she gave birth to a male child. An adivasi Binjhal couple gave shelter to Kamala Sati and her son. Latter with the help of the Binjhals the boy became the ruler.

The Bhunjia myth of Aala Udel reflects their culturally defined meaning of life, their emotions and their territoriality. The myth reflects how zealously the Bhunjias try to preserve their traditional institutions and *adivasi* self-image simultaneously claiming *adivasi raja* an exalted *kshyatria* status. This also reflects their patriarchal value. The escape of pregnant woman is a common motif; it permits claims to exalted antecedents when positive evidence to that effect is lacking. Furthermore, in a matrilineal society, the woman is only the carrier; it is the son who continues the line. Even the Gond, the Paharia and the Chauhan myths have similar escape story. In the above instance, the widow gave birth to boy who later showed extraordinary and supernatural power.

The story of Bhunjia folk drama Aala –Udel

Raja Jaisal, the ruler of *Gudaraij* or Raimado kingdom left behind four sons; Aala, Udel, Derah and Malkham. Each of them was endowed with good qualities of life. Aala, the eldest son inherited his father's throne of *Gudaraij*. He was a great horse rider. He could cross the great waterfall Kharaldhas (A waterfall in Sunabeda hills) on horseback. His brothers helped in the smooth management of the kingdom. Under their able supervision all important hills of *Gudaraij* were connected with artificial roads. The formidable forts Manikgarh, Cheliagarh and Jumlagarh (ruins of these forts are in Sunabeda hills) were built during his reign. *Gudaraij* was well protected by the blessings of the presiding deity Sunadei and her six sister deities and one brother deity Budharaja. Once Udel proposed for a pilgrimage to Purvi Mela (A sacred festival) held at Balgokhar in his father-in- law's kingdom. He wanted to take Inder, the only son of Aala along with him. Aala and other two brothers were reluctant to leave Inder as he was the only son in their family. But Udel insisted and finally reluctantly Aala allowed his son to accompany Udel.

Udel along with Inder reached Balgokhar, the kingdom of Abhinda and entered the palace. From the first floor Chitrarekha, the princes of Balgokhar, saw Inder and fell in love and wanted to marry. The next day they visited the *mela*(festival) on the river bank of Ganga. After sometime Inder was found missing. All attempts to locate Inder became futile. Udel became worried because he had brought Inder in spite of objection from his brothers. He was much worried that his brother might suspect him of a foul play. He became almost mad and was in tears when Inder could not be traced in spite of all possible attempts. Fortunately, his mother- in- law Rani Jamuna informed him confidentially that Inder had been kidnapped by Chitralekha by her magical power and had kept him in a secret place. Chidralekha had mastered magical *sadhana*. Udel in disguise of a *sannyasi* visited Chitrarekha's apartment, but could not trace Inder. Finally, he came to know from the *Bandi* or friends of Chitralekha that Inder and Chitrarekha had entered into Guptabiha or secret marriage. They also informed that Chitrarekha, by her magical power had transformed Inder into an insect and had hidden somewhere beyond their knowledge.Udel made last attempt to search but failed. He returned to his kingdom and revealed the truth to his brothers. They finally decided to attack

Gokhar kindom of Avinda. The great battle took place between to formidable sides for days together at Lodra, Tikrapada, Dadhibaman, Manikgagh etc. There was great loss from both sides and finally both the parties agreed for the peace treaty and agreed to arrange *Parkatbiha* or open marriage of Inder and Chitralekha. A grand marriage ceremony was performed with song, music and dance. Everybody including their deities blessed the new couple on the occasion of their marriage. Thus, the play ends with a happy note. A folk drama is played in the open theatre by the Bhunjia tribe (Fig-5&6). The story of the drama is based on the myth entitled "Ala Udel". The story begins with the description of Raimado kingdom, its prosperity, its strong hill-fort Manikgarh, it's just king Jaisal and his four sons. The play ends in a happy note of marriage between Inder, the son of Aala and Chitralekha, the princes of Balgokhar.

This type of myths does not constitute reliable narratives of events; yet their structure has much to tell us. A careful study of these reveals internal developments and conflict in society, which can be tested in the framework of validated historical findings. We may however ask, what purpose do such myths serve? At what point, does it become necessary to convert the myth to folk drama or to a written *rajapurana*?

Dramatic Performance

The play begins with the invocation of *Mait Maa* (the mother Earth), Sunadei (the presiding deity) and Budharaja (another significant male local deity). The musical instruments are placed together and a short ritual is performed in which the audience actively participates. They offer coconut and incense stick and seasonal fruits. The local Bhunjia Jhankar (priest) initiates the ritual, and then song and dance in praise of local deities begins.

Then the main plot of the Aala Udel folk drama unfolds in the form of energetic songs, dances and dialogue. The dialogues are delivered in *amittrakshyar chhanda* (blank verse) and the actors use local Bhunjia dialect. While some portions are sung by the background chorus the performers use elaborate gesture to act out the text. An overt influence of Chhatisgarhi *Nacha*, Pandwani and Kosli folk dramas *Ushabati Haran, Bilanka Ramayan* and *Dandnach* are noticeable. It is performed on the village square under the open sky and the performers mingle with the audience. The play normally begins at the sunset and continues up to past midnight and sometime till sunrise. Earlier *mashal* or torchlight and Patromax light were used. Now a days they hire generator light in villages where electricity is yet to reach. Instruments such as *dholak, madal, gini, jhanj, and harmonium are* played to make the play more lively. The actor performers are naturally gifted talents. All the characters of the play including the female roles are played by males. They use face powder and jink on the face and hands. The actors use special costume to match the character they represent. As we have observed above, the story is based on an imaginary local history and rich folk tradition which they have conserved and fostered. Aala Udel myth glows with heroism and revenge but Aala Udel folk play is all about compromise and amicable settlement. The marriage scene of Inder and Chitralekha are applauded by the audience. When the marriage ritual of tying of hands of the bride and the bride-groom takes place in the play the audience actively participates by entering the play area. They pour some water on their hand and offer their blessings and present token money as if it was not a play but a real marriage ceremony, a real-life situation. In the process Aala Udel myth has perhaps lost the original moor and purpose, and even at present represents just the opposite of earlier version. But it reflects the changes the Bhunjia society has undergone over the years. This play is an integral part of their life and culture. In the last twenty years this folk drama has not been enacted due to the presence of left-wing extremists in the Sunabeda hills. The script is now worshiped as a *purana* or a religious text. The young generation has not even viewed this folk play.

CHAKUTIA BHUNJIA WOMEN DANCING   CHAKUTIA BHUNJIA

FIG-5 &6: Chakutia Bhunjia Tribes and Dance

References
- C. B. Patel,1995, 'Maraguda Valley, Archaeological Project Proffile', Orissa State Archaeology, Bhubaneswar, Dept. of Culture, Govt. of Orissa.
- Collected during 1991, Indian Council for Historical Study project granted to Lokdrusti, Khariar, for Exploration, Survey and Photographs the ruins of Maraguda Area before the completion of Patora Dam. Survey Report was submitted to ICHR, New Delhisin 1991.

- R.V. Russel,1916, *The Tribes and Castes of the Central Provinces of India*, vol. II, p.325.
- F. Deo, 1984, "Tribal-Non-Tribal Interaction", M. Phil Thesis JNU, P.-56; "Study on the Difficulties Faced by the Children of Bhunjia Tribes", Lokadrusti supported by OPEPA, p.1.
- K.C. Dubey,1961, "Possible Origin of Bhunjia and their Ethnic Relationship: A New Hypothesis", *Eastern Anthropologist*, XIV,1, p.49.
- F. Deo, 2009, *Roots of Poverty*, Ameadeus, Bhubaneswar.
- Collected from sunabeda village in 2006.
- Ala- Udel, a Chhattisgarhi drama, this book was collected from Bijay Bhunjia.

Indigenous Ethno-medicinal Practices and Healing Method in Baiga Tribe of Sonebhadra District of Uttar Pradesh

Dr. Shiv Kumar

Assistant Professor, Department of Anthropology, Model Degree College Nuapada, Odisha, Affiliated to Maa Manikeswari University, Bhawanipatna
Email: shiv.anthro@gmail.com

Abstract:

According to the Botanical Survey of India, 46000 species of plants exist and 705 tribal communities reside here, who are rich in indigenous knowledge. These tribal communities living close to nature have unique indigenous knowledge of using and protecting the plants present around them (Jain, 1998). For centuries, the knowledge of indigenous medicine has been transferred orally to different generations (Ganasen, 2004). These medicines have been used indigenously by the tribal community for centuries, but due to the influence of modern medicine, the use of traditional medicine and traditional healing knowledge have declined to a great extent. Being connected to the borders of four states, Sonebhadra district of Uttar Pradesh is rich in natural wealth. Most of the Sonbhadra district is filled with rivers, mountains, prehistoric places and natural resources. The Baiga tribe consisting of 30006 populations (2011 census) found living in Myorpur, Babhani, Ghorawal blocks of Sonbhadra district. For a long time, the Baiga tribal community has been using this natural wealth for the treatment of various diseases on the basis of indigenous knowledge.

The present research paper focuses on the use of traditional medicinal practices of the Baiga tribe of Sonebhadra district of Uttar Pradesh. Following mixed method, data have been collected from 125 women and 250 men through structured schedule and from 10 indigenous Baiga practitioners and

Vaidyas through interview method. Various plants and their usage for curing various diseases have been documented. An attempt has also been made to show the various methods of preparing ethno-medicines prevalent in the Baiga community and the importance of different plants. It has also been found that the Baiga tribe uses many types of healing methods for the same disease.

Key words: Baiga tribe, Healing method Indigenous ethno-medicinal practices, medicinal plants, Sonebhadra district.

Introduction:

Illness and health are common human experiences in primitive and folk communities and every society has a conceptual method of defining them. Since the 19th century, a lot of work has been done in the field of diseases. In this sequence, Rudolf Virchow (1848) tried to look at medicine from a socio-cultural perspective. He said that social conditions act as factors of disease. He published a journal 'Die Medizinische Reformin' (1848), in which medicine was completely described as a subject of social science. Since the 19th century, indigenous knowledge became a subject of enthusiasm, in which various social scientists propounded many theories from their study and research. Many different indigenous knowledge practices have been considered among rural and tribal communities. The study of indigenous or local knowledge has proved effective for the development of communities. Indigenous knowledge is closely related to the medical practices in the different tribal communities, which reflects the unique healing practices through their indigenous ethno-medicinal practices.

Ethno-medicine, which is the study of traditional medical methods, is concerned with how different cultures perceive health, illness, and disease as well as how people access healthcare and engage in healing rituals (Krippner, 2003). Since ancient times, people have found healing through the complex multi-disciplinary discipline of ethno-medicine, which incorporates the use of plants, spirituality, and the natural world (Lowe et al., 2000). The study of traditional medicine, or ethno-medicine, is concerned with how different cultures see health, illness, and disease as well as how people access healthcare and engage in healing rituals (Krippner, 2003). Since ancient times, people have found healing through the complex multi-disciplinary discipline of ethno-medicine, which incorporates the use of plants, spirituality, and the natural world (Lowe et al., 2000). Indigenous medicine practices are following by traditional healing method which has cultural importance. The cultural dimension of traditional healing practices indicates the fact that the continuing and socially accepted heritage contains both the material and non-material aspects used within the context of sickness.

Anthropologists believe that culture affects the activities of all humans both biologically and non-biologically. Therefore, it is universal for every human to take care of illness and health. Every community has its own distinct culture. The culture of that community determines to a large extent why people of that culture suffer from certain diseases and what type of treatment is required. This has led to the development of Medical Anthropology as a sub-discipline of Socio-cultural Anthropology. Anthropological interest in the study of ethno-medicine practices grows out of the fact that health is not only a function of medical care but also an important aspect of the overall underlying development of individuals in a society. Health is related to the socio-cultural and economic status of an individual, family composition, customs, beliefs and values, life-style, type of household and use of medical resources available in the society. Thus, the study of socio-cultural influences on health and diseases in anthropology not only involves a subject of immediate medical relevance but is also of special interest because of their impact on the foundations of human ecology and human evolution. It is not only the diseased and the medical personnel who are the subject of medical anthropology but also the beliefs and practices relating to health as a socio-cultural system in different societies in the present times. Nature had produced various types of herbs and plants even before the emergence of humans. These herbs contain all the qualities that are necessary to prevent illness and cure the disease. There is no authentic document available as to when and which plant was first used by humans as medicine, but in our country, the Rig Veda is the first authentic text to provide information about medicinal plants. Through the *Rig Veda*, we come to know that in ancient times, the Aryan sages used a plant called 'Som' as medicine for the first time. In the ancient Indian system of medicine, there is more description of medicines made from herbs. One of the main reasons for this is that as soon as humans fell ill, they first used those plants as medicine which they could easily find near them. This is the reason why Vedic practitioners and authors concluded that the patient can be cured only by the herbs growing around him. In this, the important role of indigenous knowledge of tribal communities can be seen since ancient times. Description of tribal and *adivasi* groups is also found in our ancient texts and literature. Baiga is most common tribal community which is found in many states. Baiga tribe is unique to their indigenous medicinal practices. Baiga known as the son of the earth is a primitive tribe of India. The Baiga tribe is known for its unique culture and social system.

This research article focuses on the medical system and indigenous medicinal practices of the Baiga tribe living in Ghorawal, Myorpur and Babhni blocks of Sonbhadra district of Uttar Pradesh state. Sonbhadra in Uttar Pradesh is famous for its minerals, power plants, cave paintings, Fossil Park, tribal identity, mines and mostly natural beauty. The whole population of this district is 1862559 (census-2011). The whole tribal population of tribal communities is 20.67% of total population of this district (census-2011). The major tribes found in Sonbhadra district, include Baiga, Kharwar, Khairwar, Parahiya, Pankha, Panika, Agariya, Patari, Chero, Bhuiya, and Bhuinya. The most famous and common tribe is Baiga, which is known as the ethno-medicinal healer of natural therapy and practices.

The Baiga tribal's dress up in colorful costumes on festivals, and celebrations, which reflect their indigenous tradition. Their livelihood and lifestyle is based on the forest. Their main means of livelihood is collecting herbs, food items and wild produce from the forest and earning livelihood from *bewar* (shifting cultivation) farming. The Baiga tribe is completely influenced by natural biology and environmental friendliness. The Baiga tribes have many different beliefs. Their indigenous medical system is also included in these beliefs. Due to the factors of social, cultural, economic and medical changes are constantly seen in Baiga society. Since prehistoric period, man has been using plants as medicines, for which many evidences have been found. There are 46000 species of plants in India and 705 tribal communities with 160 linguistic groups live, who are rich in indigenous knowledge. These tribal communities living close to nature have unique indigenous knowledge of using the plants present around them (Jain, 1998). Tribal Medicine various tribal communities around the world are the protectors of natural wealth and are experts in botanical medicines. The knowledge of indigenous medicine has been orally transferred from one generation to another (Ganasen, 2004).

Indigenous ethno-medicinal practices are the traditional and ritualistic method which the tribal society associates with its socio-cultural beliefs and values. The Baiga tribe has also been transferring this belief from generation to generation. This research paper investigates these values and beliefs. This research paper is also important because in today's changing times, all forms of society are being influenced directly and indirectly by modernization and westernization, but the Indigenous traditional medicinal practice prevalent in the Baiga society in the form of Indigenous knowledge system still holds its place. Direct evidence of this was seen when all allopathic medicines failed during the period of Covid-19, then the traditional medical system protected the values of life in the local society.

Objectives:

The objective of this article was to observe the various indigenous ethno-medicinal practices prevalent in the Baiga tribal society, who lives their lives through indigenous medical system based on their indigenous knowledge system in the natural environment in a tribal district of Uttar Pradesh known as Sonebhadra and to document the methods of use.

Methodology:

For a long time, the Baiga tribal community has been using this natural resource for the treatment of various diseases on the basis of indigenous knowledge. For this, a structured schedule was prepared by the author, which included questions related to the indigenous medicinal practice and healing techniques of their use. This schedule was asked to various women, men and indigenous medicinal practitioners of the Baiga tribe. In this article, information and evidence have been collected through interview method from 125 women and 250 men and 10 indigenous Baiga practitioners and *Vaidyas*.

The Baiga: Indigenous Medicinal and Healing Practitioner

The Baiga tribe is considered the Particularly Vulnerable Tribal Groups (PVTGs) community. This tribe is found in Madhya Pradesh, Chhattisgarh, Jharkhand, Bihar, Odisha, Uttar Pradesh, Maharashtra, and West Bengal. The Baiga community is the regular medicine practitioner for the neighboring tribal community. The word Baiga is derived from the Vaidya, which means 'medicine man' (Bhagabati et al. 2019). The Baiga community mainly resides in the dense forest area in a scattered manner.

In the form of Indigenous medicine, Baiga Ethno-medicinal practitioners traditionally inherit from their ancestors or through dreams. The healing techniques of traditional medicine mainly consist of religious beliefs, witchcraft, spells, rituals, exorcism and herbs and barks of trees and plants obtained from the forests around them.

Baiga people easily believe in witchcraft, exorcism (*tantra-mantra*) and ghost obstacles. They have an unshakable belief that the exorcism of practitioners *Dewar, Ojha and Gunia* has the power to cure all diseases. They have knowledge of many types of herbs and barks in the form of indigenous knowledge, through which they have the power to cure various diseases and disorders of people in their society. During field work, the author observed that *Dewar, Gunia, Ojha* do not take money for treatment. Their belief behind this is that if any *Dewar, Gunia, Ojha* takes money, then their *Tantra-Mantra* (spells-rituals) power (*Guniyapan*) ends. The Baiga follow many social, family and community rules to maintain the success of their traditional indigenous knowledge of *Tantra-Mantra*, exorcism. Patients voluntarily give gifts to them. If the medicine works on the patient, then goat, chicken with reverse wing, pig, coconut and liquor made from Mahua flower has to be given. In this way it has been seen that Indigenous ethno-medicinal practitioner and healer experts get a special place in the local Baiga society.

Indigenous Medicinal Practices and Healing Techniques:

The present attempts to highlight the most commonly used medicinal plant through indigenous practices by local healer on the basis of ritual believes. Baiga healers have a different type of techniques and method which is runs inside the local society. Sonebhadra district of Uttar Pradesh is rich in natural resources, which is naturally connected to the border of four states. Most of the Sonbhadra district is filled with rivers, mountains, prehistoric places and natural resources. The area of Sonbhadra district is 6,788 square kilometers and it is the second largest district of Uttar Pradesh. The Baiga tribe living in this district is found in Myorpur, Babhani, Ghorawal blocks of Sonbhadra, whose population is about 30006 (2011 census). In the present research, about 26 plants and 11 healing methods have been documented, which are easily available in the natural environment and local fields of Ghorawal, Babhani, Myorpur blocks, which the Baiga people use in their medical system. It was also found that the Baiga tribe uses many types of methods for the same disease.

Various plants used as medicines have been documented. Along with this, it has also been described which part of these plants is used for which disease. An attempt has also been made to show the importance of various ethno-medicines and methods of preparation of plants prevalent in the Baiga community. It clear that different parts of plants are used for different problems and plants of the same species are used for different problems. Medicines are prepared by indigenous practitioners by mixing either one or several plants. These plants treat minor problems like headache to serious problems like snake bite. This knowledge is indigenous and beneficial as well as less expensive, but due to the influence of modernity and lack of plants, today this indigenous knowledge is in a state of extinction. Tribal societies have a lot of knowledge about medicinal plants and related information.

Table No. 1 Medicinal Plants used by Indigenous Medicinal Practitioner of Baiga Tribe

Sl. No.	English Name	Scientific Name (Botanical Name)	Useful Part of Plant	Medicinal Uses
1	Bamboo	Bambusa vulgaris	Stem & Leave	Antioxidant properties. Bamboo leaf extracts may help prevent cardiovascular diseases. Anti-inflammatory properties
2	Hibiscus	Hibiscusrosa sinesis	Flower	Treating colds, inflammation, Weight loss, Cholestrol and high blood pressure
3	Lemon	Citrus limon (Linn.)	Fruit	Treating infections, reducing inflammation, and improving digestion etc.

4	Oriental Cashew or Nut Tree	Semecarpus anacardium	Fruit, Oil & Seed	The oil is applied on wounds and sores to prevent pus formation. The juice of the nut is used in ascites, rheumatism, asthma, neuralgia, epilepsy, and psoriases
5	Butternut tree	Madhuca indica Madhuca longifolia	Fruit, Flower, Leave & Seed	Mahua oil is used for skin, hair, and massage. Treating anti-inflammatory, anti-ulcer, anti-oxidant, analgesic etc. Formation of alcohol
6	Pot marigold	Calendula officinalis Senna occidentalis	Seed	Treats menstrual irregularities, eye problems, peptic ulcers etc
7	Cassia	Cassia occidentalis	Seed	Treatment of fever, typhoid fever, malaria, and hepatitis
8		Cissampelos pareira	Seed, root & bark	Treat Ulcers and wounds, fever, asthma, and inflammation. It has been used to treat snakebites.
9	Mexican poppy, Argemone	Argemone maxicana	Seed	Treat skin infections, psoriasis, insect and scorpion bites

10	Crown flower or Giant milk-weed	Calotropis gigancia	Root	Skin diseases, Pain, inflammation, leprosy, and dysentery
11	Cowhage or Cowitch	Mucuna prurtia	Root, seeds, leaves & stems	Increase sperm count, regulate ovulation,
12	Pala indigo or Dyer's Olean-der	Wrightia tinctoria	Stem, bark & stem	Used in treat-ment of diar-rhea, various skin disorders
13	croton	Codiaeum variega-tum	Stem	Treating diar-rhea, stomach aches, and ex-ternal wounds, malaria, pain, and weight loss
14	Mugwort	Artemisia vulgaris	Stem	Treat irregular menstruation, hypertension, & Itching
15	Black oil plant or Intellect tree	Celastrus paniculatus	Stem	Treat pain, inflammation, osteoarthritis & cuts for healing
16	Bishop's Weed, or Ca-rum	Carum copticum	Seed	Digestive issues, respiratory prob-lems, Asthma, Coughing and joint pain
17	Castor bean	Ricinus communisl	Seed	Treat a variety of conditions, including in-flammation, constipation, liver disorders
18	Broad bean or faba	Vicia faba	Seed	Treat Diabetes, Stomach ulcers, Anemia, aller-gies

19	Pongam tree or Indian Beech Tree	Pongamia pinnata	Seed, leaf, flower, stem & bark	Treat skin diseases, ulcers, tumors, piles, bronchitis
20	Purple tephrosia	Tephrosia purpurea	Seed, leaves, stem & bark	Used to treat asthma, Wound healing, piles.
21	Indian coral tree, tiger's claw, and coral tree	Erythrina variegate Madagascar periwinkle	Flower & leaves	Relieve pain and inflammation in rheumatic joints, Anti-asthmatic and anti-epileptic
22	Cayenne Jasmine Or Madagascar Periwinkle	Catharanthus roseus	Flower	Treating cancer, diabetes, and skin conditions
23	East Indian ebony	Diospyros melanoxylon	Fruit, leaves & bark	Used to treat diarrhea, diabetes, cooling and astringent effect
24	Neem	Azadirachta indica	Fruit, leaves, seeds & peel	Treats fungal, bacterial, viral infections, blemishes, eczema, heals wounds, Increases immunity, antioxidant
25	Bedda nut	Terminala bellirica	Fruit	Used as an astringent, laxative, antipyretic, Menstrual disorders, Wound healing, Antioxidant & Respiratory issues
26	Portia tree	Thespesia populnea	Fruit	Skin ailments, brain and liver disorders, and wounds & antibacterial

(Source: Collected and compiled by Researcher from first hand data)

Table No.2: Healing Methods related to Indigenous Medicinal Plants

Sl. No.	Disease	Name of Medicinal Plant	Useful Part of the Plant	Healing Method
1	Diarrhea	Cowhage & Crown flower	Root, seed, bark & leaves	The roots or leaves or bark of cowhage and crown flower are grinding and mix with water.
2	Diarrhea	Butternut tree (Mahua)	Fruit	The juice of Mohua is poured into a plate and the sick child is made to sit on it.
3	cold and cough	Bishop's Weed, or Carum	Seeds	Roast carum and make pills with honey and feed it
4	Snake Bite	Neem	Bark	Neem's bark is grinding and given continuously.
5	hot wind or Loo	Cassia	Seeds	Cassia seeds are soaked for 5-6 nights and are chewed and eaten in the morning.
6	Headache	Pot marigold	Seeds	Fresh marigold seeds are fed.
7	Tooth ache	Neem	Fruit	Neem fruit is burnt and applied to teeth.
8	Tooth ache	Mexican poppy, Argemone	Seeds	Grind the seeds and press them into the teeth.
9	Eye infections	Mexican poppy, Argemone	Roots	The root is tied around the child's neck.
10	Weakness	Black oil plant or Intellect tree	Stem &bark	After delivery, the mother is given a toothpick.
11	Scorpion bite	Cowhage or Cowitch	Roots	It is applied on the scorpion bite.

(Source: Collected and compiled by Researcher from first hand data)

Indigenous Healing Practices and Socio-Cultural beliefs:

Many diseases are treated by using wild seeds, stem, leaves, herbs and barks on the basis of their indigenous knowledge. Every disease has its own herbs and barks. Some indigenous herbs and barks are known to every person in the village, some such herbs and barks are known only to the indigenous practitioners like *Dewar, Ojha, Gunia, Vaidya* of Baiga who has indigenous knowledge of those herbs and barks of wild trees and plants. There are practices of treating various types of big and small diseases with the herbs and barks of wild trees and plants found in the surroundings. In the Baiga community, there are practices of curing diseases by using herbs and barks obtained from the forests around them, even for the major diseases, whether related to gynaecological diseases, general diseases related to teeth, ears, nose, eyes, major diseases and diseases related to wild animals and pets in their homes. Before giving the herb to the sick person, the herbs and ulcers are awakened with mantras, after which the *Dewar, Ojha, Gunia* grind the herb and make it drink with water or Mahua flower liquor. The dosage of Dewar medicine is given to the patient according to the disease. If the patient has a long-term illness, then he is given medicine for a longer period. While awakening the herbs and ulcers, a coconut, Sarai Lasa incense, a bottle of Mahua flower liquor is given as a gift to the *Dewar/ Gunia/Ojha*. The herb does not work without awakening the Dewar. This is the belief of the Baiga practitioners *Dewar, Gunia, Ojha*. There are some such herbs too, which are given to the patient immediately when the disease occurs. Due to which there is no possibility of the disease increasing, immediately after that the treatment is done by the practitioner *Dewar, Gunia or Ojha* in a proper manner.

Conclusion:

Since prehistoric times, humans have been using various plants present in their local environment for medicinal purposes. The Baiga tribe has a close relationship with their local forests. The Baiga community living in Ghorawal, Myorpur and Babhani blocks of Sonbhadra district of Uttar Pradesh has indigenous ethno-medicinal knowledge of various plants, which they use in various indigenous healing methods. There is a need to collect the various indigenous methods present in the Baiga tribe and get them recognized by indigenous practitioners like *Gunia, Dewar* and *Ojha*. The Baiga tribe has also been transferring this belief from generation to generation. This research paper is also important because in today's changing times, all forms of society are being influenced directly and indirectly by modernization and westernization, but the Indigenous traditional medicinal practice prevalent in the Baiga society in the form of Indigenous knowledge system still holds its place. Direct evidence of this was seen when all allopathic medicines failed during the period of Covid-19, then the traditional medical system protected the values of life in the local society.

References:

- Ahirwar R K. (2017). "Ethno-medicinal investigations among the Baiga tribes, district Anuppur, Madhya Pradesh, India". Nelumbo,59(2):181-186.

- Ahirwar, Ramesh Kumar (2015). "Indian Folk Medicinal Plants of District Mandla Madhya Pradesh" LAP LAMBERT Academic Publishing GmbH & Co. KG, Heinrich-Bocking-Str. 68,66121 Saarbrucken, Germany. ISBN: 978-3-65942534-9

- Bhagabati K, Chandel VK, Yadav A. (2019). Marginalisation of the elderly amidst changing social dynamics: A case of Baiga tribe. Research & Development Journal, HealpAge India.;25(01).

- Bhasin, V. (2007). Medical Anthropology: Healing Practices in Contemporary Sikkim. Delhi. India. (Pp. 56-64) in V. Bhasin and M. K. Bhasin (eds), Anthropology Today: Trends, scope and Applications. Delhi: Kamla-Raj Enterprises

- Bhosle SV, Ghule VP, Aundhe DJ, Jagtap Suresh. (2009). Ethnomedical knowledge of plants used by the tribal people of Purandhar in Maharashtra, India. Ethnobot. Leaflets.;13:1353-1361.

- Boas, Franz. (1920). The methods of ethnology. American Anthropologist. Vol. 22 (4): 311-321.

- Chopra, R.N., S.L. Nayar and I.C. Chopra, (1958). The Glossary of Indian Medicinal plants. CSIR. New Delhi

- Clements, F.E. (1932). Primitive Concepts of Disease. Anthropology Publication: University of California in American Archaeology and Ethnology. 32: 185-252

- Dwivedi T, Chandra Kanta, Singh LR, Sharma IP. A list of some important medicinal plants with their medicinal uses from Himalayan State Uttarakhand, India. Journal of Medicinal Plants Studies. 2019;7(2):106-116.

- Jadhv, Dinesh. (2008). Medicinal plants of Madhya Pradesh & Chhattisgarh. Delhi: Daya publishing house.

- Jain, S.K. (2002). Bibliography of Indian Ethnobotany.Jodhpur: Scientific Pblisher.

- Jose Boben, K. (1998). Tribal Medicine: Continuity and Change. New Delhi: A.P.H. Publishing Corporation.

- Joshi, P.C. and Anil Mahajan (1990). Studies in Medical Anthropology. New Delhi: Reliance publishing house.

- Kleinman. A. (1980). Patients and Healers in the Context of Culture: An

Exploration of the Borderland between Anthropology, Medicine and Psychiatry. Berkeley: University of California Press.

- Kumar P, Dangwal LR, Uniyal P, Lal T. (2022). Ethno-medicinal uses of some aquatic plants in district Haridwar, Uttarakhand. International Journal of Botany Studies.;7(1):388-93.

- Kumar, K. Anil. (2006). Ethno-medicine, indigenous healers and disease healing practices among the Kolam of Adilabad district of Andhra Pradesh. Journal of social anthropology, vol.3No.1 (june-2006): 75-88.

- Russell, R.V. and Heera Lal. (1916). The Tribes and Caste of Central provision of India, Macmillan & Co, London.

- Tiwari, S. K. (1997). Baigas of Central India: habitat and culture of a primitive tribe. New Delhi: Anmol Publication.

Business-Society Interface: *Implications of CSR in Socio-Economic Empowerment of Tribal Women in Odisha*

Dr. Manosmita Mahapatra

Assistant Professor in Sociology, Ravenshaw University, Cuttack
Email: manosmita1065@gmail.com

Abstract

Much is being written regarding the contribution of companies to the interest of community development as a part of their social obligations. Corporate Social Responsibility (CSR) is the prism through which the companies route their initiatives for developmental activities in the social sectors often on a sustainable basis. The present paper represents a modest endeavour to comprehend the CSR contributions of the Vedanta Aluminium Limited (VAL) company to community development in general and the promotion of healthcare, education and livelihood of women in particular especially among the Dongria Kondh, Kutiya Kandha, Lanjia Saora and Santhal tribes located in Lanjigarh, Jharsuguda. in Odisha. Further, it's equally significant to make sense of the overall efforts of the company in the direction of women's empowerment in these tribal communities. In addition, the study opens up further lines of inquiry to unearth the constitutive linkage between company and community in particular and business and social sector in general. The arguments of the paper revolve around the data reflected in the CSR annual sustainability reports of the said company.

Keywords: Corporate Social Responsibility, Women's Empowerment, Healthcare, Livelihood, Tribal Development.

Introduction

Business as a component owes its existence to the larger society.

Corporate Social Responsibility (CSR) brings an interface of business and society by focusing on the socio-economic development of the underprivileged. According to The World Business Council for Sustainable Development (WBCSD), CSR is defined as the commitment of business to contribute to sustainable economic development, working with employees, their families, the local community and society at large to improve their quality of life (WBCSD, 2002). The new dimensions of development include not only the narrow domain of economic growth and profit rather on the larger social dimension by making the community as their significant stakeholder. Social involvement of corporates in society is not just a reciprocal or business relationship; rather community participation provides companies the opportunities to invest in fostering, trusting and understanding community relationships (Green and Hunton, 2003). Although earlier it was included only an a management concept but later on CSR is seen as an umbrella concept which includes all the elements of business-society relations such as business ethics, corporate citizenship, corporate governance, sustainability, and stakeholder theory. Realizing the corporate sectors constraints in playing the roles as agents of development, the CSR initiatives need to be implemented with the involvement of the government agency to assist community development. Moreover, they are encouraged to embark into partnership with government agencies to effectively implement CSR programs and initiatives as their CSR strategy (Ideamudia, 2007).

Large corporations have begun intensifying their CSR engagement under pressure of meeting the societal obligation (Jamali, 2008). Wood (1991) recommended that companies should integrate CSR into their business strategy and operations and that CSR should be monitored by the board of directors. The report also emphasized the importance of transparency and accountability in CSR reporting. Hence, community as a stakeholder and hence community development as a business strategy, CSR has moved from a philanthropic approach to have a sociological perspective by addressing issues pertinent to social development especially in rural areas like health care practices, street lights, infrastructure development, livelihood generation, education and environmental sustainability.

CSR in Community Development

Many companies in the name of development grab the land of the tribal people and debar them from their basic rights and heritage culture. It affects their livelihood making them almost homeless. The precarious situation of the development induced displacement is rampantly growing in India and the most vulnerable target has always been these marginalized tribal people. It is only recently that there has been a transformation of the focus of the Multinationals to extend the hand of help to the community being displaced for the establishment of firms and the development of the peripheral areas of the location of the firm as well. William Frederick argued that business resources should also be used for broad social good and corporations assume certain responsibility to society which extends beyond their economic and legal obligations (Fedrerick, 1960). In order to bring a balanced business perspective and sustainable development of the community, the concept of business in community has gained ground where more and more companies are seen to behave in a socially responsible manner with an ethical display of concern towards community sustainable development. The companies make such policies that keep the community as its most important stakeholder and enhance the development both in terms of economic growth and sustainability. In this venture, there has also been the involvement of Government and NGOs in the new forms of public private partnership. Thus, the corporate display of social responsibility has become widespread over the past two decades (Vogel, 2006). Moreover, transparency and accountability of corporations to the community gives an enhanced way of carrying a trustworthy relationship of Business Corporations with the society as an important stakeholder.

Since the year 2000, over 5000 business firms have subscribed to the UN Global Compact call to emerge in self-regulation in order to fill the gap that has emerged as a result of the process of globalization. A few times it has been seen that the companies prefer to go beyond philanthropy and engage in true CSR activities, whereas other companies were seen only to engage in community for their brand image and enhance their business for profit motive. It is only recently that companies are facing a mandatory policy for community development. The Companies Act 2013, any company having a net worth of rupees 500 crore or more or a turnover of rupees 1,000 crore or more or a net profit of rupees five crore or more, those companies have to spend at least 2% of last three years' average net profits on CSR activities as specified in Schedule VII of the Companies Act 2013, and as amended from time to time. Following are the areas where CSR promotes investments:

1. Eradication of extreme hunger and poverty.
2. Gender equity and women's empowerment.
3. Promotion of education.
4. Reducing child mortality and improving maternal health.
5. Combating HIV/AIDS, malaria, and other diseases.
6. Environmental sustainability.

7. Social business projects.
8. Employment enhancing vocational skills.
9. Contribution to the Prime Minister's relief fund and other such state/central funds.
10. And such other matters as may be prescribed.

There has been an increase in public awareness of corporations' impact on societyfor which corporate social reporting has been maintained through their annual sustainability reports mostly in their websites to create transparency and run an ethical business-society interlace. Among the various social responsibility activities, it is often seen that many companies prioritise the local needs of the community and create CSR strategies which are often need-based to bring social change. They are often seen to have a basic focus on the health care practice, education and income generation through livelihood strategies. For instance, a study conducted by (Mahapatra, 2018) depicts the concept of explicit CSR where the communities are taken as stakeholders to influence the social structure through the CSR programs. The company provides economic assistance, bank linkages to help the rural women to form SHGs and carries responsibility towards their capability building and skill development. It also enhances the income through market connections and by providing training in tailoring, local crafts, animal husbandry and organic farming which promotes women entrepreneurship. Also, Sharma (2011) opines that CSR programmes not only economically empowered women but also made them united at community levels. It bridged income disparity. The study highlighted how the marginalized women suddenly got some meaning of life. Their community bond increased through their newly found livelihood activities. Chapple and Moon (2005) conducted a study they found there has been various works of CSR with importance to its community development. Its community participation basically focuses on education and training, and health, community development, girls' education and disability. Saleh et al (2010) have conducted a study and viewed that CSR agenda is the way to initiate the involvement of the companies in socio economic development of the society. Through the CSR agenda the companies can provide relevant training programs and workshops to improve individual knowledge and skills. Companies provide a mode of communication and educational sponsorship to elevate the standard of education of the individual. Companies also provide financial aid to underprivileged sections especially women to elevate the standard of living.

Aim and Focus of the Paper

The study focuses on the role of corporate social responsibility on enhancing the socio-economic empowerment of tribal women for community development. It attempts to depict the ethical role of business in society by adopting business strategies to bring a transformation in the health care practices, education and livelihood generation of tribal women. The study is carried out by secondary sources of data collection by the reported information of the company. The paper emphasizes the CSR of Vedanta Company located in Lanjigarh, Jharsuguda in Odisha. The objective is to understand the CSR initiatives of Vedanta Company on the tribal women empowerment with regard to health, education and livelihood generation. The research gap shows CSR has always been dealt with as a concept mostly in management academic literature and very few studies have focused on the community development approach especially from a marginalized gendered perspective. It is in this context; the present study becomes relevant as it analyses the CSR initiatives taken by the Multinationals towards tribal women empowerment thereby depicting "explicit CSR" and sustainable development.

Tribal women's precarious scenario depicts that they face lots of socio-cultural barriers in health care accessibility, educational facilities and income generation sources. With survival in remote rural areas, healthcare infrastructure is minimal or non-existent. It is even worse for reproductive health care thereby increasing the mortality rates in Odisha. Traditional healers over modern medical treatment have limited access to skilled healthcare and inadequate Governmental facilities are another challenge. Patriarchal norms and gender inequality debars them from income generation sources making them a lifelong dependent person except for few engaging in agricultural related activities. Educational barriers are even greater including their socio-cultural situations which require an early marriage and pregnancy and language barrier forms another challenge for accessibility of education. Economic constraints and gender discrimination for girl child education at household level is considered normal. Keeping these issues of tribal women in the backdrop, the paper attempts to depict the role of CSR in tribal women empowerment through community development and focusing largely on health care, educational facilities and livelihood generation programs.

Findings and Discussions

Tribal communities in India, particularly in regions where Vedanta operates, are experiencing significant benefits from various projects aimed at enhancing their socio-economic conditions. In Odisha, Vedanta Aluminium

Limited (VAL) has implemented a variety of initiatives focused on community development, health, education, and sustainable livelihoods. The company's operations in Jharsuguda and Lanjigarh have led to substantial investments aimed at improving the quality of life for local communities. Vedanta Ltd. has made significant contributions to community development through its Corporate Social Responsibility (CSR) initiatives in Odisha. These initiatives focus on sustainable agriculture, skill development, healthcare, and women's empowerment, leading to improved livelihoods and overall community wellbeing. Notable tribes benefiting from these projects include the Dongria Kondh, Kutiya Kandha, Lanjia Saora and Santhal tribes. The total investment in Odisha for the fiscal year 2023-2024 amounted to Rs 3,90,000 million, directly benefiting over 1,32,996 individuals across various sectors, including healthcare, education, women's empowerment, skill development, and sustainable livelihoods.

Healthcare Initiatives

In Odisha, Vedanta's healthcare initiatives have been pivotal in improving community health outcomes. The Aarogya project which operates both in Jharsuguda and Lanjigarh, provided essential healthcare services to over 76,247 individuals. The project included mobile health units that conducted health camps, reaching more than 37,754 people. Additionally, the Nikshay-Mitra initiative supported over 700 tuberculosis (TB) patients with nutritional aid and medical assistance, ensuring comprehensive care for those affected by the disease. The focus on preventive healthcare through awareness campaigns has also been instrumental in addressing common health issues in the region. Healthcare is a critical area of focus for tribal communities, and the FACOR Sathi Aarogya project addresses this by providing essential medical services and health education. The initiative has conducted 246 mobile health camps, offering free checkups and consultations to 15,238 beneficiaries in operational areas, including members of the Dongria Kondh tribe. Additionally, the Nikshay-Mitra initiative supports 30 TB patients with diagnostic, nutritional, and vocational aid, ensuring comprehensive care for vulnerable populations.

Education Initiatives

Vedanta has prioritized education through various programs aimed at enhancing learning outcomes for children and adolescents. The Project Vidyagraha initiative in Jharsuguda improved secondary education, achieving a remarkable 100% pass rate in 5 out of 6 schools. This initiative supported over 7,500 students from Class 6 to Class 12, providing essential resources and training for teachers. Furthermore, the Vedanta Mini Science Centre was established to promote STEM education, benefiting over 3,000 students by providing hands-on learning experiences and access to modern educational tools. Education is another vital aspect of community development. The FACOR Sathi Shiksha Amrit Pariyojana project aims to enhance educational opportunities for children and adolescent girls in rural areas, including those from the Santhal tribe. This initiative has supported 158 students with educational materials and established 3 science labs, benefiting 288 students by improving STEM education. Furthermore, the project promotes menstrual hygiene management through Kishori clubs, conducting 26 sessions and distributing 590 kits to 694 adolescent girls.

Sustainable Livelihoods

Sustainable livelihoods have been a key focus area for Vedanta in Odisha. The Jeevika Samriddhi initiative promoted sustainable farming practices, benefiting 545 farming households and increasing productivity by 45%. This project emphasized the importance of modern agricultural techniques, including the use of solar-powered irrigation systems and crop diversification. Additionally, the Nand Ghar project established over 6,000 centres across 14 states, benefiting 2, 40,000 children and 1, 80,000 women, with a focus on nutrition and early childhood education.

The company has made significant strides in empowering women through the Sakhi initiative, which has positively impacted 1,880 women involved in micro-enterprises. This project has facilitated financial literacy and skill development, enabling women to secure loans and improve their economic independence. In Odisha, the Sakhi program has helped women save a cumulative total of Rs 14.5 million, with Rs 12.8 million in loans secured for various income-generating activities. The initiative has fostered a sense of community and collaboration among women, enhancing their social standing and decision-making capabilities.

Vedanta's commitment to skill development is evident in its various training programs aimed at enhancing employability among local youth. The Vedanta Skill Development Initiative in Lanjigarh trained 280 students in various trades, achieving an impressive 80% placement rate. The training programs focus on providing practical skills relevant to the local job market, ensuring that graduates are well-prepared for employment opportunities. The Zinc Kaushal initiative further supported over 1, 00,000 individuals across Odisha, equipping them with essential skills for sustainable livelihoods.

With regard to the sustainable agriculture initiatives, one of the key projects benefiting tribal farmers is the WADI initiative, which promotes orchard-based development. This project has directly supported 500 tribal farmers from the Dongria Kondh tribe across 8 villages in the Chas and Chandankiyari Blocks of Bokaro District. The initiative has converted 450 acres of barren land into cultivable land, resulting in increased productivity and income. Farmers involved in the project have reported an average income of ₹13,000 per season through intercropping, which includes seasonal vegetables and other crops. Additionally, the project has developed 10 poultry yards, 10 piggery units, and 15 vermicompost units, providing new income opportunities for landless farmers.

The skill development initiative shows the Vedanta ESL Skill School is another significant initiative that has trained over 150 unemployed youths, including members of the Santhal tribe, in various trades, including Sewing Machine Operation and Solar PV Installation. The program has achieved an impressive 80% placement rate, with graduates securing jobs at companies like Adani Power and Mahindra Techno Ltd. This skill development initiative not only enhances individual livelihoods but also contributes to the local economy by producing skilled workers who can meet industry demands.

Empowering women through self-help groups depicts the Sakhi program is dedicated to empowering women in tribal communities, including the Kutiya Kandha tribe, by enhancing their socio-economic status through Self-Help Groups (SHGs). This initiative has succeeded in enabling hundreds of women to obtain loans, secure savings and attain some degree of financial independence. The program also provides entrepreneurship training, enabling women to establish and sustain their businesses, thereby improving their social standing and community participation.

Conclusion

Corporate Social Responsibility (CSR) plays a vital role in fostering sustainable community development. By aligning business objectives with social and environmental goals, companies can contribute positively to local communities through initiatives like education, healthcare, infrastructure, and environmental protection. Through targeted CSR initiatives, companies can support education, vocational training, and skill development programs tailored to the needs of tribal women, enhancing their employability and income-generating potential. CSR can also focus on improving access to healthcare, sanitation, and clean water, which significantly impacts the overall well-being of women in tribal communities. By fostering entrepreneurship, providing microfinance opportunities, and supporting women's cooperatives, CSR can empower tribal women to become financially independent and self-reliant. Effective CSR practices not only enhance a company's reputation but also build strong relationships with communities, promoting social equity and economic growth. When corporations invest in the well-being of the communities they operate in, they help create a more inclusive and sustainable future, benefiting both the organization and society at large.

References

- Chapple, W., & Moon, J. (2005). Corporate Social Responsibility (CSR) in Asia: A Seven-Country Study of SCR Web Site Reporting. *Business & Society*, 44, 415-441.
- Frederick, W.C. (1960) The Growing Concern over Business Responsibility. *California Management Review*, 2, 54-61.
- Green, A. O., & Hunton-Clarke, L. (2003). A Typology of Stakeholder Participation for Company Environmental Decision-Making. *Business Strategy and the Environment*, **12**(5), 292–299.
- Ideamudia, U. (2008). Conceptualizing the CSR and Development Debate: Bridging Existing Analytical Gaps. *Journal of Corporate Citizenship*, 29 (Spring), 91-110).
- Jamali, Dima.2008. A Stakeholder Approach to Corporate Social Responsibility: A Fresh Perspective into Theory and Practice. *Journal Of Business Ethics*, Vol 82. Pp 213-231.
- Mahapatra.M. (2018). CSR and Social Entrepreneurship: Role of Multinationals in Empowering Rural Women. *International Journal of Economics and Management Studies* 5(9):1-8.
- Mohapatra, Ashish. (2017) Economic and Political Empowerment of Women in Tribal Communities of Contemporary Odisha. *International Education & Research Journal*, Vol 3(5) pp 191-193.
- Mustaruddin Saleh, Norhayah Zulkifli, Rusnah Muhamad (2010) Corporate Social Responsibility Disclosure and Its Relation on Institutional Ownership: Evidence from Public Listed Companies In Malaysia. *Managerial Auditing Journal* 25(July):591-613
- Sharma, S. (2011). Corporate Social Responsibility: The Case of ITC Limited in Uttar Pradesh, *Indian Journal of Social Development*, 11(2), 683-698
- The Business Case for Sustainable Development: World Business Council for Sustainable Development Making a Difference Towards

the Earth Summit 2002 And Beyond, *Corporate Environmental Strategy,* Volume 9, Issue 3, pp 226-235,

- Vogel, D., 2006. The Market for Virtue. Washington, DC: Brookings Institute.
- Wood, D.J. (1991) Corporate Social Performance Revisited. *The Academy of Management Review,* 16, 691-718.

Podha Kedu – Symbol of Cultural Identity of the Kondh

Dr. Gouranga Charan Dash
Retired Professor, PG Department of Odia
Ravenshaw University, Cuttack

Dr. Shreekanta Kumar Barik
Assistant Professor of Odia (OES-I), Model Degree College Nuapada,
Khariar, Odisha, Email: shreekantakumarbarik@gmail.com

Abstract

Kedu is a 'Kue' word and the exact synonym in Oriya is Balibhoga, the sacrifice. The Kondhs offer this kind of sacrifice to appease the Penu or God. Here, sacrifice means an offering by killing one's dear most animal to appease the deity. This sacrificial object may be a hen's egg. a chick. a cock. a goat, a hog. a buffalo, a monkey. and even a human being. The reason behind this kind of offering never meant for any self-gain. but for the common welfare of the community as a whole. Along with his sacrifice of his dear animal, he also offers his consciousness, his emotion, and all his soul's experience. This kind of offering is so dear to his heart that one could understand it as the offering of his 'self' itself. Podha Kedu can be said as an institution shrouded in mystery of primitive thought and faith. This paper focuses primarily on Podha Kedu which represent the cultural identity of the Aboriginal Kondh community spread in the districts of Kandhamala, Boudh, Kalahandi. Ganjam and Angul of Orissa.

Keywords: Kedu, Sacrifice, Kondhs, Kandhamala, Podha, Dharanipenu

I

At the outset of my discourse on *Podha Kedu*, I feel obligatory to introduce myself with you all. I am a student of literature and mv profession is mainly academic. My interest lies in the field of anthropology, which many may brand as an occupational adventure. Here, I discuss primarily on *Podha Kedu* which represent the cultural identity of the Aboriginal Kondh community spread in the districts of Kandhamala, Boudh, Kalahandi. Ganjam and Angul of Orissa. Their cultural life. their religious faith. their dance. song and music: and their love for art could be understood through this kind of discussion, in other words. I may say that this may be accepted as a treatise on the cultural identity or life style of a community.

It is really very delicate on the part of any outsider to have a discussion on the culture of any community and the emotional attitude which is intricately associated with it. Unless one is very much objective in deliberations, this could lead to misreading of the lifestyle and culture of the concerned ethnic group. Without any prejudice one ought to have love to study the life and culture of a particular community.

The eminent anthropologists like E. B. Tylor, J. G. Frazer. J. D. Unwin. Bronislaw Malinowski have made many preliminary studies on the culture of many Aboriginal communities. They had gone to the fields, collected first-hand information about the life and culture of those groups, but their studies were mostly prejudiced and whatever conclusion they have drawn were based on their own yard-stick and therefore biased. This happened only because their analysis lacked the love for the people's life they studied, while they considered themselves to be civilized. educated and enlightened. they felt these tribes of their study were barbarous. primitive, uneducated and undeveloped human species (Tylor:1871, Frazer: 1910-14, Malinowaski: 1926). But the modern anthropologists deliberating on the findings of Tylor. Unwin and others from new perspective have succeeded in discovering new aspects of fellow-feeling and love for life among the so-called uncivilized tribes.

I have tried to discuss the lifestyle of this community without any bias. I have travelled to many of these inaccessible areas dominated by Kondh community in the district of Kandhamala in 1995 10 make a first-hand study on the mystery shrouding the *Podha Kedu*, the Buffalo sacrifice and fortunately in course of my field study. I could associate myself in this festival in Baliguda and G. Udayagiri. I have tried to come nearer the truth of the mystery. But how far I have succeeded in my venture is left to the members of the concerned community.

II

Kedu is a '*Kue*' word and the exact synonym in Oriya is *Balibhoga*, the sacrifice. The Kondhs offer this kind of sacrifice to appease the *Penu* or God. Here, sacrifice means an offering by killing one's dear most animal to appease the deity. This sacrificial object may be a hen's egg. a chick. a cock. a goat, a hog. a buffalo, a monkey. and even a human being. The reason behind this kind of offering never meant for any sell-gain. but for the common welfare of the community as a whole. Along with his sacrifice of his dear animal, he also offers his consciousness, his emotion, and all his soul's experience. This kind of offering is so dear to his heart that one could understand it as the offering of his 'self' itself. *Podha Kedu* can be said as an institution shrouded in mystery of primitive thought and faith.

All the creative activities of every Aboriginal tribe in this world springs from their faith and necessity. Their need-based endeavours are never commercial like that of the so-called - modern civilised men but those are meant for self-realisation and joy of living a community life. Any personal., or commercial or natural adversity is always considered as something caused by the *Penu*: their faith and their God. For each adversity. particular Gods or Goddesses are born whom they consider responsible for certain happenings. And for that reason, they appease Him/her by offering those things dear to him. But after the period of diversity is over; the particular God no more exists for them. For that reason, many *Penus* are born and die, which can be considered as something of the creative imagination of the Kondhs. These people are the staunch believers in animism and are firm nature worshippers. They consider the hills., the mountains. the wind. the sky. the water beds. the hillocks. the rocks, the trees and various birds and beasts to be having the souls of different Gods, and. they are manifested as *Penus* on different occasions. And. these *Penus* regulate their day-t0-day life, their faith and fear, their joy and sorrow etc (Tylor:1871, Frazer: 1910-14). They are also the driving forces in their individual lives. Among these *Penus*. the earth, the sky. the mountains are considered the primordial forces and they are accepted to be eternal and ever-living *Penu*. That is the reason for which they observe particular festivals on different days of the year in honour of them as prophesied by the Jani, the priest. Therefore. the ritualistic practices during the *Podha Kedu* may appear to some as inhuman, ugly and vulgar. But for the Kondhs. it is a truth without any alternative, and, thus is an indispensable necessity.

III

The Kondhs say the reasons and the history of *Podha Kedu* are related to their own birth and that of the creation of the Earth. In this myth, the history of the Earth is mentioned. They say, the first creation of this Earth was a woman, Naranthali. who is considered as the Culture Hero. She is created out of the Earth and therefore. she is the Earth Mother or the mother of the Earth (*Dharani Penu*). After her. other Gods and Goddesses were born. and, then the man. She chose *Bura Penu*. the sky God as her companion. Then, Devi Mungudi, the mountain Penu joined them. These newly created entities came down to the foot-hill from the mountains. The foot-hills were covered by clay or water. To harden the soft soil. Naranthali demanded sacrifice from the Kondhs who claimed themselves as the first human being born of the Earth. Kondhs offer different sacrifices. the trunks of the trees. the tropical Bija tree, the squirrel, the cock. the cow etc. The deity was not satisfied with these sacrifices and demanded the blood of human being. The Kondhs did not agree to this demand. As a result, there occurred many natural calamities. There was no rain. no vegetation. The land was parched, the streams dried up. There was neither crop and or water. At last, a young girl willingly offered herself to be sacrificed for the sake of the suffering people of her community. Thus, started the first human sacrifice of one's own child to appease the *Dharani Penu* by a Kondh. As a result, there was rain and the earth became suitable for cultivation. The people lived happily thereafter (Elwin:1954, Baily:1960 and Boal:1982).

But afterwards, the Earth become impure and unsuitable because of their evil deeds. And again, there was the need of appeasement of *Dharani Penu*. Even these superstitious people believed that besides the *Dharani Penu*, there are many other divine forces in different natural forms and the souls of their fore-fathers were angry on them (Felix:1995/2000). And, they used to satisfy them by offering the blood of any birds or animals. F. G. Baily and Verrier Elwin have discussed this and many versions of the tale quite familiar among other groups of tribal people. There is another story where one finds that *Dharani Penu* demanding from Jani offerings of blood of a Lohar boy of Patmari desa (Kalahandi district). or the blood of a milk-man, or that of a man of Pan community. But there is no historical truth of this custom. But one thing is very clear that *Dharani Penu* was the embodiment of the soul of the Mother Ear1h accepted by all Kondhs and she can be appeased with human blood. And. only then. she will bless the land to be full of vegetation. On the other hand. there are certain other evil forces which create diseases and unnatural deaths but are easily satisfied with the blood of birds and beasts. *Podha Kedu* may be recognised as the alternative of human sacrifice (Elwin: 1954).

If one goes by history. human sacrifice by the Kondhs was banned in 1859 by an enactment by the British. This suggests that the then government was aware of human sacrifices as a ritualistic practice prevalent among the Kondhs prior to 1859 (Das:1969). There are, of course. many stories about "why' and how' the human sacrifice was considered as evil, vulgar: and the reasons which led to the ban of such practices. As per one of the stories, the Kondhs say, there were two Sahibs Mukman and Keramal who first opposed this Meriah custom. There, the Sahibs were exercising their power and authority in different manner on the Kondhs. They freed hundreds of Meriahs kept as captives by them for meant for sacrifice. The consequence was, the Mother Earth got angry on the Sahibs and as a result the children of those two officers become victims of unnatural death. The Sahibs suffered physical and mental agony. And, to appease the angry deity, they introduced buffalo sacrifice instead of human sacrifice. Of course. the deity accepted this alternative arrangement. but was never happy as before. From that period onwards the Kondhs have been subject to anger of the deity and they have been affected by many epidemics. They were facing crop-failure and then have a feeling that the *Dharani Penu* has been waiting to taste the blood of the Meriahs. The also feel their knifes and axes are crying to taste blood (Felix: 2000).

However, the historical truth of this story is highly controversial. One cannot accept certain historical records to be full proof. For example. we have suspicions about this particular even. The British rulers in reality. wanted to bring the Kondhs under their power and authority as they considered them as most barbaric. Ignorant and indomitable. As it is, the Kondhs were very much emotionally attached to the ritualistic sacrifices which the British knew, and, therefore, taking the plea of stopping a heinous and evil practice, they struck at the sentiment of the Kondhs by enacting low putting an end to human sacrifice. But the truth was something else which has been discussed by Felix Padel at length (Felix: 2000). So one may conclude based on the remark made by Felix Campbell and Mcpherson (Keramal and Mukman as described by Kondhs respectively) were truly the representatives of British imperialis1m and their intension was to spread a sense of fear among the aboriginals living in the jungles elsewhere in the empire by subjugating the Kondhs as responsible for human sacrifice, and also for woman-infanticide with an enactment in 1859, And. the British colonists branded the religious faith of the Kondhs as 'animism" and their rituals to be most primitive, barbarous and inhuman. Further, to achieve these objectives, they have butchered hundreds of innocent Kondhs and set fire to their villages which gave birth to the rebellious attitude among them. To suppress such uprisings of the Kondhs, the Britishers did adopt many inhuman ways which the Kondhs also encountered bravely. However, the oppressed did ultimately surrender. There was a kind of understanding between the oppressor and the oppressed. This conflict was later named as 'War of Freedom for the Meriah' or War of Pacification'.

In the mid-nineteenth century the British has introduced a planned oppression which was not based on any principle, but intended to enforce a sort of political and social misrule which antagonised the natives. And. as a result. they fell victim to shrewd scheming of the rulers. Some native kings, high caste feudal lords and profit mongering traders of the plains also took the lead to exploit the Kondhs. These groups of people exercised their right on the forest land occupied by Kondhs and even claimed the products of the land as their own (Baily: 1960). Added to this, there was another political event which needs mention here. The king of Ghumusar, resisted to pay certain taxes levied by the British and in this cause the Kondhs willingly supported the stand of the king of Ghumusar and provided shelter and safety to him. This also enraged the Britishers. In this given situation the Kondhs did not have any alternative but to protest the role of the British asserting their right to their land and guard their own life and property. In reality. they sided with the king for the very fact that they were given protection by the king while offering human sacrifices. Therefore, the British, in order to control the king and bring the Kondhs under their authority. they started to launch a movement known as the Meriah Mukti Andolan in 1937 led by Campbell. Further, towards the end of the nineteenth century the Christian Missionaries have also come to these tribal lands and came to know the barbaric practices of the aboriginals. As elsewhere. these missionaries had also tried to reform and civilize these people by propagating Christianity among them. They found it convenient to preach their religion to remove the taboos associated with many tribal customs. But the innocent tribals failed to understand the cunning intention of the missionaries.

Podha Kedu is a ritualistic practice very much associated with the life of this tribe and simply observing this from a distance, certainly one cannot realise the mystery that has given birth to such a custom. The so-called educated or cultured modern man cannot dismiss this practice as something barbaric or primitive, unless he dives deep into the mystery. He will be definitely biased in his comment on this. I, for myself have tried to study these ritualistic practices associating myself with their life and culture before understanding how relevant those were in their day-to day life. A man gets drunk, sings and dances in an inebriated mood. finally offering sacrifices are something to be deeply studied. What kind of emotional changes that take place in the collective life of the community in all the more a difficult subject for study (Felix: 2000).

IV

The main purpose of *Podha Kedu* is to appease the *Dharani Penu*. This ritualistic festival is not celebrated every year in a village. But often it is seen to be repeated every three, ten or sixteen years. The year, when there used to be crop failure, natural calamity, and the defilements of the Mother Earth leading to her anger, is known to the Jani. Jani is the priest who offers prayers to *Dharani Penu, Mungudi* (the mountain-God) and *Bura Penu* (the sky-God) and other natural agents of the divine forces. The Jani informs the wishes of the *Dharani Penu* to the Chieftain of the village. And everyone in the village gets engaged to fulfil the ritual as per the advice of the Jani. They contribute to a common fund. With the collected money, a buffalo is bought, usually an adult one. No leash is ever attached to the neck of the animal. It is set free. It is considered divine, like a God. The Kondhs believe that the sacrificial animal is considered to be an offering to the deity, who is the symbol of Shakti, and, therefore is never an ordinary animal.

The animal which is sacrificed for the cause of their happiness and prosperity should be most dear to them, and therefore, they never hesitate to offer it to the Shakti. This intended sacrificial buffalo wonders around the village grazing upon anything it comes across. Even the inhabitant offers it cooked food. The Jani informs the villagers about the place of sacrifice which he claims to have been advised by the deity by his dream. He identifies the particular patch of land where the animal is to be offered. That patch of land must be a virgin land. And. for the first time. the intended buffalo and a black Oxen are yoked together and that patch of land is tilled. Before the tilling. a hog is usually sacrificed on that particular patch of land and buried there in the soil. This is the first stage of purification of the land. From that day onwards till the final ritual, the men and women of the village use to dance. sing songs on that patch of land.

Around a month before, the villagers start preparing a Kena or an image using the dough of maize as the symbol of Shakti. They keep this dough-image in a pot of *siali* leaves and allows it to be dry in the sun for about a month. After this, they grind this dough-image into powder. This powder is added to the decomposed rice which ultimately becomes the divine wine. This they consider as their *prasad*.

The last three days of *Kedu Parba* are considered most auspicious. The first day is known as the *Chhatarchauni*. That day a hog is sacrificed at a particular place in the village. A shade thatched with leaves is temporarily constructed on that place which is known as the house of the Gods. A long bamboo pole is planted by the side of the hut. Two pieces of long cloth, one white and one red, use to be tied to the top of the pole. Underneath the cloth at the top, a bunch of peacock feathers are tied to the bamboo. A ring is fastened at the top of the pole through which a long rope is lowered down to the ground. At the top of the pole a living chick is bound and five to six bronze bells are attached to the rope at different heights. And at the middle of the pole, a small bamboo basket containing the hooves. the cars, the tongue. the snout. and the tail of the pig is kept. At the bottom part of the pole, in a small basket, twelve hen's eggs are also kept. The different parts of the pig are meant as offering to the *Sarubali* (mountain-God. the Mungudi). while the eggs kept at the bottom are intended for the Dharani Penu and the chick at the top for the *Bura Penu*. The rituals are the part of fertility rites when the tribals offer living eggs for the living deities. When the rituals are associated with funeral. they offer dead eggs for the dead souls. This bamboo pole is symbolic of the life-force.

On the second day, the tribes worship the buffalo. On that day. the buffalo is brought to the newly constructed shed. It is bathed with turmeric water and castor oil. The Jani touches the head of the buffalo with knife and axe. It is given home-made cakes, porridge and hey. But this day it is given very little water. This happens to be the buffalo's last food and drink. It is then tied to a strong staff nearer to the bamboo pole. Near the staff a knife. an axe and a crow bar are kept. On the second night in every house of the village, they worship lingo, a symbol of *Dharani Penu* along with different weapons and agricultural implements.

The third day festival is *Podha Kedu*. On that day, all the villagers come out of their homes and do not enter their houses again if not especially required otherwise. They assemble at the place where the buffalo is kept. The male folk gather round the newly-thatched hut. They have the *dhola, changu,* (big and small drums) and *mahuri* (a crude wind instrument like shahnai). The female-folk stay near the buffalo, ring the bells shaking the rope attached to the ring in the pole. Some ladies produce some kind of music playing on bird-like wooden toys. All the ladies sing in chorus to the accompaniment of ringing of the bells, sound of the bird-toys, the blowing of *mahuri* and the beating of the drums. Amidst all the din and frenzy. the helpless animal stands transfixed on its place. It is even denied a chance to lie on the ground.

The atmosphere towards the afternoon gets surcharged. Men and women attired in their festive best come from the nearby villages accompanied by various musical instruments. They come in many groups. They arrive dancing holding branches of different trees and peacock feathers to the festival ground. are welcomed by the village folk, both men and women and were treated as guests. They are received with honour with offerings of rice, turmeric powder, *mahuli mada* (a kind of wine brewed by them). It seems all the crowd have assembled there have been transformed into a community of one village. All start dancing together. sometimes in a circular fashion, and at other times in semi-circular formations. Sometimes they dance in single lines, at other time facing each other; sometimes dancing in pairs and at other times holding each other round the waist. But every time they sing and play on their instruments in unison. The dances may be frenzied because of intoxication, but never out of tune. All assembled them irrespective of age do indulge in dance and music. A novice may become an expert dancer, or. an exalted singer or a master musician. They feel whatever they are indulged in, all meant only the offering (sacrifice) and intended to satisfy the *Dharani Penu*.

I have heard in some of the area, there are men-folk putting on red sarees in dishevelled hair come to the place of *Kedu*, dance like *Dharani Penu*, holding two swords in both their hands. Other follow them from the thatched cottage to the sacrificial ground. However, I did not have the opportunity to witness any such performer in G. Udayagiri and Baliguda. However. Norman Bancroft-Hunt and Werner Forman have concluded that this kind of dance and music by the aboriginals is a sort of communication between the people of this world and the spirits of the unseen world. They say such festivals on such occasions do establish a kind of rapport between the man and his God and this may be the key or the binding principle behind all activities of creation.

Around afternoon that day, amid song and dance. some of the hefty men come near the buffalo and they take out the bamboo pole off its place. Some of the men carry the bamboo pole with all reverence to the selected ground. There, the pole is again planted as before. All the female folk again assemble and start singing there. Some other men simultaneously take the buffalo by the leash and some others control the animal with the help of a rope tied to the three legs of it. In the melee of men and women and the frenzied dance and music, the animal starts running out of fear, thirst and hunger. But the people never release it. Around the scene, the pitch of the din reaches its peak and the helpless animal out of sheer fright, attempts to run away from the crowd. But sometimes because of weakness, it falls on the ground injuring itself and at other times lies on the ground not able to get up. The merciless men drag it to the sacrificial ground. Because of intoxication the men also fail to maintain their own balance and fall on the ground and get wounded. It seems these people have forgotten their own selves. At last, the animal is brought to the sacrificial ground. The Jani generally keeps waiting for everyone to arrive there. A pit has been dug there already near 6which the buffalo is forced to stand. The Jani sanctifies the animal with turmeric water, castor oil and rice. He also touches a knife and an axe on the forehead of the buffalo. After this, the animal is forced by the men to fall on the ground. Then they cut out the snout, the hooves, the tongue, the ears. the tail etc. and take out the heart of the animal by tearing open the lower part of its belly. These five parts of the animal are kept together in a new earthen-pot and buried in the pit observing all the ritualistic paraphernalia. While all this go on, the ladies keep on singing to the tune of the non-stop music.

Soon after the whole ritual takes the different turn. The stronger male-folk with sharp knives start cutting pieces of flesh out of the body of the animal. For this, there used to be a stiff competition among them and in no time the big animal is reduced to a blood-stained skeleton. The brave heroes on this occasion with chunks of flesh in their hands rush to their companions waiting for them at a distance. After a while putting the raw flesh in *shala* leaves start running to their respective villages. This they consider as *prasad* of the Mother Earth, and not ordinary flesh. In their respective villages, they distribute the flesh ceremoniously and bury some of it in their own land, some others also eat this as Prasad. But in the evening in every village, they start sacrifices of pigs, hens and keep on feasting with song and dance throughout the night. They feel that the *Dharani Penu* has been appeased and there would be good crop in the next season. No deity would be angry on them. there would be no epidemic, and the dumas (the soul of the dead) would be happy. And, there will be peace and prosperity in the village.

Those who have witnessed the attitude and behaviour of the Kondhs when they would be cutting the flesh of the animal, it would be difficult to believe how could such simple, innocent and kind-hearted tribals turn into such hard-hearted, violent competitors among themselves. This proves how conscious they are of their self-prestige and dignity who never want to surrender before the opponents. Although, most of them in this deadly competition get wounded and even there are instances of death, no one ever surrendered in this combat. From this we can deduce that the Britishers really recognised the bravado and the heroic character of the Kondh which they deliberately wanted to suppress and planned accordingly to bring them under their control.

After the guests of the nearby villages have left, the male-folk of the locality assemble where the sacrifice was conducted, carry the carcass of the animal from the sacrificial ground and bury it under the earth nearby in their land. On the surface. they sow the seeds of crops and start dancing. Afterwards the women of the village bring their male-folk to their own houses from that place and in the night, one notices absolute calmness and serenity prevailing in the village through the night as if the village itself has gone into a deep slumber. Of course, the villagers use to sacrifice goats on the particular place of sacrifice followed by feasting. But the ladies do not take part in it.

The next day happens to be the day of *Sudhikriya* (purifying rites). In the morning, the bamboo pole and the other pieces of wood, rope, baskets. different parts of the newly-thatched hut and everything else associated with the festival are collected and carried to a place where no one ever frequented. All the things are cut into small pieces and made into a heap. All these things now considered in auspicious and even to touch them is forbidden. Returning to the village, the Jani use to sprinkle the charcoal and tur1neric water chanting certain mantras in the village. After that, they all take bath and gather where the buffalo was first tied to a staff. The Jani touches castor oil and grass on the heads of everyone. Again, they offer sacrifices of pigs and hens seeking blessings of *Dharani Penu*. There used to be a communal feast on that day. Everyone rinks wine, sings, dances. There is no distinction of age, sex and no one seems to be tired. This seems a sort of rejoicing of a free. simple and innocent community. Usually. This *Podha Kedu* as a religious festival is observed sometime between spring and summer season. The ritualistic significance of this festival is that they thatch their own houses after this festival, start tilling their own lands for the ensuing seasonal cultivation. After that they also start sowing seeds wishing for a good harvest. Especially the ladies, having their monthly periods and the sick are not allowed to participate in this ritualistic festival. They keep themselves indoors.

V

I have already cited in the beginning that the *Kedu Parampara* of the Kondhs have been accepted many of us as something of a primitive faith or a taboo in the tribal society (Steiner: 1956). It may be termed as of a brutal or ugly custom. But nonetheless, it has a tradition of its own. We cannot certainly assume something and dismiss it outright by simply branding it to be improper. superstitious, unscientific and without any background. The pure, divine behaviour of a group who live with a strong ancient faith that is age-old, cannot be discarded from their ethnic inheritance. Franz Steiner, Margaret Mead, Ian H Porter, Richard G Skalko, Nigel Davies. and few other anthropologists and psychologist like Sigmond Freud have discussed this basic question at length. There is definitely some sort of meaning of any strong faith associated with the cultural life of any ethnic group. And behind any religious and cultural activity. we always discover a positive mental attitude (Frazer:1890, Hurbert:1889, Nigel:1981). Therefore, we cannot condemn their act to be heinous and term them as senseless killers. Many anthropologists of the world have accepted the human sacrifice as a holy act of a tribe for their self-defence and territorial expansion. In later times, this merciless killing of human beings has become part of the character of the powerful to perpetuate their hegemony over others. Even in the modern world, the powerful groups are bent upon subjugating the weaker group by applying their military force, power and money. Even sometimes, they pollute the whole environment with different type of poison to eliminate particular communities. Some other times. the leaders of many powerful nations even encroach upon the integrity and sovereignty showing their big brotherly attitude. There are examples of others those who consider the people of the other areas as underdeveloped, superstitious, barbaric and even terrorists. There, they forget that they are more dictatorial than others in exercising their authority and committing oppression. There are the people who take the lead in killing other and destroying the natural wealth of the weaker society. Should we not brand these people as barbaric? Are they really civilised, enlightened and cultured? Do they think of the common welfare of the human society as whole? Are we truly thinking of a better world? In this context, one can certainly say that we are constantly under the threat of the pseudo-humanistic authoritarian leaders. Now judge for yourself, who is barbaric, the people of *Podha Kedu* culture or the war hungry dictatorial leaders.

We accept the practice of sacrifice by the Hindus, the Christians, the Muslims and many other religious groups to be a necessity because they have institutionalised it. It is really hard to understand why the practice of the Kondhs should be consider as inhumane and corrupt (Stall:1993/1996).

If we study the sings and the rituals, certainly, we can understand how deeply the Kondhs are attached to their society and its age-old practices. Their songs express the joy and suffering of 8both their individual and communal life (Bowra:1962). I, myself, have realised this listening to their songs and associated rituals during the *Podha Kedu* festival. On the whole, we may conclude that the basic truth behind such ritual is faith. and, faith alone.

The women-folk of Kondh community never learn any song from any teacher. They only assemble and sing together. The theme of their songs relates to their past, their joys and sufferings of the present and the dreams of their futures. Their memory and experience are narrated in their songs. They invoke the souls of their dead ancestors, and the *Dharani Penu* -informing them about the change in the seasons, the failure of crops, the sufferings they have endured, the death of their live-stock. the drying of the streams, the denudation of the forests etc. In the songs, they. too, solicit the blessings of the *Dharani Penu* to help them overcome their miseries while they make their dear-most offering to Her. This is in form of propitiation of *Dharani Penu* where they sacrifice the animal in her honour. The following songs one often hears during the festival.

> Come, Oh friend, Dear
> come, beating the drums
> and blowing the *mahuri*
> Let us sing
> Drink *Chauli* and *Mahuli* and be merry.

> Look, the new year has come
> There are flowers in the mango trees
> But the mother earth weeps
> Weeps the mother earthen-potWhy does she weep?
> Call the priest.
> Ask the exorcist.

> Oh, exorcist
> Can you tell
> Why are they weeping?
> All our seeds have been destroyed
> All our cows, buffaloes and oxen are dying
> The insects despoil our crops
> The forests are caught by fire

> He, Exorcist
> Come, you know the black magic
> Tell us
> Show us
> Why all these happen

> He comes
> And, tells everything
> We brought the bamboo
> And, the straw and the ropes
> Thatched our huts
> Brought the pig
> Brought the chick
> Brought the unboiled and half-boiled rice.

The exorcist said
He would please the Mother Earth
There won't be crop failure
And, death of the live-stock
Call all the brothers, uncles and other elder-fathers
Summon all the friends and relations
Bring the long bamboo pole
Plant it vertically on the earth
Make the parrots of wood
We will converse among ourselves
Will sing songs and dance
Then give a buffalo sacrifice
Mother Earth would be happy
Our suffering would be over.

The female-folk producing a kind of music out of the wooden parrots, ring the bells, sing the songs in a serene voice. They repeat the refrains of the song round the buffalo as if to force the animal to listen their woeful life. They expect the soul of the buffalo would go to the Mother Earth and tell her about their pain and suffering. Once the soul of the buffalo escapes from this mundane life it would be free from sin and emerge as something divine and pure. And, once the soul of the animal finds its happy abode, the community believes they would lead a happy life on this earth.

And, the people, who have come from other villages as guests to participate in the festival also join in singing. dancing and merry making. All of a sudden. the whole scene is transformed into a theatrical stage where all those present. men, women and children alike are all assumed-characters of the march of events of the whole ritual that has been described. The events move on as the changing scenes of a drama with variety of characters in an open-air-theatre. There are some Kondhs who could be distinguished from their costumes from others do participate in this festival, although. they may be the converts of other religious groups living with some occupation other than cultivation elsewhere. But once they are here during the festival. they are one with other natives gathered there. They too sing and dance with others. From this. one can conclude that the social affinity of this particular cultural ethnic groups all the more stronger during such festivals.

Again, the different materials used in this ritual are the symbolic agents of the faith of the Kondhs. As they have accepted, the egg and the chick as the symbol of rebirth. The different colours like white (corn powder). black (the charcoal). saffron (the earth) and yellow (turmeric powder) with which they decorate the sacrificial ground are also consider representatives of different elements of human body. They have a belief that the Mother Earth has created man using all these materials Nayak;Boal; Soren:1990). The fresh blood is considered as the life-force and the long bamboo pole is symbolic of prosperity.

Therefore, the anthropologists have reckoned this as a fertility rite. But to my mind the ritual, from the beginning till the end, appears to be a religious play with a fertility theme intended to end in a point of contentment. To give the play a composite structure, there is the moving theme, an open-air stage and innumerable characters. There are elements of fear and apprehension mixed together., and, therefore the difference between the performers and the onlookers is totally eliminated. The sacrifice, the gratification of the deity, the invocation of the souls of the dead ancestors accompanied with song. dance and music - all create an absolute mystery beyond the understanding of any ordinary man. And, probably. for that we can term this as a play based on the faith of a tribal community -the Kondh. where their life and art. joy and suffering. expectation and dreams, desires and creativity, culture and reality are intricately intermingled. Possibly, this is the identity of *Podha Kedu*.

The Sacrificial Buffalo

The Sacrifice of Buffalo and Dancing during the sacrifice of Buffalo

Notes and References

- The Anthropologist, E.B Tylor (Primitive Society:1871), J.G. Frazer (Golden Bough: 1910-14), Bronislaw Malinowski (Crime and Custom in Savage Society: 1926 and Myth in Primitive Psychology in Magic, Science and Religion and Other Essays 1948), J.D. Unwin (Sex and Culture: 1934) have always thought themselves more culture and enlightened than the Primitive Communities and try to give their own comments in their own way. Unwin has remarked in his books "Sex and Culture" that "Uncivilised men and women are more tactful than truthful. They are anxious to make a good impression on their distinguished visitor and are extremely careful not to cause him pain and displeasure (Oxford University Press, London PP. 7)," Charles A. Valentine has not accepted the views about Anthropologist mentioned above in the book "Culture and Poverty" in different way. (Culture and Poverty, 1968, The University of Chicago Press, Chicago).

- In this Context one can accept the view discussed by E. B. Tylor, J.G. Frazer and Norman Baneroft - hunt and werner Forman.

  (1) "Spirits are personified causes"., "Everything in this world had a soul". in, Primitive   Culture (1871).

  (2) "After man peopled with multitudes of individuals spirits, every rock and hill, every tree and flower, every brook and river, even breeze that blew and even cloud that fleeted with silvery while the blue expanse to the heaven. in, Golden Bough (1910-14).

  (3) "Everything possessed power, or a spiritual force, be it a pebble on the beach, a rock, tree, animal or man himself; abstract qualities, such a beauty, had a similar force, as deed the sun, moon, and stars and the lakes and the rivers. Although this power originated in the spirit world, it manifests in a realm man occupy. in, People of the Totem (1969/1985) Orbis Publishing Ltd., London.

- There are varieties of description in the stories about the human sacrifice of the Kondhs. These varieties in the stories have been discussed by Verrier Elwin, 1954, Tribal Myths of Orissa, Oxford University Press, London; Maria Murder and Suicide, Oxford University Press, London; F.G. Baily, 1960, Tribe, Casteand Nation; A study of Political Activity and Political Change in Highland Orissa, Oxford University Press, London; Barbara Boal, 1982, The Kondhs: Human sacrifice and Religious Change, Warminister, Aris and Philips, London.

- The sacrifices by the Kondhs are meant to satisfy the spirits of unseen world. And for their appeasement blood is considered as sacred offering. In the language of Felix Padel, "The blood sacrifice of animals is basic element in human relationship with spirit world. In tribal view (as in Hinduism and Christianity) sacrifice is far more than simple propitiation is an action essential for life. in, Felix Padel, 1995/2000, The Sacrifice of Humane being British Rule and the Konds Orissa, Oxford University Press, London, Page 129.

- Verrier Elwin, 1954, Tribal Myths of Orissa, Chapter - XXVII and Page - 544 - 551.

- Das, Anirudhha, 1969, Meriah (In Oriya), Vidyapuri, Cuttack-2, Chapter- I II and IV.

- In his books Felx has described, having seen the buffalo sacrifice and heard of the Jani, the priest that "Axes and Knives weep" Felix, 2000, PP- 119.

- Felix Boal, has depended on the information provided by F. G. Baily, Verrier Elwin, Barbara Campbell (Kondhisthan), of Ghumsar Movement. many contemporary Govt. records and books on history We can cite the remarks on the Christian Missionaries and administrators of the time made by Felix, as "Yet Briton saw their enforcement of a long-term control as bringing "Peace" and "Justice" as a "Gift". These ideas of wars to enforce a state of peace had powerful Christian association. "Pacifying" the Konds, Briton saw as the first stage to "civilising" them. XX "A conquest over their mind" X "Peace" is their prevailing condition. Among many savage tribes, the state of war is universal at a more advance stage, hostility is limited by compacts". in, Felix, 2000, PP - 12 55

- To F. G. Baily "Meriah wars seen a period of anarchy XX Konds fought not so much because they wanted to preserved the Meriah right, but because they feared their land Would be taken or taxed. X X Their villages were burnt, stores of grain destroyed. X Leaders of the konds, flogged or hanged, 960, PP - 181.

- Felix has given a lively description of the scene of Podhakedu in his book. in, Felix, 2000, PP-115.

- During the ceremonial's dancer displayed the dances and songs, they have obtained from various supernatural spirits. As to do so required "Possessions" either real or "stimulated". Then took place at a time when communication with the spirits could be easily established. in, Norman Bancroft - hunt and werner Forman, 1978-1985, People of Totem, Orbis Publishing Limited, London, PP- 104.

- Discussion on Taboo by Franz Steiner and Margaret Mead can be cited here.

(1) "Taboo is concerned, 1) with all the social mechanisms of obedience which have ritual significance; 2) with specific and restrictive behaviour in dangerous situation. One might say that taboo deals with the sociology of danger itself, for it is also concerned, 3) with the protection of the society from some endangered - and, therefore dangerous persons. X X Taboo is an element of all those situations which attitudes to values are expressed in terms of danger behaviours. in, Taboo, 1956, Cohen and West Ltd., 30 Peray Street, London, PP-21.

(2) Taboo may be defined as a negative sanctioned, a prohibition whose infringement results in automatic penalty without human or superhuman mediation. in, Taboo 1937 Encyclopaedia of Social Science, Vol. -3, MaC Millan and Co. PP -502-505.

- Depending on the observation of William Robertson Smith and Frazer -
(1) "Sacrifice at the alter was the essential feature in the ritual of the ancient religions. XX It was nothing other than act of fellowship between deity and his worshiper. X X The oldest form of sacrifice, then, older than the use of fire, or the agriculture, was the sacrifice of animals whose flesh and blood were enjoyed in common by the God and his worshipers. It is essential that each one of the participants should have the share of the meal" (W.R. Smith).

(2) "Sacramental killing and communal eating of the totem animal at a solemn festival once in a year, after which it is mourned and its skin and feathers were preserved. (Golden Bough, Chapter - X, XIII, XIV - Vol. - 2), Sigmound Froued has dealt the sacrifice of birds and animals among the ancient tribes and feasting thereafter has commented thus. "It confesses, with a frankness that could hardly be excelled, to the fact that the object of the act of sacrifice has always being the same - namely, what is now worshiped as God, that is to say the father. The Problem of the relation between the animal and the human sacrifice, thus admits of a simple solution. The original animal sacrifice was already a substitute for human sacrifice - for the ceremonial killing of the father, so that, when the father -surrogate once more resumed its human safe, the animal sacrifice too could be changed back into human sacrifice. in, Totem and Taboo, 1913/2001, Routledge, London, PP -175-176.And, "Civilisation has been achieved by sacrifice in the gratification of innate desire.

- J. G. Frazer has dealt with the human sacrifice as part of the fertility rite, as "The idea that human sacrifice was virtually a universal feature of Primitive Society". in, Golden bough, 1890/1941, Mac Millan, PP. 134.

And, Joseph Campbell has supported this view of Frazer, in his book, "The Mask of God, Primitive Mythology, 1959, Viking Penguin, New York. Depending on the views of Hurbert, H. and Mauss (1889), and Nigel Davies' commendable work, "Human Sacrifice in History and Today", 1981, Mac Millan, London. Padel has accepted that "Sacrifice as mediation -the victim and his death form a bridge between the human and the define worlds that generates life giving sacredness. in, Felix Pade, 2000, PP-135.

- It is necessary to add here that the practice of sacrifice has not prevalent among 16. the tribes of the ancient world, but they were much in Vogue in the Vedic society. There is discussion in Yadurveda, Brahmanas, Epics and Puranas. There are examples of sacrifice practised by the people those were indulging in "Tantra". In the later period, Mahavir, Buddha and many saints have opposed such practices. Different objects of nature like trees, flowers, fruits etc. have been substituted for different religious practices. in, "Frits Stall, Ritual and Mantras, 1993/1996, Motilal Banarasidass, New Delhi, in, Chapter II, PP. 61-182". And there are also evidences of practice of sacrifice in Mahengo-Daro and Harppa Civilisation. in, Marsal, Mahengo-Daro and Indian Civilisation, Vol-I, PP - 81 & Vol. - 3.

- There are scenes of song of dance often seen on tragic occasions such as separation, diseases, death etc. In the words of Bowra, C.M. "Primitive songs which is burned from elemental dramatic rites is a ceremonial activity. In a world where ceremonies provide a, main focus for social life, song is among chief of them and each used both to communicate with the supernatural and to express joy or grief or other strong emotions" X X All Primitive songs are records of immediate reactions to events or belief or feelings aroused by some unexpected change or need, and therefore, still vivid and powerful in the mind, of a full personality thrown into the task of songs with all its strength communicated to it. In, Primitive song, 1962, Weidenfeld and Nicolson, London, PP - 38, 88.

- Nayak, Radhakanta; Boal, Barbara; Soren, Nabar, 1990, The Kondhs, Indian Social Institute, New Delhi, in, Chapter - Ritual.

Indigenous Beliefs and Practices: The Kandha Tribe of Kalahandi, Odisha

Dr. Nalinikanta Rana

Assistant Professor, Department of History
Maa Manikeshwari University, Bhawanipatna
Email: nkrana@kalahandiuniversity.ac.in

Abstract

This study explores the indigenous beliefs and community practices of the Kandha tribe in Kalahandi, Odisha. The Kandha tribe, known for their rich cultural heritage, exhibit a unique blend of traditional customs, rituals, and socio-economic activities deeply rooted in their environment. This research focuses on understanding the tribe's spiritual beliefs, agricultural practices, hunting and fishing traditions, and their reliance on forest resources for sustenance and medicinal purposes. Fieldwork conducted through interviews and observations in various Kandha villages provides an in-depth look at how these practices are intertwined with their daily lives.

The study highlights the importance of festivals and rituals in maintaining social cohesion and cultural identity among the Kandha. It also examines the impact of modernization and external influences on their traditional way of life, revealing a dynamic process of cultural adaptation and resilience. By documenting the Kandha's indigenous knowledge and practices, this research aims to contribute to the broader understanding of tribal societies and their ongoing efforts to preserve their cultural heritage in the face of changing socio-economic conditions. The findings underscore the need for policies that support the preservation and promotion of tribal cultures, ensuring their sustainable development and cultural continuity.

Key Words- Community Practices, Cultural Heritage, Indigenous Beliefs, Kandha Tribe, Sustainable Development.

Introduction

The term *tribe* has been a subject of diverse interpretations, often rooted in colonial perspectives that labeled tribal communities as "primitive" or "uncivilized." Such terminology reflected a negative bias, marginalizing the rich cultural and social systems of tribal societies (Patnaik, 2005). Despite these colonial constructs, tribes have maintained unique identities through distinct languages, customs, and lifestyles. Tribes in India are known for their vibrant art forms, traditional practices, and communal way of life. Their occupations range from food gathering, hunting, and shifting cultivation to craftsmanship and wage labor, exemplifying a deep connection to their environment.

India, home to over 400 tribal groups speaking more than 300 languages and dialects, has the world's second-largest tribal population, accounting for 8.6% of the nation's population as per the 2011 census. Odisha, with 62 tribal communities constituting 22.85% of its population, holds a significant place in India's tribal landscape. The state's tribal groups, including Kandha, Koya, Gadaba, Juang, Oraon, and Santal, predominantly inhabit the Eastern Ghats' hill ranges, showcasing diverse cultural practices and traditions.

Kalahandi district in Odisha, known for its picturesque landscapes and rich tribal heritage, is home to several tribal communities such as the Kandha, Gond, Saora, and Bhunjia. The district, with a total population of 1,576,869 (2011 census), has a substantial tribal population, among which the Kandhas hold prominence, numbering 449,456. This district's geographical features and cultural diversity make it a vital region for understanding the lifestyles and traditions of Odisha's tribal groups.

This paper explores the unique cultural and social aspects of the Kandha tribe in Kalahandi, focusing on their beliefs, practices, and evolving identity amidst modernization. By examining the historical, anthropological, and ethnographic studies, it highlights the importance of preserving the invaluable heritage of these communities while addressing their developmental challenges.

Review of Literature

The scholarly study of the Kandha tribe spans from early colonial reports to modern ethnographic and anthropological analyses. The first written documentation by Campbell and Macpherson in the mid-18th century was followed by E. Thurston's significant chapter in "Tribes and Castes of South India" (1909). Researchers like Herman Niggemeyer (1964), F.G. Bailey (1957, 1960), Neville A. Watts (1970), and Barbara M. Boal (1997) have offered detailed insights into the tribe's culture, rituals, and religious practices. Niggemeyer explored cultural parallels between the Kutia Kondh and other tribes, while Bailey's work provided pioneering insights into social and cultural dynamics. Watts emphasized the tribe's relationship with Odisha's topography, and Boal examined the history and impact of human sacrifice among the Kandha.

Indian scholars like N. Pattnaik, P.S. Das Patnaik, and P.K. Nayak have contributed foundational research on the tribe's socio-political structures and cultural practices. Loknath Parida and Subodh Chandra Das provided valuable narratives on Kutia Kondh origins and ecology, while Nihar Ranjan Patnaik explored socio-cultural aspects and economic life.

Further studies include Krishna Sharma's anthropometric research (1979) on Kandha subgroups, Dol Govinda Bisi's ethnographic exploration (1990) of clan and territorial divisions, and modern research from SCSTRTI and scholars like Dash and Dash (2009), Panda and Pandhy (2007), and Mahendra Kumar Mishra. These studies have enriched the understanding of Kandha ethnobotany, dietary habits, and oral traditions. Recent ethnoarchaeological efforts by Rana (2022) have sought to correlate Kandha practices with archaeological evidence.

This extensive body of literature highlights the multidisciplinary interest in the Kandha tribe, addressing their history, culture, rituals, and adaptations, while emphasizing the need for ongoing exploration of their evolving identity.

Culture and Custom of Kandha Communities of Kalahandi

Odisha hosts the largest number of tribal communities in India, with 62 distinct tribes influencing and integrating with non-tribal cultures, creating a composite culture. These tribes are classified into Austro-Asiatic (Mundari), Dravidian, and Indo-Aryan ethno-linguistic categories, each with unique languages and cultural practices. Odisha has one of the highest concentrations of tribal populations in India, totalling around 8 million. Major tribes include the Kandha, Santhals, Oraons, and Gonds, with some, like the Juangs and Saoras, being exclusive to Odisha.

Among these, the Primitive Tribal Groups (PTGs) face significant economic and social challenges. Thirteen PTGs in Odisha, including the Birhor, Dongria Kandha, and Juang, are recognized for their pre-agricultural economies and low literacy rates, largely subsisting on hunting and food gathering.

The Kalahandi region shows evidence of human habitation from the Mesolithic to Chalcolithic periods, with early tools scattered across river terraces and caves. As of the 2011 census, Kalahandi's population was 1,576,869, with a nearly equal gender distribution. India exemplifies unity in diversity, with cultural changes shaped by both internal evolution and external influences. Indian society has transitioned from agricultural to industrial, moving towards a casteless and classless society. Thinkers like Comte, Spencer, and M.N. Srinivas have explored these social transformations, highlighting the ongoing process of cultural adaptation and social change in India.

The Dongria Kandha inhabit the Niyamgiri hill ranges in Odisha, covering parts of Rayagada and Kalahandi districts. Situated at elevations ranging from 1,000 to 5,000 feet, their habitat enjoys a cool climate year-round. Dongria villages are typically located on gentle slopes or shelves of steep hills, featuring houses with multiple rooms and unique designs, including front and back verandas, a central living space, and attached pigsties. Mortars embedded in the floors of central and back rooms are integral to their daily activities. Primarily dependent on horticulture, the Dongrias cultivate jackfruit, banana, mango, and pineapple across the hill slopes. They traditionally practiced shifting cultivation and organized their territory into Muttahs, administrative-cum-social units serving as exogamous clans. Each village hosts a youth dormitory, called Adasbetta, where unmarried girls and visiting boys engage in singing and dancing.

The Dongria worship Dharanipenu, the earth goddess, as their supreme deity, housed in a central village shrine. Their most significant ritual is the Kedu or Meriah festival, involving the sacrificial slaughter of buffaloes to appease Dharanipenu, believed to enhance soil fertility and ensure community well-being. Rituals also include cremation ceremonies, where the dead are burned on a pyre, followed by community mourning and celebration. Their vibrant culture reflects deep-rooted traditions and harmony with nature.

The Kutia Kandha reside in the remote highlands of Belghar-Lanjigarh and Thuamul Rampur in Odisha, surrounded by dense forests of the Eastern Ghats. Their villages are located at the foot-hills or valleys, typically featuring rows of houses along a narrow street, with youth dormitories at the ends. Shifting cultivation is their primary livelihood, supplemented by hunting and forest produce collection. Although they cultivate various crops, including paddy in plains, food scarcity often affects them during the summer and monsoon transition. Barter trade remains prevalent, with high exchange rates for essential goods like liquor.

Centrally located in the villages are sacred shrines to Dharani Penu and Karumunda, while Sapangada is revered as their origin place. Traditionally single-clan, their villages now comprise multiple clans, most of which are totemic. Exogamous clans trace descent from common ancestors and are divided into Majhi and Jani lineages. Family forms the basic social unit, and the birth of a child is celebrated equally for boys and girls, who also have dormitories. Kutia Kandha are fond of music and dance, with songs reflecting themes of creation and societal changes. Their pantheon includes numerous deities, both benevolent and malevolent, propitiated by priests and shamans. Festivals, notably the buffalo-sacrificing Kedu festival, are central to their cultural life.

The Desia Kandha, the largest Scheduled Tribe in Kalahandi, inhabit both plains and hilly areas. Known for their slim, muscular build, dark complexion, and broad features, they are simple, hospitable, and cheerful. Historically, the Kandha practiced human sacrifice and infanticide, but these practices have ceased. Their mother tongue is Kui, though they also speak Kalahandi Odia.

Traditionally, Kandha held a privileged position, with the Raja of Kalahandi symbolically sitting on a Kandha's lap during accession and marrying a Kandha girl, though not allowing her to reside in the palace. These customs symbolized the Raja's derived authority from the Kandha but have now vanished due to Hinduization. This cultural shift has eroded tribal councils, dormitory systems, communal dances, and vibrant rituals, especially among the Desia Kandha, leading to a loss of artistry and traditional joy. However, these institutions persist among other Kandha groups in Kalahandi.

Social Organization Among the Kandhs Tribes

The Dongria Kandha inhabit the Niyamgiri hill ranges, where their territory is divided into Muttahs, each functioning as an administrative-cum-social unit and exogamous clan. Prominent Muttahs include Jakasika, Wadaka, Pusika, Sikaka, and Kadraka. Marriage within the same Muttah is strictly prohibited, ensuring exogamy. Historically, Muttahs were homogenous, but over time, they have become heterogeneous, with people from other Muttahs settling in different territories. Dongria villages have youth dormitories for unmarried girls, called Adasbetta, where they interact with unmarried boys from affinal villages through singing and dancing.

Among the Kutia Kandha, the nuclear family is the smallest social unit, comprising parents and unmarried children, with the father as the head. Married sons establish separate households. Clans, such as Andanja, Bandanaka, and Gujika, are totemic, exogamous, and trace descent from a common ancestor. The tribe is divided into two lineages: Majhi and Jani, often residing in separate rows within a village. Intermarriage occurs between lineages but not within the same row.

The Desia Kandha also maintain nuclear families and trace descent patrilineally. Their lineage is the next larger unit, traditionally living together in villages or Muttahs. Marriage holds significant social importance and includes various forms, such as arranged marriage, marriage by capture, marriage by service, and love marriage through elopement. Across these Kandha groups, clan, lineage, and family structure play central roles in shaping their social and cultural lives, ensuring cohesion and maintaining traditional practices.

Subsistence System

The Kandha of Odisha have a multifaceted economy that includes agriculture, shifting cultivation, hunting, fishing, and gathering wild food resources such as roots, fruits, tubers, and leaves. They also collect honey and have extensive knowledge of medicinal plants. Their agricultural tools, such as ploughs, sickles, and spades, as well as hunting implements like bows, arrows, axes, and spears, are kept within their homes. Small game hunting includes squirrels, rabbits, and birds, while larger animals like wild boar and deer are occasionally hunted, especially during rituals. Although hunting is now restricted, it remains part of their cultural practices. Fishing is practiced occasionally, with many Kandha now working as daily wage laborers or engaging in trade for their livelihood.

The Desia Kandha, a sub-group, focus heavily on agriculture and forest resources. Forests provide essential food sources, including fruits, leaves, mushrooms, and honey, and materials for building homes and crafts. Key forest products like timber, bamboo, Kendu, and Siali leaves are sold for making plates and cups, supplementing their income from agriculture. Unlike the Dongria and Kutia Kandha, who practice shifting cultivation, the Desia Kandha have adopted ploughing from non-tribal communities and cultivate plains. Their economy revolves around agriculture, forest products, wage labor, and trade.

The Kandha community continues to rely significantly on a food-gathering economy, reflecting their origins as hunters and gatherers. They collect roots and tubers for both food and medicinal purposes, favoring traditional herbal remedies over modern healthcare. Their staple diet comprises various millets (such as rice, maize, great millet, finger millet, little millet, Kodo millet, fox-tail millet, Kangoo, and barn-yard millet) and pulses (Biri, Kandul, and Jhunga). They supplement their diet with natural foods like mangoes, tubers, Khursa, Mahua flowers, Kardi, and wild mushrooms, collected mainly during the rainy season. These mushrooms, known as Chati, are selected for edibility with great care, demonstrating the Kandha's indigenous knowledge. Collected tubers, referred to as Kanda, are prepared by boiling or roasting based on their taste.

The Kandha also gather a variety of wild fruits, including Amba, Kendu, and Panasa, integral to their traditional diet. Food gathering is an ancient practice for these hill-dwelling tribes, who have developed effective techniques for processing and preserving wild produce. This reliance on natural resources sustains their diet, provides resistance to diseases, and endows them with the stamina required for their agrarian lifestyle. These practices underscore the Kandha's enduring connection to their environment and cultural heritage.

Hunting has been a significant occupation across societies, and the Kandha of Kalahandi are no exception. Traditionally, they planned hunts based on animal habits, targeting small game like pigeons, doves, mynas, parrots, jungle fowl, peacocks, squirrels, rabbits, and langurs, which were prepared as special dishes. They also hunted reptiles like dhamana and godhi for their skins, used in musical instruments. Occasionally, they hunted larger game, including wild boar, sambar, kutra, bear, porcupine, wild goat, and deer. Hunting provided meat and had religious and spiritual significance, although it is now less central to their economy.

Fishing is another common practice among the Kandha, often pursued as a hobby during leisure time, especially in rainy and winter seasons. They use various methods, including weirs, nets, hooks, arrows, and traps, to catch fish, tortoises, and crabs. Fishing and hunting reflect the Kandha's deep connection to their environment and traditional livelihood practices.

Belief Systems and Ritual Practices

Festivals in Kandha society are deeply rooted in history and rituals, offering occasions for cultural renewal and fun. These events foster connections with deities, ancestral spirits, and supernatural forces, believed to ensure prosperity and protection from diseases. Celebrations are also aimed at agricultural welfare, household life, and livestock breeding.

The Kutia, Desia, and Dongria Kandha identify various powerful deities and spirits influencing their lives. Illness, misfortune, and unusual occurrences are often attributed to these spirits, believed to reside in hills, forests, streams, and dwellings, with their numbers growing through the inclusion of deceased ancestors. The Kandha revere "Dharni," the Supreme

Earth Goddess, represented by a stone or wood pillar, responsible for vegetation and land productivity. Historically, human sacrifices were offered to her, a practice now replaced by buffalo sacrifices. Ancestor spirits, called 'Dumbas,' are also worshipped, appearing in dreams to request offerings. The Kandha's religious beliefs encompass various deities, spirits, ghosts, and magics, reflecting their fatalistic worldview and reliance on chance and luck.

Meriah festival is a significant event among the Kutia and Dongria Kandha, held every 5 to 10 years to honor Dharni with buffalo sacrifices, replacing the earlier human sacrifices. This festival, known by various names such as Kedu and Meriah Puja, spans 3 to 5 days. The Desia Kandha also perform buffalo sacrifices but without human brutality. Dongria Kandha, being animists and polytheists, invoke a pantheon of spirits during the Meriah festival, while Kutia Kandha's spirits inhabit natural sites. Desia Kandha's magico-religious practices include creating artifacts with symbolic significance, worshipping multiple deities, and performing buffalo sacrifices for agricultural success, reflecting their evolving religious practices influenced by non-tribal assimilation.

Conclusion

Tribal festivals in Odisha are rooted in a deep belief in supernatural forces regulating human existence, celebrated at domestic, community, and regional levels. These events aim for good farming, health, and safety. Ancestors, alongside gods and goddesses, are worshiped with equal respect, intertwining religious and socio-cultural aspects of tribal life. The Kutia and Dongria Kandh celebrate the Meriah festival every 5 to 10 years, now using buffalo sacrifices instead of humans to please the Earth Goddess, Dharni Penu.

Odisha's geography, divided between advanced plains and tribal highlands, shaped distinct social systems. This led to three inhumane practices: Sati among high-caste Hindus, and Meriah (human sacrifice) and infanticide among the Kandh. Meriah, rooted in superstition, aimed to ensure abundant crops and avert disasters by offering human blood to the Earth Goddess. It also sought success in inter-tribal conflicts through human sacrifices.

These practices highlight the strong influence of socio-religious customs and superstitions in Odisha's tribal communities. Despite their brutal nature, they were deeply embedded in the belief systems, reflecting the intertwined nature of religion, superstition, and socio-cultural identity in tribal life.

The British government abolished the Meriah sacrifice practice in 1861 through forceful interventions and established measures to supervise the affected areas. They provided education and training to the saved Meriah, enhancing the prosperity of the Kandh by integrating them into various trades. This intervention led to significant social and economic reforms, raising the Kandha's standard of living and reducing the need for costly sacrifices. British reforms also improved the Kandha's economic status through road construction, fairs, and schools, facilitating trade and cultural exchange with advanced Hindus of the plains. Consequently, the Kandha adopted some Hindu customs, deities, and festivals, leading to a reduction in superstitions and a cultural transformation.

Despite the official ban on human sacrifices, secret practices continued, as revealed by an eyewitness account of a girl's sacrifice in the Kutia Kandha community. The informant described the brutal ritual performed to appease the Earth Goddess, Dharni Penu. These events indicate that such sacrifices may still occur unnoticed in remote areas. The British reforms significantly influenced Odisha's socio-economic landscape, bringing progress and transformation. While driven by colonial motives, these efforts eradicated inhumane practices and paved the way for modernization and prosperity in the 20th century.

References:

- Bailey, F.G. 1960. *Tribe, Caste and Nation*. Oxford University Press. London
- Bisi, D. G.1990. Kandha Jatira Bibah Pratha (Odia), Saintala, Balangir.
- Boal, Barbara M. 1997. Human Sacrifice and religious change, the Kondhs, Inter-India publications, New Delhi,
- Das, M.N.1956. Suppression of human sacrifice among the Hill Tribes of Orissa, *Man in India*, Vol. 36(1). P. 21
- Dash, B and N. C. Dash. 2009. Kondhs: An Ethnobotanical Study, Amadus Press. Bhubaneswar.
- Mahananda, R. 2011.Tribal communication technology: A case study of Kondhs of Kandhamal of Odisha. Orissa Review. December. pp.50-60.
- Mahapatra, S.1993. The Tangled Web: Tribal Life and Culture of Orissa. Bhubaneswar. Sahitya Akademi. Bholanath Press. pp. 10-114.
- Niggemeyer, H.1964. Kutia Kond, Klaus Renner Verlag, p. 244
- Ota, A.B. 1996. Changing Demographic scenario of the scheduled tribes in Orissa. Tribes of India: Ongoing Challenges (Rannsingh Mann eds.), Delhi: M.D. Publication Pvt. p. 151.
- Panda, T & Padhy, R.N. 2007. Sustainable food habits of the hill-

dwelling Kandha tribe in Kalahandi district of Odisha. *Indian Journal of Traditional Knowledge.* Vol. 6(1), pp. 103-105

- Patnaik, N. 2005. Primitive Tribes of Orissa and their Development Strategies, D.K. Print world, New Delhi, p.20
- Patnaik, N.R. 1992. History and Culture of Khond Tribes, New Delhi: Common Wealth Publishers.
- Primitive Tribes of Odisha. 2013. Scheduled Castes and Scheduled Tribes Research and Training Institute, Bhuabaneswar.
- Rana, N. K. 2019. Tribal Culture of Kalahandi: Particular References to Kandh Tribes, Kunal Book, New Delhi, p. 195
- Rana, N.K. 2022. Prehistoric Cultures of Odisha: A study of Tel River valley, Sharada Publishing House, Delhi
- Risley, H. 1969. The People of India. Delhi: William Crooke.
- SCSTRTI. 2010. *Kutia Kandha,* Bhubaneswar: Scheduled Castes and Scheduled Tribes Research and Traning Institute.
- Senapati, N. and D.C. Kuanr. 1981. District Gazetteers, Orissa: Kalahandi, Bhubaneswar, p. 72
- Sharma, K. 1979. The Konds of Orissa, New Delhi
- Taylor, E. B.1958. Primitive Culture: Researches in to the Development of Mythology Philosophy, Religion, Art and Custom, Gloucester, Mass Vol. 2.
- Thurston, E. 1909. Castes and Tribes of Southern India, Madras, Vol. II, p. 358
- Watts, Neville. A.1970. The Half –Clad tribals of Eastern India, Calcutta, Orient Longmans.

Understanding Religious Beliefs and Practices among Oraon Tribe in Odisha: A Sociological Study

Pujarani Behera

Ph.D. Scholar, Department of Sociology,
Ravenshaw University,Cuttack
Email: pujaranibehera1606@gmail.com

Abstract

Tribal community is considered to be the indigenous group in India. They are the asset of our society. They are rich in indigenous knowledge. Indigenous knowledge is used by tribal community in different spheres, like-agriculture, health and handicrafts. Tribal population has seen in all parts of India and majorly in Odisha. There are 62 types of tribes in Odisha and Oraon tribe is one of the leading tribes in them. Their religious practices, custom, tradition and rituals are changing day by day. In this paper there is an effort to analyze the religious practices& rituals among Oraon tribe living in Burla, Sambalpur District of Odisha, how the custom & tradition of Oraon tribe is changing due to modern practice and various festivals followed by them. This study is based on both primary and secondary sources of data. The paper broadly reflects, Sarna religion is the original religion of Oraon tribe, but presently they practice Hindu religion, celebrate various festivals like-karma festival, nawakhani festival, Holi, Diwali, puspuni etc.

Key Words: Tribe, Indigenous knowledge, Religion, Rituals, Festival.

INTRODUCTION:

The Oraon tribe has been nomadic and migrated one place to another place. Due to the advancement of communication, modernization, globalization and industrialization their culture and traditions have developed day by day. Traditionally Oraon men and women used to wear lion-cloth and paria or khanria respectively. The bachelor's dormitory among the Oraons named Dhumkuria. It is a non-formal training center of youth in the art of singing, dancing, drumming and handicrafts. The Oraon women enjoy relatively high status within their own community (Bara.m, 2023). The Oraons were born of the blood from the chest of a holy man. They themselves use the name Kurukh, possibly after a mythical Oraon king called Karakh. Traditionally they were depending upon forest and farms for their ritual practices and livelihood but now days they are considered as settled agriculturalists. Before attaining adulthood, every boy and girl considered tattooing as a religious ritual. Their belief system is God will be angry upon dying without having tattoos on their body (Sinha and Tirkey, 2024).

Kurukh is another name of Oraon tribe. They belong to Austro-Asiatic linguistic family. Their history is considered by cultural diversity and environmental compliance. The Chotanagapur Plateau is the home of Oraon tribe since early times. Their ancestors were hunting and food gathering for fulfillment of their basic needs. Day by day they moved into permanent agricultural settlements and produce crops like- rice, maize, lentils, Dahiya and kutcha. The name Oraon originated from two words "Ora" and "On" means "man" and "our" respectively, which represents their shared identity and community feeling. (Kumari. U, 2024).

The changing patterns in rituals of Oraon tribe:

Due to the impact of modernization and urbanization the customs and traditions of tribal is speedily eroding. The tribal religion, custom and tradition have under gone changes by the influence of town culture. There are also positive sides, due to the modernization the exploitation of tribal has lesser and they maintain the better living condition with better education and health facilities (Kumari. N, 2018).In the era of 21st century, the social status of Oraon tribe remains unchanged. Due to their caste & creed they are unacceptable by their community. Several facilities like- tribal rehabilitation, security, grants, safeguards, welfare etc. is not fully success because lack of practicability. Still the tribal community lacks the equality due to our class based social system. Their society is treated as agricultural society, but in recent trends it is shown that they are involved within the industrial sector like- mining, quarrying, manufacturing, servicing & repairing (Maitra. R, 2016).

The various religious practices followed by Oraon tribe people:

Traditionally Oraon's Dharma was Sarna Dharma. Due to effect of

Hinduism, they started Sarna Dharma in Hindu way. Festival is part of the Oraon life. Sarhul and Karma are two most important festivals of them. In Spring season when Sal tree is come into flower Sarhul festival is celebrated. In their belief, this festival is a symbolic marriage between sky and earth, this leads to fertility of mother earth. They celebrate seasonal festivals which are linked to agriculture such as- Basundhara in month of Baisakhi, Bhadri in Bhadra, Jejuti in Agrahayan, Itu in Falgun and Sarhul in Chaitra (Purkayastha. N, 2018). The Oraon tribe divided into 8 clans, which is based on animals & plants that is called traditional clan. Traditionally while the crop harvest is not over cremating a dead body was observed as taboo but at current time such type of practices has not been observed. Presently they cremate the dead body like- Hindu through burning ghat. They believe on supreme power name sun or Suraj. All the festivals divided into 3 categories such as- family, clan and community. Velofari, Lakshmi puja are family festival, maghebasi is a clan festival and karma are treated as community festival. Parab is a festival where all the people of Oraon clans meet together & everyone share monetary support. The Karam, maythan, maa puja are treated as Parab (Biswas. C, 2020).

They celebrate various festivals which is linked with their agricultural practices, spiritual beliefs and community life like- Sarhul (festival of flowers), Karma (festival of youth and nature), Sohrai (the harvest festival), Tusu parab(the harvest celebration), Bhagat parab (the festival of strength and devotion). There are many traditional dances such as- Chhau dance, Santhal dance, Paika dance, Jhumar dance, Dhomkach dance. They use various traditional musical instruments like- Madal, Bansuri, Nagara, Shehnai (Tiwari. S & Phalachandra. B, 2024).In marriage ceremony the Oraon people invite the community members and relatives in traditionally. Traditional way of invitation is called newta tikhil, which is made with smearing of turmeric and sun-dried rice. Before the marriage ceremony the newta tikhil is brought by women in her anchol whereas the same rice is carried by men in paper packet. The way of invitation of head of the family is the same rice is thrown on the roof of the home. In this ceremony there is always seen a mutual cooperation within both the family of bride and groom. (Toppo. C, 2023). Festival is part of the Oraon life. Sarhul and Karma are two most important festivals of them. But now a days due to the influence of Hinduism, they are celebrating several local festivals- Durga puja, Kali puja, Laxmi puja etc. In their society there is the restriction of inter-tribe marriage so they prefer to marry Oraon only. Child marriage and married men and women are not allowed for second marriage but second marriage is allowed for a divorced, widow and widower. But now, due to the assimilation of other caste people there is found of inter caste marriage in some Oraons. (Purkayastha. N & Bhattacharyya. K, 2017).

Research Gap:

After going through various literatures, it has been observed that most of scholar focuses on the major religious practice which they followed like Sarna Dharma, major festival they celebrated such as, the Sarhul & Karma festival, the impact of modernization & industrialization on the pattern of worship. But they have not analyzed that, at present time or recently which sources of livelihood they follow or the changing patterns of livelihood, the impact of changing livelihood options on the socio-cultural life of tribe and which religious practices they follow & which festivals they celebrate.

Significance of the Study:

Tribal community is considered to be the indigenous group in India. They contribute a lot for the progress of nation because their regions are rich in natural resources. They are also rich in indigenous knowledge. Indigenous knowledge is used by tribal community in different spheres, like-agriculture, health, handicrafts etc. But they are not receiving so much support to expand their traditional knowledge. So, there is the need of sustenance to preserve their traditional knowledge, their customs, culture and traditions. Tribal use indigenous knowledge in various areas, like health, agricultural practices, on art & crafts, etc. Tribal have rich indigenous traditional knowledge on medicinal plants to cure various diseases by using various plants parts.

Theoretical Framework:

The French Sociologist Emile Durkheim developed the theory of religion in his work *The Elementary Forms of Religious Life* by studying the Arunta tribe of Australian aborigines. Religion is a unified system of beliefs and practices relative to sacred things. Religion has two parts, like- beliefs & rites and sacred & profane. Beliefs are a set of ideas & attitudes in relation to sacred things. Rites are a system of action towards the religious things. Sacred refers to extraordinary things which is relate to religious beliefs, rites, duties etc. Profane refers to those practices which is relate to everyday attitude and utilitarian things. He analyzed their belief system of totemism. Totem is the simplest and most primitive form of religion. The stone, tree, animal all are considered as totem for them. In this paper the Oraon tribe practices Sarna religion, which binds people of their community together and maintains we feeling between them. They belong to one totem which means they share one identity.

Methodology

In the present study the research design is exploratory & descriptive, the sample design is simple random. This study was carried out in Oram Praha, university campus, Jyoti Vihar, Burla, Sambalpur. The researcher took both primary & secondary source for data collection.Primary data are collected through Interview Schedule and Observation tool. Secondary data are collected through Article, Journals and Internet browsing etc.

Findings and Discussion

The researcher has tried to analyze the socio-economic profile in the present chapter. The Social profile of the respondents includes gender, Age, Caste, Religion, Marital status, educational qualification, Family type & Economic profile of the respondents includes Occupation, Income. Religion of the respondent plays a significant role in the study purpose.

The researcher took religion as a variable to study the tribal people on the basis of various religions. All the respondents in the area belong to Hindu Religion. The level of education has a direct impact on the activities or reactions of the people. Educational qualification of the sample respondents is an important social variable. Because education helps to improve the knowledge, advance the economy and social development. In this study, the male literacy is higher than female literacy. Family plays an important role to socialize children. Considering this vital role of the size of family, the present study has been made to document the family size of the respondents. Here maximum of the respondents belongs to nuclear family. The occupation of the tribal people also affects their living standard. Here, half of the respondents are laborers.

Income plays a vital role in livelihood of a person. When income is high people lead a better standard of living, but when income is low people lead a worse condition of living. So, the study has been made to know the condition of the respondents. It is observed that economic condition of the respondents is not very well. Most of the respondent's income is between 1000-5000.

Respondents' opinion on beliefs and practices

Indicators (Belief and opinion of respondents)	Yes	%	No	%	Total
practices of Sarna religion	1	5%	19	95%	20
believes in blood sacrifice	18	90%	2	10%	20
beliefs in witchcraft.	6	30%	14	70%	20
believes in one supreme god	4	20%	16	80%	20
Belief on celebrates sarhul festival	2	10%	18	90%	20

This study highlights that, the people of Oraon tribe practices both cremation and burial for disposing the dead body. They practice burial because poverty is the reason behind this. The rituals follow for dead body are after three days of the death, the family members eat non-vegetarian food, only fish. But after 10 days there are no restrictions to take food. In 11 days, the head man of this community performs the role of priest for ancestor worship. In this community there is no role of Brahmin. Sarna religion is the original religion of Oraon tribe, due to the influence of Hindu religion, maximum respondents practice Hindu religion. They worshiping the tree namely: karma tree, Sala tree, neem tree etc. the animals namely: cow, sheep etc. there is no such restrictions to enter into the local temple. Maximum respondents believe in blood sacrifice. They sacrifice hen, goat etc. before harvesting & after harvesting. In the belief system some respondents believe in witchcraft and one supreme god. Before the harvesting they sacrifice hen, goat, sheep etc. in that agricultural field for bumper crop and they celebrate various festivals like-karma festival, nawakhani festival, Holi, Diwali, puspuni etc.

The following insights are found in regard to contemporary religious practices and rituals among Oraon tribe.

The changing patterns in rituals of Oraon tribe:

After data collection & analysis researcher have found that, there are some changes in rituals followed by oraon tribe people for dead body, like-after three days of the death, the family members were eating non-veg but now due to the impact of Sanskritization, they eat non-veg after ten days. Most of the respondents' follows the practice of cremation for disposing of the dead body & some respondents follow the practice of burial.

The religious practices followed by Oraon tribe community:

Sarna religion is the origin of tribal religion, but most of the respondents are following Hindu religion. Maximum respondents believe in blood sacrifice. In early days, there were some blinds believes like-witchcraft, evil spirit etc., but now due to the developments in medical science, the role of witchcraft slows up, some respondents believe in witchcraft. The oraon tribals worshiped stone, tree etc., but in present times they are worshiping the Hindu deities.

The various festivals followed by Oraon tribe:

In early days, they were celebrating Sarhul festivals. But now a days, only some of respondents are celebrating this festival. They are celebrating Holi, Dusshera, Ganesh puja, Saraswati puja, Diwali, puspuni, Nuakhai etc.

Conclusion

Tribal community is considered to be the indigenous group in India. The Oraon tribe is one of them. Due to the impact of modernization and urbanization the customs and traditions of tribal is speedily eroding. The tribal religion, custom and tradition have under gone changes by the influence of town culture. In the era of 21st century, the social status of Oraon tribe remains unchanged. Due to their caste & creed they are unaccceptable by their community. Government grants various scheme for their upliftment still they are not treated as equal with the other sections of society. Several facilities like- tribal rehabilitation, security, grants, safeguards, welfare etc. is not fully success because lack of practicability. Still the tribal community lacks the equality due to our class based social system. In early days they believed in the evil spirit and also believed in witchcraft but at present there are some changes in believe system. Another change is they believed in blood sacrifice, like- animal sacrifice, now days this believes system is reducing. There are no such restrictions to enter into local temple.

References

- Bara. M (2023), "Ethnographic Study of Oraon Tribe of Lodhma Village, Jharkhand" *Journal of Humanities and Social Science,* Vol.28, Issue.4, Pp-36-54.
- Biswas. C (2020) "Impact of Modernization and Continuity of Oraons of North 24 Parganas, W. B, India: An Anthropological Study" *American Research Journal of Humanities and Social Sciences,* Vol. 6, No. 1, Pp-1-3.

- Kumari. N (2018) "Impact of Modernisation on Tribal Religious Customs and Traditions: A Case Study of Rourkela" *International Journal of Scientific Research in Science and Technology,* Vol. 4, No. 8, ISSN-2395-6011.
- Kumari. U, (2024) "The Oraon Tribe of Jharkhand: Their Art and Culture" *Journal of Arts, Humanities and Social Sciences,* Vol. 7, No. 7,ISSN-2581-6241.
- Maitra. R (2016) "Tribal Communities of India: A Case Study of Oraon Community" *International Journal of Research,* Vol. II, No. I, ISSN. 2455-1503.
- Purkayastha. N & Bhattacharyya. K (2017) "Effects of Tea Industry on Tribal Life: A Sociological Study" *International Journal of Multidisciplinary Research,* Vol. 3, No. 7, ISSN-2455-3662.
- Purkayastha. N (2018) "Tribe in Making: A Study on Oraon Tribe in Barak Valley Region of Assam" *Global Journal of Interdisciplinary Social Sciences,* Vol. 7, No. 1, Pp-7-12.
- Sinha and Tirkey (2024), "A Tribal Community in Eastern India: A Case Study of Oraon Tribe" *International Journal of Creative Research Thoughts,* Vol.12, Issue.1, Pp 989-994.
- Tiwari. S & Phalachandra. B (2024) "Culture of Tribal People of Jharkhand: An Overview" *International Journal of Research Publication and Reviews,* Vol. 5, No. 6, Pp-150-159.
- Toppo. C (2023) "Marriage among the Oraon Tribe of Chotnagpur (Jharkhand)" *International Journal of Creative Thoughts,* Vol. 11, No. 8, ISSN-2320-2882.

Shakti Worship in Kandhamal: An Ethno-Historical Study

Bishnu Prasad Rath

Lecturer in History, A.M.C.S COLLEGE,
Tikabali, Kandhamal
Email ID: bprath1969@gmail.com

Abstract:

Shaktism is a cult of Hinduism that focusses on worship of the Goddess or the divine feminine. At times the Shakti is praised as serene and bounteous, while at other times fierce and destructive, which is because She is 'Soumya' to her devotees and 'Ghora' to the enemies of her devotees. She is both Prakriti and Shakti. As Prakriti or Creatrix or Nature She is the principle of the materiality, the ground of all being. The Devi Bhagavatam clearly asserts that all goddesses have the same cosmic source representing the power of creation or "Primal Nature" described as "Prakriti". "The village Deities are also parts of Prakriti and all the female sexes, everywhere in the universe are all come from the parts of Prakriti. So, to insult any women is to insult the Prakriti" (Devi Bhagavatam 9.1.140). As Shakti She is the creative power impelling manifestation. She is both form and without form and is termed variously. She is called Prakriti by the follower of Sankhya, Avidya by the Vedantins, Power of words by the grammarians, Shakti of Siva by the Shaivites, Vishnu by the Vaishnavas, Mahamaya by the Shaktas and Devi by the Pauranikas. She is untransformed. The Agamas, Nigamas, Shakta Puranas and Upapuranas reveal the significance of Shakti worship through ages. The female aspect of the divinity has been venerated since antiquity. Shakti is worshipped in the forms of Stambeswari, Mahishamardini Durga, Parvati, Chandi, Chamunda, Kali, Vimala, Dasamahavidya or Transcendent knowledge, Varahi, Saptamatrika, Sixty-four Yoginis etc. The aim of the present paper is to focus on the hinduisation of autochthonous goddesses of Kandhamal manifested in the form of Stambheswari, Patakhanda, Barala Devi, Bhima Devi, Brahmani Devi, Andhari Bauti, Kandhuni Devi etc. It also aims at the integration and assimilation between the tribal culture and Brahmanical Hinduism. Here, both the primary as well as secondary sources have been utilised for writing of the present paper.

Keywords: Saktism, Kondh, Tribal, Ethno-History, Dharani Penu

Introduction:

Shakti is the source of cosmic evolution and the controller of all forces and potentialities of nature. Being feminine in gender She has long been associated with the various male deities as their energy but in Shaktism the energy of each God becomes personified as his consort, and thus, if a god is separated from his consort or Shakti, He is powerless and inert. To justify this statement, Sankaracharya, the propounder of monistic theory, in the Saundaryalahari has eulogised the greatness of Shakti in the following manner:

Sivah saktya yukto yadi bhavati saktah prabhavitum
na ced evam devo na khalu kusalah spanditumapi;
ata stvam aradhyam Hari-Hara-Virincadibhir api
pranantum stotum va katham akrta-punyah prabhavati

(Saundaryalahari, sloka I)

Types of Shaktism:

Shaktism can be divided into three denominations depending on the origin and use; i.e., tribal or folk, Tantric or yogic and devotional or Bhakti strands. The tribal or folk strand involves in possession, healing, and animism; the Tantric or yogic strand encompasses meditation and visualization; and the devotional or Bhakti strand relates love for a specific Goddess. In combined form, they like a rope of strands interwoven together.

Tribal or Folk Shaktism:

The Tribal or Folk Shaktism is perhaps the oldest form of Shaktism in India. It involves the worship of both tribal and local Goddesses. The local Goddesses are generally rocks or other natural objects who have revealed themselves to villagers. The folk Shaktism is practised to heal the diseases, accord fertility to all living beings and to get rid of spirits of the ancestors. In Odisha, the Goddesses are generally worshiped in several forms. The Goddess may be the tribals' dark and powerful Kali, the hunters' Chandi; the snake goddess Manasa; the smallpox goddess Shitala, etc. She is also worshiped as Grama Devatis and Yoginis.

The folk tradition is primarily an oral tradition, handed down from village elders or priests to the followers. Likewise, the traditions of goddess worship are passed down to next generation. Few elements of Brahmanical Hinduism (such as Sanskrit mantras or brahman priests) are also found in Shaktism. In few cases, the tribal shaman-healers (Ojhas) and Shakta Tantrikas perform meditation and worship in burning ground.

The multitude of deities with a tribal origin form a characteristic and at the same time fascinating and distinguishing feature of the religious landscape of Odisha. Although most of these deities have found their way into the realm of pan-Indian Hindu gods and goddesses, their character and the rituals and 'texts" associated with them continue to reveal more or less traceable features of their tribal origin (Beltz &Frese, 2004).

It is believed that Shakti worship is directly originated from the primitive mother-goddess cult and that it gradually crept into the tribal and folk culture and subsequently into the mainstream of Indian religions. It is an admixture of heterogeneous elements of the non-Aryan and Aryan origin pertaining to customs, rites, worship patterns, myths and legends of multifarious nature.

The popularity of Shaktism, in contrast to other Indian religions, lies in its prolificity and universality by throwing its doors open invariably to the people of all castes, creed and sects. As a result, the Shakta religion could have devotees or followers from all strata of the society and had wider acceptability to other religions. Tantricism in particular, a well-known trend in religious efflorescence, finds its flowering in amalgamation with Shaktism. At a particular time of history, indeed, both the trends of thought were so inextricably integrated that one could not possibly be separated from the other (Brighenti,2001). When the Goddess was made to proclaim that the Vedas were derived from Her, her assimilation was complete. The complexity and multiformity of the Goddess presented a number of possibilities at adjustment with Brahminism at different levels (Chakrabarti, 2021).

Shakti cult plays an important role in the socio-religious life of the Odishan people. The archaeological as well as literary sources prove the prevalence of Shakti cult in Odisha to an early age. Both in paintings and engravings of Odishan rock art several instances of bisected triangles resembling female genital have been encountered (Donaldson & Behera, 1988). One of the earliest references appears in the line six of Rock Edict XIII of Asok which alludes to the mother-worship by the Atavikas who lived in the forest regions of Kalinga (Hultzsch, 1925). Every day, as pointed out by B.C Pradhan, the Divine Mother, usually in the form of a post or a pillar, is worshipped in virtually every forest (Atavi) region in Odisha while the concept of Vana Durga became especially popular in the medieval period (Pradhan, 1983). Non-Aryan tribes like the Savaras, the Pulindas and the Sailajas who were the inhabitants of the forest area of the Mahendragiri Mountains, as indicated in the early Odishan inscriptions as well as in the Sanskrit works such as Kathasaritsagara (Tawney 1924), were great devotees of the Divine Mother. Like the phallus-worship resembling Lord Siva, the worship of Shakti in the form of a log of wood, a post, or a stone pillar (Stambha) most likely evolved from primitive tree worship. In Odisha this form of the Divine Mother is often designated as Stambhesvari (Khambhesvari), or as Kandhunidevi i.e. the deity of the aboriginal Kondhs (Pradhan, 1983).

The earliest epigraphic reference to the tribal goddess in Odisha appears in the Bhadrak inscription of Maharaja Surasarma, dated on Palaeographical ground to the 3rd century A.D., where the goddess Parnnadevati (goddess of leaves or forest) received donations of three pieces garments, one pedestal and two pieces of gold, the gold given being 80 Panas from a lady named Ranghali, wife of Sri-Pava. The tradition of worshipping the goddess of leave under the name Patarasuni is still prevalent in the rural areas of Odisha (Panigrahi, 1981). By the 4th century A.D. due to the influence of south Indian campaign of Samudragupta (Das, 1978), Brahmanical form of Hinduism penetrated into the tribal hinterlands of ancient Kalinga, Kangoda and Kosala, the historical sub regions of Odisha, leading to the transformation of the tribal Stambha or Khamba or the pillar to Stambhesvari or Khambhesvari. Before Samudragupta's South Indian campaign, Odisha had remained untouched by Brahmanical influence. Moreover, the Terasinga copper plate of Tustikara of the Sulki dynasty refers to Bhagavati Stambhesvari as the tutelary deity of Maharaja Tustikara, whose mother Sri Sobhini Kaustubhesvari was a committed devotee of Stambhesvari. The charter was issued at a place named Parvatadvara (gateway to mountains) (Rajaguru, 1985). The Stambhesvari cult still survives at the village level in Sonepur, Boudh, Angul, Dhenkanal and Ganjam districts. Temples are also erected in the honour of Stambhesvari at Sonepur and at Aska.

Kandhamal District is nearly synonymous with goddess worship. Popular memory has it that the origin of goddess worship is traced back to the hoary antiquity. In the tribal community of Kandhamal most of deities belong to feminine line. They worship Earth Goddess, River Goddess, and Mountain Goddess etc. All the sources of nature are worshiped as Goddesses in tribal societies. At the end of every village in Kandhamal we can witness a place dedicated to Mother Goddess, known under different names. Although they may be represented in diverse ways and vary in importance, collectively they are the religious fabric of the settlement. Practically, the goddess provide succour in times of trouble and a barrier to ward off any negative influences that may threaten the village or town's inhabitants. They are believed to be the guardian deities of the villages and eradicate all evils. The tutelary deities gradually assumed the form of *Istadevatas* of the ruling family of Odisha during the early medieval period. However, in the later medieval period some local goddesses of Odisha also rose to prominence as the tutelary deities of some feudatory families. They are being Hinduized in name and process of worship and Brahman priests are engaged by the state.

Stambhesvari

Stambhesvari, the Goddess of the Post or Pillar, is one of the famous formless autochthonous deities widely worshipped in the hill tracts of south and western districts of Odisha. She also goes by the local colloquial name of Khambesvari. She is worshipped as a manifestation of Shakti in the forms of wooden posts or pillars and also threw stones. She was the tutelary deity of some ruling dynasties like those of Tushtikara, the Sulkis, the Bhanjas and the feudatories of the Somavamsis like Ranaka Sri Jayarnnama in the early medieval period. The antiquity of the Stambhesvari cult may be traced back to the 5th century A.D. Since, then the cult of Stambesvari alias Khambhesvari is wide spread and popular particularly in western Odisha and the Ghumusar region of south Odisha. She is still the presiding deity in most of the villages of Ghumsar, Boudh, Sonepur, Angul, Talcher and Dhenkanal regions (Patnaik, 1922) which consist mostly of hill and forest tracts.

The aboriginal Goddess worshipped by the non-Aryan tribes of hinterland Odisha, in course of time, were absorbed in the Hindu pantheon. They were adopted and worshipped by the Aryan invaders who had settled amidst the non-Aryan tribes. Gradually when the Aryan chiefs established small kingdoms of their own, they had to depend upon the sturdy tribals for the consolidation and the defence of their newly established kingdoms. The Aryan kings also needed the lands of different tribes and their services for promotion and extension of peasant agriculture which would yield enough surplus crops to meet the requirements of the increased civil and military personnel. Thus, the kings were dependent upon the support and the loyalty of the tribes. Therefore, they kept them in good humour through the gradual process of inclusion of tribal groups into the Hindu caste system and the absorption and adoption of some aspects of the tribal religion and culture into the Aryan fold (Majumdar, 1911). Pargiter had observed that "the Aryans met with the religious practices and beliefs among whom (the tribes) they ruled over or came into lasting contact with, and have assimilated some of them gradually thus modifying their own religion to a certain extent" (Pargiter,1922). In this process the dominant tribal deities like Stambhesvari were Aryanised and patronized by the kings as their tutelary deities. Patronage of the dominant autochthonous deities enabled the kings to consolidate their power and its legitimation in the Hindu tribal zone of the hilly hinterland of Odisha(Kulke & Tripathi ,1978).

In this process of Aryanisation the Brahmanas who were granted rent free lands in the tribal area, played an important role. They settled in the forest tracts through land grants and came into contact with the forest tribes which resided in the dominion of the Aryan kings (Kosambi, 1962). The Brahmanas defined and codified the duties of the tribes which were to lead a recluse living in the forest and serve their king by digging wells, by giving water to thirsty travellers, giving away bed and other reasonable presents upon Brahmanas. Prof. R.S. Sharma has rightly stated that " the significance of land grants to Brahmanas is no difficult to appreciate. The grantees brought new knowledge which improved cultivation and inculcated in the aborigines a sense of loyalty to the established order upheld by the rulers" (Sharma, 1965). The coexistence of Brahmanical and tribal cultures led to the inter-action between these two[21]. So much so the deities like Stambheswari worshipped by the non-Aryan tribes entered the Brahmanical pantheon. It may be mentioned that the hill tribes who believed in matriarchy were worshippers of Shakti. Stambhesvari is also worshipped as a manifestation of Shakti in the hill tracts of Odisha or at least in tribal surroundings. Stambhesvari is the best example of the aboriginal goddesses of Odisha which underwent the process of Aryanisation in earlier times.

So much so mother Goddesses worshipped by the non-Aryan tribes entered the Brahmanical pantheon. It may be mentioned that the hill tribes who believed in matriarchy, were worshippers of Shakti." This explains why the temples of autochthonous Goddesses are found in the hill tracts of Kandhamal or at least in tribal pockets. These Goddesses, Hinduised in course of time, were ultimately transformed into Shakti cult. The practice of human sacrifice which was prevalent among the hill tribes was adopted in earlier times by the Aryans, who assimilated their system into their religion in the Naramedha. This gives us an idea of how the Hindu religion became a blending of heterogenous cults embodying the precepts of different tribes in different times. In Kalika Purana we come across the name of Savaras as the worshippers of Goddess Kali (Rath, 1987).

Like Stambeswari (Khambhesvari in Odia), Vyaghradevi and Tara-Tarini the aboriginal Goddesses of the Ganjam district of Odisha (Rath, 1987), Goddesses Patakhanda, Baraladevi, Andhari Bauti, Bhima Devi etc of Kandhamal underwent the process of Aryanisation in earlier times. These deities do not possess any specific iconographic features, nor do they appear in all Indian Brahmanical theology. However, R. N. Nandi has said that "they were acknowledged as members of the documented theology of the society in whose contact the tribes lived" (Nandi, 1978). Worshipped in the form of stones these deities have been anthropomorphised and converted into images. Most of these Goddesses were kept in open space under the bushy groves or under a tree on the road sides or hutments in the middle of the village or at one end or in the close vicinity of the village or in the caves. But in course of time temples were also constructed to install these Goddesses. The tribals had a conviction that sacrifices were essential to please the Goddesses. Hence animal and human sacrifices were offered to them. This explains the reason why the temples of these tribal Goddesses are generally found at secluded places (Rath, 1987).

In most of the temples of these aboriginal Goddesses in the Kandhamal district stones or pebbles are worshipped along with the main image in the sanctum sanctorum to which Gandha (sandal paste), Pushpa (flowers), Dhupa (incense), Dipa (oil wick lamp) and Naivedya (eatable articles) are offered. Sometimes Snana (bath) is also offered. Goats and cocks are sacrificed before the Goddesses round the year, preferably on the Sankranti day and more ceremoniously in the months of Chaitra and Aswina to fulfil wishes. The priests, both males and females, of these temples are non-Brahmans. They are affiliated to different tribal groups. The male priests call themselves Jakeri, Guru, Dehuri, Sudra Muni, Muni, Jani, Mali, Devata, Raula etc. The Puja is performed in some temples every day and in some others only once in a week, i.e., on Tuesday or Thursday.

It is believed that these tribal Goddesses protect human beings, cure diseases, save the tribes from epidemics such as pox and cholera and ascertain fertility. The Kondhs, Savaras and other aboriginal hill tribes of Kandhamal believed that their Goddesses cause famine as punishment for their sins. Hence, they feared to commit a sinful act. They also believed that their Goddesses were unconquered and although they were the sources of all evils. They could confer every form of mundane benefit. Besides, they thought that the Goddesses appeared on earth to restore peace and introduced the art of agriculture as well as other blessings into the world (Rath, 1987).

Goddess Pattakhanda

The deities of Pattakhanda and Baral Devi of Kandhamal district have a tribal root, in course of time they have developed to the status of regional fame being patronized by local chiefs and worshipped by both tribals and non-tribals which helped the chiefs to subdue the tribal subjects and to gain control over them.

The word Pattakhanda literally means 'chief sword or main sword'. Pattakhanda worship indicates worship of weapons. Weapons are regarded as Goddess Durga, which is prevalent in the Hindu society of Odisha since hoary past. The deity of Pattakhanda installed at Baliguda, Mahasinghi and elsewhere is represented by a piece of crude stone, having no shape of any living being. A sword is being placed near the deity known as Pattakhanda. It may be presumed that the sword had been presented by any local chief many years ago. Placing of a sword indicates that the deity was regarded as war deity in remote past and gradually people regarded her as guardian deity of the village as well as the region. Non-Brahman, mostly Kshatriya caste priests are employed for worship of the deities of Pattkhanda. Except Baliguda, in other places a curved pole is posted named as Chhatkhamba where the sacrificial animal is tied. It reminds us the worship of Khambeswari by the tribal Kandhas in the early times.

People of Baliguda region regard Mahasinghi as the first seat of Goddess Pattakhanda, where she was worshipped by the Kshatriyas belonging to the Nala dynasty. They were regarded as the Rajas or kings of the area. When their family expanded, they were sent to rule in different Muthas and they also established Pithas of Pattakhanda at each Mutha headquarters. In this way Pattakhanda worship extended from a village cult to a regional status.

The legend attached to the temple narrates that the original seat of Pattakhanda is Jarasinga in Bolangir district. From Jarasinga the deity was brought by the first Raja of Mahasinghi to his capital. Those plain-lander people started worshipping the tribal Goddess Pattakhanda. Since then, the Goddess has been venerated by both tribals and non-tribals. The Goddess is offered Prasad two times a day and Arati (Light offering) is done daily in the evening, which has been introduced by Brahmanical Hindu priests. But other tribal systems are still prevailing there. Even the non-Brahman priests have not been changed till now. Nuakhai, Kandul Bhaja Parab and Dasahara festival are being observed in Pattakhanda Pitha at Baliguda. Dasahara is observed with much pomp and veneration. Kandul Bhaja Puja is observed in a day in the month of Phalguna. Arhar is locally known as Kandul. People are restricted not to eat Kandul till observation of Kandul Bhaja Parab.

Bonda tribals of Mudulipada area also observe Pattakhanda worship on the first Monday in the month of Magha (Rath, 2009). A sword known as Pattakhanda kept in a hole of a banyan tree is brought down and worshipped by the Dehuri and a goat is sacrificed. The blood of the sacrificed animal is mixed with the seeds to be planted next year and distributed among all. We could not find any link between the Pattakhanda of Mudulipada and Baliguda. But a legendary link could be observed with Pattakhanda of Jarasinga of Bolangir district and Mahasinghi. As per the legend surrounding the Goddess mirrors that about 13 generations ago there lived Adivasi chiefs named Nagbura and Kanabura, who used to worship Goddess Pattakhanda. They both committed innumerable offences, which enraged the Goddess. The deity became angry as a result the streams also dried up, the land and all human beings became barren, and the Kandhas suffered from hunger and drought.

If legends have to be believed, people felt that such calamities occurred due to the anger of Goddess Pattakhanda. Hence all of them prayed the Goddess and begged apology. The Goddess appeared to them in a dream and told that She would not accept offering from the chief priests because the chief priests had become polluted by eating meat and consuming alcohol. Hence, she was not satisfied with their worship. So, people were asked to search for another priest. There upon the people prayed Her to know the name of the priest.

There upon the Goddess appeared to them in dreams and instructed that they should tie two pieces of black yarn and yellow yarn to two arrows and shoot them high into the air. The place where these two arrows would fall there would be a man and he was to be brought and make their king. Then Nagbura and Kanabura shoot the arrows and followed the arrows. The arrows went and struck the ground near a spring at Jorasingi. At that place a man named Madan Singh was bathing. Then the Kandhas physically carried him to Mahasinghi and kept him with royal honour. Then the Kandhas assigned him with some hard work in order to test him and miraculously Madan Singh came out successful. Then the Kandhas crowned Madan Singh as their king. Madan Singh, the new king was entrusted with worship of Goddess Pattakhanda. There after all their miseries vanished and their land became fertile again and their barrenness came to an end. Pattakhanda is also worshipped at G.Udaygiri, Daringbadi, Kainjhar etc with great veneration.

Goddess Baraladevi

A further example of tribal goddess subject to the process of Hinduization is, from the hill area of Kandhamal district, Baraldevi. Goddess

Baraldevi is the presiding deity of village Balaskumpa, which is situated at a distance of 15 kms from Phulbani, the headquarters town of Kandhamal district. A temple has been built for the deity now. Before the construction of the temple there was a thatched hut meant for the Deity. The Deity is in the form of three to four small stones buried under the ground and smeared with vermillion. In front of the temple a pole is posted, where the sacrificial animal is tied before sacrifice. Since 1999, animal sacrifice has been banned.

Baraldevi is also worshiped at G.Udayagiri, K.Nuagam and Mahasinghi of Baliguda sub-division and Bandhagada, Menia, Gochhapada etc. of Kandhamal sub-division. Goddess Badarauli Devi, who is worshiped at Baramul in Nayagarh district, is perhaps a changed version of Baraldevi who has connection with Sri Jagannath temple (Rath, 2009). Before cutting of timber for making of chariot of Lord Jagannath, the Goddess Badarauli is being worshipped with the offerings of seven sarees, Mahaprasad, sandal wood and Ajnamala or authorisation garland sent from the Sri Jagannath temple. Hence the importance of Goddess Baraldevi, which is a cult of tribal society needs more research.

At the main seat of Baraldevi at Balaskumpa, Durgapuja is observed from the second day to the tenth day in the bright fortnight of the month of Aswina, which is locally known as Navami Yatra. On the beginning day of the festival the sword, gun, Tangi and knife which were presented by the then Raja of Boudh are placed near the shrine and offered puja by the Dehury and a goat is sacrificed. Navami or the ninth day of bright moon of Aswina is celebrated with pomp and spirituality. On this day people of the area gathered at Balaskumpa and offer their devotion to the Goddess. In addition to the main buffalo, other buffaloes which have been dedicated to the Goddess are tied to the posts in front of the temple before being killed directly in the sight of the Goddess. After the sacrifice of the main buffalo, other buffalos are sacrificed. The pole where the main buffalo is tied is known as Chhatkhamba. When the old Chhatkhamba is destroyed a new one is installed. To install a new post some rituals are observed which have resemblances with Navakalevar of Lord Jagannath.

As per the legends surrounding the Goddess, Mahasinghi was the original seat of Baraladevi. The Raja of Mahasinghi used to worship the deity. The Raja of Boudh was also a committed devotee of Mother Goddess. He wanted to bring the Goddess Baraladevi to his kingdom. Hence, he fought against the Raja of Mahasinghi which was a part of Sanakhemundi kingdom. The Boudh Raja fought for twelve years. But he could not get victory. Hence for a long time he prayed Goddess Baraldevi. Finally, Goddess pleased with the king of Boudh and asked for a boon. The Raja prayed to the deity to take her to his kingdom. The Goddess appeared to the king in a dream and announced if the Raja appeased Her with human blood She would go with him. The Raja fulfilled the wishes of the Goddess and returned with the Deity. On the way where they halted there became a Pitha of the Deity. Accordingly, at Bandhagarh and Menia, Baraldevi Pithas are found even now. Then the Raja and his party reached at Balaskumpa. The Raja witnessed that a dog was being chased by a rabbit. He considered that place as heroic soil and felt that the soil of the place is auspicious to install the Deity. There upon he installed the Deity at Balaskumpa and engaged non-Bramhan priests. After some days the Raja left Balaskumpa for his kingdom. On the way he installed the Deity at Purunakatak under the name of Bhairabi. Then the Raja entered his kingdom and installed the Deity by the name of Durga.

Barala Devi is also worshipped at Bandhagarh. Bandhagarh is a village in the extreme south of the Kandhamal subdivision close to the source of the river Bagh. It contains a shrine of Goddess Baraldevi. At this shrine the annual worship of the Goddess takes place in the month of Jyaista (May-June) and is visited by a much larger number of people than of Balaskumpa. The deity, in the shape of a block of stone, is said to have been unearthed by a Kandha while ploughing his field. The Hadgarh Kandhas of the Ganjam district hearing of the discovery, demanded the stone by way of compensation for the Deity which was also formerly taken away by the local Kandhas from Mahasinghi and was being worshipped at Balasukumpa. But their efforts to remove it proved futile as the more they dug the ground round it the deeper it sank. The local Kandhas regarded this as intended for the themselves, took up arms against the Hadgarh people and drove them off. A large embankment, close to the site of the village, was fortified and some of the Odia people from the adjoining village of Kandagarh took up their residence near it for better protection of the Goddess. The village has been named as Bandhagarh after this embankment, its name meaning the "embanked fort"(Senapati & Kuanr, 1983).

The Sudhas of the adjoining villages in Ganjam district are allowed to take part in the worship of the Goddess. The first offering was made by Dadra Kanhar, the descendant of the Kandha who discovered the stone, and the rest of the ceremony is the same as at the Balaskumpa shrine. The man who slays the victims offered to the Goddess is called Bahuka. He is Sudha by caste.

Goddess Bhairabi

Goddess Bhairabi is the presiding deity of the Purunakatak. Previously deity was being worshipped in a thatched hut. Durga puja is observed for 16 days just opposite to the Bhairabi temple in the newly constructed temple of Maheswar Mahadev.

Andhari Bauti of Gochhapada

Together with Barala Devi, a look should be taken at the Goddess Maa Andhari Bauti. Maa Andhari Bauti chooses to occupy a position outside the inhabited area of Gochhapada. She resides peacefully under the shade of a large banyan tree. Her aniconic features resplendent with thick glossy vermillion paste and two silver piercing eyes attract devotes. Rather than being at the centre of village life, Maa Andhari Bauti draws the world to her.

There is a lot of rich folkloric history attached to the deity. The local legend speaks that the Goddess is called Andhari Bauti because Maa Andhari Bauti is worshipped in the darkness. The Dipa or lamp is installed or offered opposite the Goddess instead of placing the face of the lamp towards the Deity. The Dehuri or the priest of the temple belongs to Sudha Caste or Khandayat feudal militia. Andhari Bauti was first worshipped at Mahasinghi, the epicentre of Shakti cult in Kandhamal. There upon the Goddess was brought from Mahasinghi to Bandhagarh and from Bandhagarh to Banduli then to Gochhapada.

Regarding the origin of Andhari Bauti a legend mirrors that the Raja or king of Boudh fought against the king of Khemundi Gada or Khemundi kingdom for twelve years in order to expand the physical boundary of his kingdom. But he was defeated time and again. Later on, the king of Boudh came to know that the king of Khemundi was being protected by the Goddess. So, the king of Boudh offered prayers to the Goddess Andhari Bauti for her blessings. There upon, the Goddess became pleased and blessed the king with grace for victory. The king again launched his war against the Khemundi kingdom. The deity changed her side with the king of the Boudh. The soldier of Boudh kingdom stood behind the Goddess and attacked on the soldiers of Khemundi kingdom. On the other hand, the soldiers of Khemundi kingdom could not see the soldiers of the Boudh as they were fighting by remaining in the darkness.

The local legend speaks that the deity was formerly worshipped by a Kondh priest. But the deity refused to accept offerings from him since he had become polluted through eating meat and drinking alcohol. So, the goddess appeared to the people in a dream to appoint a new priest. There upon a new priest was entrusted with a duty of worshipping to the Goddess belonging to the Sudha caste of feudal militia. The priest of the temple says that their family originated from Budhipadar in Boudh kingdom. They came to this area 13 generations i.e. 500 years ago as stated by Sri Sripati Bhukta of Gochhapada.

Thursday is considered extremely auspicious in Maa Andhari Bauti Pitha. Puja or worshipping is offered once a day in the morning. It is restricted to open the door again once the door is closed after the offerings. The first Thursday of bright moon in the month of Jyaistha is celebrated with much fanfare and spirituality. The festival takes place before Raja Sankranti or Mithuna Sankranti. As an offering to the goddess fruit, milk and home-made sweets are given which then consumed in the form of Prasada or consecrated food. Earlier on, the Goddess was offered with human sacrifices. Later on, devotees would also sacrifice buffalos, goats and cocks. It is believed that those who come to seek the blessings of the goddess don't return barren. Goddess Baraladevi is also worshipped at Gochhapada. Baraladevi is enshrined at the centre of the village. It is unique that offerings are made to Baraladevi before the offerings to Andhari Bauti. It is interesting that, there are three swords kept in a separate sacred room. The three swords are brought out on three occasions and worshipped by the priest.

Goddess Pitabali

The temple of another goddess called Pitabali is situated at Dimbriguda 5 kms away from Phiringia. Goddess Pitabali originated at Dimbriguda. Goddess Pitabali is imagined in a group of crude stones, having no stone similar to any other living beings. Non-Brahman priest, particularly a Kshatriya male (Sudha Odia) priest worships the Goddess. People of Phringia have a great fear, faith and chant the name of Goddess in prosperity and diversity.

Another Pitha of Pitabali is embodied at the out skirt of the village Phiringia. Formerly it was opened once in a week only that was on Thursday. Thursday is the most auspicious day of the Goddess Pitabali.

Pitabali Shakti Pitha is also enshrined at Pasara village. It is about 300 years old Shakti Pitha. A small temple has been built for Devi under a large banyan tree. A local legend surrounding the temple mirrors that Devi was brought to Pasara from Dimiriguda, the cradle of Pitabali. Further the legend speaks that formerly Kandha priests worshipped the deity. But the Goddess refused to accept the offerings from the Kandha priests because they had polluted themselves through consuming meat and drinking alcohol. The Bisoyees of the Suddha caste was invited to perform priestly work. Since then, the Bisoyees have been performing the duty of the priest.

Pitabali temple opens every day. The people of nearby villages visit the shrine to worship the Goddess. They come with Puja materials like flowers, fruit, and coconut etc. for the Devi. Sometimes the devotees offer goats and cocks. The main festival of Devi is held in the lunar month of "Baisakha". It is known as "Latha puja". Pitabali is given offerings once at seed time, the other at harvest. The Devi is accordingly offered the first harvest of crops as is the tradition in most agriculturally led regions, where she is worshipped and offered milk. In this puja all seeds of different crops are offered to the Devi. After Latha puja the farmers show their seeds on Akshaya Tritiya. In Latha puja, numbers of goats and cocks are sacrificed. The Devi is offered Annabhoga by the local communities.

Goddess Brahmani Devi

Goddess Brahmani Devi is worshipped at Bellapadar in Chakapada block of Kandhamal district. A local legend has it that the people of Bellapadar area found a Kalasa (Kalasigada) or a vessel on the top of a hill named Brahmani Devi hill which is situated in the Brahmanapada area. The people of Bellapadar area worshipped Her on the hill for some years. There was a well near the worshipping place. The legend further speaks that there was a well near the worshipping place. In the earlier times, a woman during menstruate period went near the well. There upon the well dried up. The well is found till now. The people could not go to the hill to worship due to long distance and hilly road. So, Goddess Brahmani Devi threw the "Kalas" or vessel from the top of hill which fell to the ground in the middle of seven villages of Bellapadar area. The seven villages are Bellapadar, Nudigada, Saramundi, Bajragada, Sadapadar, Thengajhola and Hatibadi. Earlier on, the people of Kanhar title belonging to Kandha community worshipped the Goddess. But the Devi refused to accept the offerings from the Kandha priests as they had consumed meat, drank alcohol and polluted themselves. Brahmani Devi appeared to the people in dreams and instructed the people that a new priest should be appointed. Accordingly, a new priest was appointed belonging to Sudha caste.

The shrine of Brahmani Devi is located in an open field. The Goddess is worshipped in aniconic form. Some pieces of crude stone are worshipped as Devi. There is an old musical instrument "Nisham" placed in front of Goddess. It is kept in an inverted way. It faces towards the ground. The main festival takes place in the lunar month of Baisakha. Women are restricted to enter the shrine during the worshipping of the Devi. On the Puja Day the puja starts in the afternoon. The devotees and their wives do fast on that day. The Devi is offered with Deepa, Dhupa, Chandana, Puspa, sundried rice, milk and coconuts etc. In Kandha tradition pure wine made from Mahua flowers is offered on every auspicious occasion. Besides, cocks and goats are sacrificed and their blood is offered to the Devi. During the worshipping of Devi, different musical instruments are played. After the performance of Puja, the offered or consecrated food was distributed among the devotees. The devotees were not allowed to take Bhoga to home. Goddess Brahmani Devi is also worshipped at Pururnagarh near Tikabali.

Dhungia Dei of Mahasinghi

Another important aboriginal goddess underwent the process of the aryanization is Dhungia Dei. A folk tale surrounding the Goddess narrates that a tribal person went to the forest to collect sacrificial wood. He saw a dream at night that a Goddess had manifested in the form of a stone on the top of the hill. The next morning, he went to the forest and saw the Goddess. He returned to the village and narrated the whole story to the people in detail. There upon people started worshipping the deity. In order to spare Her devotees, the tiresome climb Maa Dhungia Dei threw a vessel from the top of the hill and the vessel fell to the ground. At the point at which the vessel landed the main temple stands. The vessel rolled down on the foot of the hill at Mahasinghi or Kakaguda near Baliguda. Since then, the goddess has been venerated as Maa Dhungia Dei. The Dhungia Dei forms a red-coloured head, covered all over with silver eyes and protruding tongue. The Goddess is worshipped by a non-Brahman priest belonging to tribal community. It is believed that nobody goes to the hill except for the priest. If anybody goes to the top of the hill he disappears and never returns home. The Deity goes by the local colloquial name Dhungia Dei or Nasakhia Thakurani as She is offered Nasa along with Gandha (Sandal paste), Pushpa (Flower), Dhupa (Incense), Dipa (lamp) and Naivedya (eatable articles) which is unique in its features. In local colloquial Nasa or snuff is called Dhungia. What is particularly unique about the Shakti Pitha is that 'Danda Nata' is not celebrated in Mahasinghi area because beating of drum is prohibited there. Besides, Mahuri is also not played on the auspicious occasions.

Bhima Devi of Tumudibandha

Another tribal goddess of Kandhamal is Bhima devi. She is worshipped on the Bhima Dangar or Parvata or hill two kms from Tumudibandha. The Goddess' face is coloured vermillion and marked with three glazing eyes and a striking mouth. The priest belongs to Paik Community. The adoption of Puranic and Brahmanical nomenclature of Bhima Devi mentioned in the Devi Mahatmya is clear evidence of Hinduization of a tribal deity. It is a non-iconic deity. The shrine is called Bhima Gudi.

Goddess Kandhuni Devi

The goddess Kandhuni Devi is another example of tribal deity being Hinduised. Her origin may be assigned to the hoary antiquity. But she is the patron deity of the royal house of the Nalas of Surada. She has no iconography, but is worshipped as a Hindu goddess by the Kandha priests. She is revered by the people of all castes and creed and has a wide popularity in Ganjam and Kandhamal districts. It is interesting that she is venerated by the royal houses of Surada, Ranaba and Karada besides she is also worshipped at Kainjhar. As the name indicates she is originally the goddess of the Kandhas. The nomenclature of Kandhunidevi indicates that the goddess had a tribal root.

Brahmacharini of Manipadar

Another shrine in Kandhamal is dedicated to the Hinduised deity Brahmacharini or Tarini. The shrine is situated at Manipadar four kilo meters away from Sarangagarh. Blood sacrifices are not offered to the Goddess. The deity is offered with Dhupa, Dipa, Gandha, Puspa and Naibedya. Coconuts, bananas and fried pressed paddy are offered to the Goddess as Bhoga or consecrated food. Female are restricted to visit the shrine. Most of the puja procedure is conducted in local Kui language by the priests belonging to Kandha community. Together with Brahmacharini, other tribal goddesses at Manipadar subjected to the process of Hinduisation are Kali, Bauridevi etc.

Manikeswari of Kotagarh

Maa Manikeswari another Hinduised Goddess is the patron deity of the house of the Gangas of Gadapur and Kotagarh in Kandhamal district. She is adorned by garlands of flower brought by devotees far and wide. What is particularly unique about these Shakti Pithas are observations of rituals like fire walking and thorn swinging. In the thorn swinging ceremony the priest sits on a flat board studded with iron nails or spikes. Thus, the mother Goddess is made to sit on a thorn swing, which has been prepared in advance and gives Darshan to devotees. In early times, human sacrifices were offered but it was prohibited. Then buffaloes were sacrificed but now the sacrifice of lamb is offered.

Narayani of Phulbani

Narayani or Power of Narayana is another important goddess of the tribal district of Kandhamal. She is worshipped in Phulbani town. Various oral traditions go around the Goddess. Maa Narayani is worshipped in the Vaishnavite way. Non-Vegetarian food is not offered to Her.

Lankeswari of Bisipada

Another aryanised Goddess of Kandhamal is Lankeswari venerated at Bisipada. Lankeswari has been worshipped at Bisipada since 1838. The Lankapodi yatra or festival is celebrated with much fanfare and festivities which is older than Daspallah Yatra.

Metaphysical Goddess of Darni Penu

The most recurring feature of the Shakti cult of Kandhamal is metaphysical goddess or Darni Penu. She is worshipped almost in every village. Six stones are installed in the shrine. People worship her before doing any auspicious work. She is also known as Dharani Devi. It is very intriguing that the Darni penu has been associated with Tantric cult based on Vedic tradition. Six stones are installed in the middle of village. These six stones have been associated with Sat Chakras or Six nodal centre on the spinal cord of our body. These nodal centres are energy centres as stated by Sri Pradyumna Pradhan from Makabidingia, Tikabali, Kandhamal.

The high priest of the Goddess is called Jakeri. He maintains severe austere life. He never takes his food outside his home. He takes his food only at home. A Jakeri returns home on same day if he goes outside for any work with social responsibilities. Women are not allowed to the shrine where the goddess is worshipped. Women are strictly prohibited to visit the shrine during their menstruate period. There is no temple for Darani Penu. She is worshipped under the open sky. She is also worshipped on the Varandas of the priest.

Conclusion

The present paper analyses different forms of legends and folklores and their role within a given context. These legends reflect the context of establishment, consolidation and legitimation of political power by feudatory families or Hindu little kings in Hindu tribal border regions or in predominantly tribal areas(Schnepel, 2002). The throwing of vessel from the top of the hill to the plain area is clearly indicative of the diffusion of tribal culture from the forest to the plains. The story of the journey of the Pattakhanda from Mahasinghi to Jarasinghi mirrors the movement of tribal culture to the plains. Similarly, the march of the King from Boudh to Mahasinghi indicates the movement of frontier Hindu civilization into the hilly tracts. Besides, the adoption of puranic or Brahmanical nomenclatures is clear evidence of Hinduisation of tribal deities. For other lesser deities also, for tribal religious system there is a special god for every need. The

Kandhas had adopted Brahmanical sounding names such as Pattakhanda, Manikeshwari, Bhima Devi, Brahmacharini etc. The earth mother, so widely worshipped particularly by primitive cultivators is called Dharti Mata or Pruthvi Mata. She is very often also identified with such Puranic deities as Parvati, Durga, Kali etc. The adoption of Brahmanical nomenclature of Bhima Devi mentioned in the Devi Mahatmya is clear evidence of hinduisation of tribal deity.

Odisha is an excellent example of interdependence of various levels of Hindu religion. The influence of tribal culture was particularly strong when Hindu kings patronised tribal deities as their tutelary deities. Kandhamal is not an exception to this generalisation. The tribal goddesses of Kandhamal have been worshipped by non-Brahman priests and these goddesses have become the deities of the Hindus. The deities like Pattakhanda, Baraladevi, Manikeswari, Bhairavi, Bhima Devi etc. have gradually become deities and become the patron deities of royal houses. Temples have been built though most of the tribal deities are still worshipped by tribal priests and not Bramhanas. The integration of cultures shows the acceptance of tribal deities in Odian context and influence of tribal deities and tribal culture on the Hindu cult co-exist. Berkemer says "the cutting of the jungle, foundation of temples, villages and towns, providing land for cultivation and tanks for irrigation and patronizing local cults were major tasks for kings. In this way, the frontier Hindu civilization moved into the hilly tracts"(Berkemer,1993). Despite the assimilation between the tribal culture and Brahmanical culture, the tribal deities have retained their primary characteristics.

REFERENCE

- Cornelia Mallebrein in a Malinar, J Beltz, H Frese (eds), Text and Context in The History, Literature and Religion of Orissa, New Delhi, 2004, P. 273.
- Francesco Brighenti, Shakti Cult in Odisha, New Delhi, 2001, p. 4.
- Kunal Chakrabarti, Religious Process, New Delhi, (9th Imp.) 2021, p.192.
- Thomas Donaldson and K.S. Behera, Sculpture Masterpieces from Odisha, New Delhi, 1988, p. 33.
- E. Hultzsch, 'Inscriptions of Asoka', Corpus Inscriptionum Indicarum, Vol. I, London, 1925, p. 66.
- B. C. Pradhan, Shakti worship in Odisha, Ph. D. Dissertation Sambalpur University, 1983, p. 18.
- S.N. Rajaguru, Inscriptions of Odisha, Vol. I, part II, Berhampur, 1958, pp. 195-96.

- Katha sarita sagara of Somadeva, tr. By C.H. Tawney, (Ed.) N.M. Penzer, London, 1924, Vol. I. pp. 102-136 and Vol. II, p. 141.
- K. C. Panigrahi, History of Odisha (Hindu Period), Cuttack, 1981, pp. 348-9.
- M. N. Das, (Ed). Sidelights on Odishan History and Culture, Cuttack, 1978, p. 351.
- S. Patnaik, Kodala Mandala O Stambjesvari, Utkala Sahitya (now defunct Oriya monthly), Vol.XXVI, Nos.3 & 4, pp.7-15, 1922.
- B.C. Majumdar, Orissa in the Making, p.107 ff; J.A.S.B., New series, Vol. VII (1911), pp.443-47.
- F.E. Pargiter, Ancient Indian Historical Tradition, 1922, p.3.
- Eschuann, Kulke and Tripathi, The Cult of Jagannatha and the Regional Tradition of Orissa (1978), pp.128-129.
- D.D.Kosambi, Myth and Reality: Studies in the formation of Indian culture, 1962, p.91.
- The Mahabharata, Santiparva, LXV (Translated by PC Roy, 1950,VIII, p.146).
- R.S. Sharma, Indian Feudalism, c. 300-1200, p.281, Calcutta, 1965.
- R.N. Nandi, Religious Institutions and the Cults in the Deccan, p.120, Delhi, 1978
- A.K Rath, Studies on Some Aspect of The History and Culture of Orissa, Kolkata,1987, pp.101-110.
- Raghunath Rath, Two Shakti Pithas of Kandhamal District, Orissa review, September-2009, pp.154-157.
- Nilamani Senapati and D.C Kuanr, Orissa District Gazetteers, Boudh-Khondmals, 1983, p.374.
- Personal Communication with Sri Sripati Bhukta, the priest of Andhari Bauti of Gochhapada, Brahmananda Kanhar, priest and member of Temple committee of Gochhapada, Birendra Kanhar, youth president of temple committee, Andhari Bauti of Gochhapada in Kandhamal District.
- Personal Communication with Sri Sripati Bhukta, the priest of the temple of Andhari Bauti.
- Personal communication with Sri Pradyumna Pradhan, an octogenarian tribal scholar of Kui language of Makabidingia Village in Kandhamal District.
- Burkhard Schnepel, The Jungle Kings, New Delhi, 2002
- G. Berkemer, Little kingdoms in Kalinga, 1993, p.7.

Ashram School in India:
A Review Study

Dr. Subal Tandi

Assistant Professor, Department of Sociology
Maa Manikeshwari University
Email: -subaltandi@gmail.com

Rashmita Sahu

Ph.D Scholar, Central University of Jharkhand
Email: rasmitareema@gmail.com

Abstract

Considering the importance of education and low educational status among tribals, the concept of Ashram school started across the country in all tribal sub-plan areas since third five-year plan with an aim to promote education among tribal. The customized rule which provided the poor to access the education with basic help in livelihood. Exiting Ashram schools are found with inadequate infrastructure. Besides that, shortage of teachers seems to be very common phenomenon of Ashram school. In relation to Ashram school, the other residential school like Model Residential school, Adarsha Vidyalaya and Sainik school etc. are growing over the state with conducive educational atmosphere. However, the Ashram schools have been neglecting by government over the decades.

Key Words: Tribal, Ashram School, Infrastructure, Educational Atmosphere, Livelihood

Introduction

Indian has a large number of tribal populations as compared to any other nation states of the world. In spite of being considered as the first inhabitant of the nation tribal are deprived of their basis requirements in their day-to-day life. They are not only socially, economically and educationally backward but also face discrimination at a large scale. They have been exploited in various forms, from land alienation to the force displacement from their dwelling place in the name of development. Tribal life has always been tied with the nature or forest and their culture, custom and tradition, and their livelihood has a close connection with the forest. But very often the act government seems to be eliminating them from the access to the forest which is like a fish without water as the tribal identity lies with water forest and land (Jal, Jangal and Jamin). Although the Forest Rights Act 2006 gave the provision for certain rights to the tribal with regard to access the forest and its product. But the provision seems to be more in pen and paper only and a big gap has been observed in the part of implementation. Even after 72 years of independence the condition of tribal community is not up to the mark as the country is growing in a rapid growth. The development process of tribal community is growing at a snail's pace. A number of policies and programmes have been made by both union and state government from time to time, yet it looks as if it has a long way to go where tribal community would be strengthen enough to walk hand in hand with the rest of the world.

Tribes are considered as the first origin of the earth. They are considered as the indigenous people living in the society in different groups or communities who have more or less same pattern of living with different culture, customs, traditions, language and faith from one group to another. Tribals are also often called as "Adivasi" which means the first inhabitant of the mother land. The term "tribe" originated around the time of the greek city states and early formation of the Roman Empire. The Latin term "tribus" has been transformed to mean "A group of persons forming a community and claiming descent from a common ancestor" (Lal 2019: 2). The google search engine describe tribe as "A social division in a traditional society consisting of families or communities linked by social, economic, religious, or blood ties, with a common culture and dialect, typically having a recognized leader" (Google 2022). Similarly, Cambridge dictionary define tribe as "A group of people, often of related families, who live together, sharing the same language, culture and history, especially those who do not live in towns or cities" (Cambridge 2019).

Scheduled Tribe in India

Tribal population in India is around 8.2 per cent of the total population living in the country. Majority of the tribal population live in the states of Odisha, Jharkhand, Chhattisgarh, Karnataka, Madhya Pradesh, Maharashtra, Rajasthan, Gujarat, Andhra Pradesh and West Bengal. These states account for about 80 per cent of the total tribal population in the country. Madhya Pradesh has the highest number of tribal populations with 14.7 per cent of the total tribal population in India. Similarly, Maharashtra and Odisha stand in second and third position in contributing to the total tribal population. Lakshadweep has a highest number of tribal populations with 94.8 per cent to the total population of the union territory followed by the state of Mizoram and Nagaland with 94.4 and 86.5 percent respectively. Similarly, Uttar Pradesh has a least number of scheduled tribes with 0.56 percent of its total population followed by Tamilnadu and Bihar with 1.1 and 1.28 per cent respectively (GoI, 2011). The ministry of tribal affairs states that there are 705 tribal groups notified by the government of India. Odisha is a state where there is maximum number of tribal communities with 62 than any other state of the country. Within 705 tribal groups 75 groups has been kept under the category of Particularly Vulnerable Tribal Groups (PVTGs) living in various parts of the country (GoI 2020a).

Constitutional Provision on Scheduled Tribe

The constitution makers were aware of the fact that the tribal community in India need special provision in the constitution to establish social justice and empowerment. Keeping this in view several special provisions were made in the constitution for overall development and to connect the tribal community to the mainstream society. The term Scheduled Tribes first appeared in the constitution of India and define Scheduled Tribes under Art. 366 (25) as "such tribes or tribal communities or parts of or groups within such tribes or tribal communities as are deemed under Article 342 to be Scheduled Tribes for the purposes of this constitution". The President of India has the constitutional power to specify or declare tribal communities or groups to be scheduled in relation to any state or union territory after consulting the governor of the concern region under Article 342. Further Article 244 and 244 (a) provide for Fifth and Sixth Schedule respectively for the special administration of the tribals. The Panchayats (Extension to the Scheduled Areas) Act, 1996 (PESA) in the Fifth Schedule Areas was introduced to secure local self-governance by the tribal people. The constitution also provides for no prohibition of discrimination on grounds of religion, race, caste, sex or place of birth (Art. 15), Equality of opportunity in matters of public employment (Art. 16), Protection of certain rights regarding freedom of speech, etc. (Art. 19), Promotion of Educational and Economic interests of Scheduled Castes, Scheduled Tribes and other weaker sections (Art. 46), Claims of Scheduled Castes and Scheduled Tribes to services and posts (Art. 335). Moreover Article 330 and 332 provides for Reservation of seats for Scheduled Castes and Scheduled Tribes in the House of the People and in the Legislative Assemblies of the States respectively. Reservation in the seats of Panchayat is also provided under Article 243 D. The National Commission for Scheduled Tribes (NCST) was set up under article 338 A to look after the affairs related to Scheduled Tribes (Tandi and Tandi, 2019).

Education of Scheduled Tribes

The colonial education policy in India was designed and implemented by Sir Thomas Macaulay, was entirely aimed at colonial British requirements. The policy was directed towards producing native administrators and bureaucrats of lower order to aid in the local administration. This was governed by the logic of downward filtration from the elites of the masses. On the other side, of the poor, marginalized and oppressed groups in India, the STs are clearly among the most vulnerable to this kind of change. Often, their tribal identity is negated and their human dignity was violated.[1] It was the Indian Education Commission in 1882, popularly known as Hunter Commission, proposed for extension of primary education in backward districts especially the areas inhabited mainly by aboriginal races. At the same time, the commission also proposed the gradual withdrawal of the Government from secondary education and to transfer secondary education to efficient private bodies by sanctioning grant in aid to it. Much emphasis of the education policy of Lord Curzon (1904) was given to English education and the vernacular was neglected.[2] Further, British appointed Hartog

1   Though, there was few commissions and enquiries initiated by the colonial adminis-tration in India, it largely focused on the mainland population. For example, a committee was constituted under Sir Charles Wood in 1854 for a comprehensive review the status of educa-tion in India generally. He recommended for the creation of a department of education in each of the five provinces. He also recommended the establishment of universities in Presidency towns of Calcutta/ Bombay and Madras. He realized the harm caused to the mass education by the Downward Filtration Theory and suggested for the increase in number of high schools/ middle schools and indigenous primary schools. The important features of the review were the adoption of modern Indian languages as medium of instruction at the secondary stage. The study recommended establishment of teacher training schools in India as in England.

2   Much emphasis was given to English education and empowerment of vernaculars was neglected. The scope for technical education was very much limited and was not useful for masses. The resolution gave suggestion for the improvement of women education through establishment of training schools for women teachers and model schools for girls. Pertaining

Committee in 1929 and Sargent Committee in 1944 to look into the aspects of education in India. Nevertheless, these committees never specifically addressed the educational backwardness of disadvantaged communities like Adivasis (Tandi, 2021).

Apart from issues pertaining with the government policies, the community's spatial isolation also exacerbated their exclusion from the modern world. In India, tribal's live in the forest-clad hills and valleys which is often far away from the mainland with poor infrastructure and other means of communications. They live mostly in scattered settlements[3] rather than villages, which makes them difficult to access education facilities for the whole communities. Teachers from mainland are often reluctant to work in schools in tribal areas because of the distance from towns, lack of infrastructure and other amenities. Moreover, tribal students also face difficulties in following prescribed text books which are not in their mother tongue, occasionally; content is not appropriately designed for their livelihood. The situation has exacerbated the dropout rate of ST students even from primary level, which ultimately culminated into their exclusion from the mainstream. In the immediate post-independence phase, as revealed from the perusal of the first four five-year plans, the establishment of hostels emerged as a strategy to improve the educational indicators among the socially and economically marginalized groups such as SCs and STs largely through schemes under the department of social welfare, department of tribal welfare and department of women and child development (Dubey and Chander, 1973).

Pandey (1981) in his study of social aspects of academic achievement and aspirations of scheduled tribe children observed that the better and negative interaction between non-tribal and tribal students and teacher's indifference towards tribal students in normal schools to their low achievement. They are notable to avail properly the educational opportunities due to their sociocultural backwardness. In this context, several commissions and organization have recommended various measures for enabling the tribal's to in overcome their disadvantages. The education commissions include

---

to secondary education the resolution opined that the standard of education at this level was far from satisfaction owing to the growth of schools under incapable teachers, inadequate furniture, lack of library, proper building etc. At the secondary stage mother tongue as the medium of instruction was emphasized.

3   The name 'settlement' is more suitable for the places where Adivasis live in India, because most of them do notfulfill the category of a typical village rather it is a colony that is newly established (maximum 30 years back), with a clear—sometimes porous—boundary with the reserve or social forests or can be called as a place or region newly settled by the government.

University Education Commission (1949), Secondary Education Commission (1952-53), and the Kothari Commission (1964-66).

The Kothari Commission[4] observed in terms of scheduled castes and tribes; —In regard to tribal education, provision of facilities at the primary stage should be improved and Ashram schools should be established in sparsely populated areas. The Medium of instruction for the first two years of the school should be the tribal language and during this period the children should be given oral instruction in the regional language and by the third year the regional language should become the medium of instruction‖ (Report of the Education Commission, 1964-66).

However, the current scenario as revealed in Census 2011 Scheduled Tribes is notified in 30 States/UTs. Number of individual ethnic groups, etc. notified as Scheduled Tribes is 705. Literacy rate for STs in India improved from 47.1 per cent in 2001 to 59 percent in 2011. Among ST males, literacy rate increased from 59.2 percent to 68.5 percent and among ST females, literacy rate increased from 34.8 percent to 49.4 percent during the same period. Literacy rate for the total population has increased from 64.8 percent in 2001 to 73 percent in 2011. Thus, there is a gap of about 14 percentage points in literacy rate of ST as compared to the all-India literacy rate. ST Female literacy rate is lower by 15 percentage points as compared to overall female literacy rate in 2011 (Tandi, 2021).

Eklavya Model Residential Schools (EMRSs)

In order to accomplish the objectives of the development of tribals, as provided in the constitution the government has made several tailor-made schemes, policies and programmes for the overall development of scheduled tribes. One of them is Eklavya Model Residential Schools which can be discussed as follows.

EMRS are set up to give quality level education to Scheduled Tribes (ST) students in remote territories of the country, not only to empower them to avail reservation in higher and professional studies but also enable them to compete for employments in government and private sector with the non-ST population. The Eklavya Model Residential Schools (EMRS) for ST students is one among the most prominent institutions like the Jawahar Navodaya

4   Indian Education Commission (1964-1966), popularly known as Kothari Commission, was an adhoc commission set up by the Government of India to examine all aspects of the educational sector in India, to evolve a general pattern of education and to advise guidelines and policies for the development of education in India.

Vidyalays, the Kasturba Gandhi Balika Vidyalays and the Kendriya Vidyalays. Eklavya Model Residential School (EMRS) are set up in the States and Union territories with grants under Article 275(1) of the Indian Constitution. The admission of students to study in EMRS is done through proper selection or with open competition where preference is given to the tribals belongs to PVTGs and first-generation students etc. The implementation of the scheme and its administration are ensured by the ministry of tribal affairs and also reviewed periodically by the implementing agency or concerning state government (GoI 2010). By the year 2019, the Ministry of Tribal Affairs has Sanctioned 271 EMRS, out of which 190 have been made functional while the rest are at different stages of completion (GoI 2019b).

Special Central Assistance to Tribal Sub-Scheme (SCA to TSS)

Special Central Assistance to Tribal Sub-Scheme (SCA to TSS) is 100% grant from Government of India since 1977-78. It is charged to Consolidated Fund of India (except grants for North Eastern States, a voted item) and is an additive to State Plan funds and efforts for Tribal Development through schemes on education infrastructure and livelihood etc. to address critical gaps. Tribal Sub-Plan (TSP) [now called as Scheduled Tribe Component (STC) at central level] is a dedicated source of funding tribal development throughout the country. The development of most infrastructures in tribal-dominated regions and the provision of basic services for tribal people throughout the country are carried out through various institutional programs of central ministries and related state governments. In this backdrop, the Scheme "Special Central Assistance (SCA) to Tribal Sub Scheme (TSS), which is part of the Umbrella Scheme for Development of Scheduled Tribes, is directed towards providing grants to States/UTs as an additive to their own efforts for accelerating tribal development and strengthening institutional arrangements. This grant is used for economic growth of Integrated Tribal Development Project (ITDP), Integrated Tribal Development Agency (ITDA), Modified Area Development Approach (MADA), Clusters, Particularly Vulnerable Tribal Groups (PVTGs) and dispersed tribal population. SCA to TSS covers 23 States viz- Andhra Pradesh, Assam, Bihar, Chhattisgarh, Goa, Gujarat, Himachal Pradesh, Jammu &Kashmir, Jharkhand, Karnataka, Kerala, Madhya Pradesh, Maharashtra, Manipur, Odisha, Rajasthan, Sikkim, Tamil Nadu, Telangana, Tripura, Uttarakhand, Uttar Pradesh and West Bengal (GoI 2019a).

Establishment of Ashram Schools in Tribal Sub-Plan Areas

The aim of the scheme is to increase education among scheduled tribes, including PVTGs. Ashram Schools offers education with residential facilities in an environment that is conducive to learning. The scheme has been in operation since 1990-91. The scheme is operated in the Tribal Sub-Plan and UT Administration. The scheme provides funds for the construction of the Ashram School for Primary, Secondary and Seniors Secondary education stage and upgrade of existing Ashram school for both Tribal boys and girls, including PVTGs. For the establishment infrastructure of an Ashram school, such as school buildings, shelters, kitchens and staff areas for girls in the TSP area, 100% funding is provided by the government through the scheme. However, for other non-recurring items Ashram schools in TSP area receives funding on basis of 50:50. Meanwhile, 100% of the funds including all recurring and non-recurring items of expenditure are provided for the establishment of Ashram Schools for students in the TSP area which is identified as naxal affected area. The implementing agencies closely supervise the progress and give quarterly report to the ministry of tribal affairs (GoI 2008c).

Ashram School

Keeping in view the peculiar problems pointed out by Kothari Commission on tribal marginality,

especially on educational backwardness. The primary objectives of these schools are to provide free accommodation, food and education to tribal students with an aim of empowering tribal communities through education. Therefore, the government provides financial assistance to tribal department for construction of new hostels and expansion of existing hostels. Apart from this, the government also provides pre-metric and postmetric scholarships to tribal students which cover tuition fees, hostel charges and allowances for books[5]. The concept of AS is derived from the term 'Ashram' which had been the hallmark of education in ancient India. It, in fact, was the teacher's household'. The 'Ashram' was in one sense, a continuation of home also when the guru and his wife offered personal affection conducive for the natural growth of tender life. It was also a new order presenting a new environment and generally new transformative forces (Chakraborty, 1958). Establishment of AS in tribal areas became the beacon of hope for the disadvantage tribal children in terms of education.

---

5   For details, See, EDU: Establishment of Ashram Schools in Tribal Sub-Plan Areas, http://tribal.nic.in/Content/EstablishmentofAshramSchoolsinTribalSubPlanAreas.aspx.

Issues regarding functioning of Ashram Schools

Issues associated with the functioning of AS are often made headlines in the media and became instrumental in the formation of several government committees but they largely failed to address the real issues regarding the schemes. There are various reasons attribute to this issue. First, in so far as the STs are concerned, the Tribal Sub-Plan (TSP) takes care of the financial aspects of their social, economic and educational problems. Taking into consideration the size of the tribal population, the state government has made substantial provisions in the TSP for the welfare of tribal's, in the form of giving scholarships to the students, running of both aided and government AS, government hostels and pre-recruitment training centers, etc. The tribal sub-plan strategy held hopes for integrated development of tribal areas. However, four decades of implementation it has not brought about any perceptible change in the life of the majority of tribal people. Further, it is alleged that the implementation of the TSP has been mostly with untrained, inefficient, insensitive and often untrustworthy hands. In general, the implementation of the policy of affirmative action has often been mindless and therefore sterile. As a major step in the realm of socio-economic empowerment of a backward community it is essential to study and critically evaluate the state's educational schemes, policies, pattern/method of implementation of these schemes by these agencies and other stakeholders like students.

Successive governments had followed strategies to address issues related to AS by considering this project as a unique one but in reality, little has been changed on the ground when it comes to the physical security of the children. In many cases instead of implementing the recommendation proposed by the studies carried out by the government appointed committees and media reports, the government continuously opted for as usual department level enquiry and corrective measures to these issues, which are often dysfunctional, loosely monitored and nibbled by corruption. Tardy implementations of TSP around AS are crippling the institution's objectives.

A recent study conducted by Centre for Budget and Government Accountability and Child Rights and You (CBGA & CRY, 2016) points out that Maharashtra stands behind Bihar and Orissa in budgetary in allocation for education. The state budgetary allocation for education in 2015-16 was merely 2.3 per cent, which even behind Bihar and Orissa. From this 1.9 per cent is allocated to AS. Interestingly, 69 per cent of the AS fund allocation siphoned as teacher's salary and 8 per cent is earmarked for infrastructure development while Rs.40, 000 is spending on each student. As a result, generally, only 23 per cent of the earmarked fund is available for curricular and welfare of students.

Here the government seems to be conveniently forgetting the rationale of TSP allocation. As the Kelkar committee (2013) pointed out that the TSP budget should be allocated for the tribal development as a principle of additionally that is over and above the regular funds for the developmental programmes and non-plan budget to the TSP areas as to other non-TSP areas. Altering the existing TSP fund allocation was yet another remarkable proposal by the Kelkar committee. It says that in line with the spirit of Panchayat Extension to Scheduled Areas (PESA)Act at least half of the funds of the TSP should be earmarked for Grama sabha which should be allowed to determine the priorities and programmes (Kelkar,2013). As per the 2014-15 budget estimate of tribal department there were 552 government run ashram Schools in the state and of which 429 were located in TSP areas and the remaining 123 in Outside Tribal Sub-Plan (OTSP) areas.

The criticism on lack of staffs in AS is primarily linked to the lack of infrastructure at school level. Though few schools are located in semi-urban areas but infrastructure facilities that can provide accommodation for teachers are not in place. Interestingly, in some area's staffs are reluctant to work even if sufficient infrastructure is in place. Yet another study by Tata Institute of Social Sciences (TISS) in 2015 pointed out that out of all the schools across Maharashtra just over 1,100 with half of them being aided and other half is state-run merely 6 per cent aided and 3.6 per cent of the government tribal schools were able serve breakfast according to the menu. Further, only 33 per cent of the schools have their gas facility and utensils in good conditions but their kitchens were found unhygienic. It also noted that merely 29 percent aided and 20 percent government AS had good drainage facilities. The rest being average or worse, magnifying the chances of water-borne diseases like malaria, dengue (TISS, 2015).

Ashram Schools and their Impact

A rigorous inspection of the educational Schemes—*Ashram Schools and their impact* is vital for this study. A study done by Tribal Research and Training Institute, Pune (TRTI) in 2002 revealed the current situation of Ashram schools, in the state. The study focuses on improper subsidy allocation, administration of Ashram schools at state and district level. It also points out the false utilization of earmarked funds, and violation of realistic physical targets for Ashram school scheme. The study furthermore points out how an Ashram school becomes the business ventures managed by the local elite for attracting government funds. Moreover, lack of cooperation and sensitiveness of TDD department often hamper the proper operation of Ashram School (TRTI, 2002).

Tandi (2019) discuses about the issues and challenges in tribal education which they categorized as external, internal, socio-economic and psychological. The external constraints are related to issues at levels of policy, planning and implementation while internal constraints are with respect to school system, content, curriculum, pedagogy, medium of instruction etc. the third set of problems relates to social economic and cultural background of tribal's and psychological aspects of first-generation learners.

Tandi (2020) focuses on socio-economic background of the students of ashram high school in comparison to education department high schools and evaluate the facilities of Ashram high schools by taking education department high school as parameter.

Government provides hostels that are desirous of taking education. In these hostels not only, education is free but food, uniform and allied requirements also provided. A TRTI report, Extent of Occupancy Rate and Utilization of Facilities in Government Girls Hostel (1994) concludes that the improvement in the standards of hostel can be brought about by developing the hostel atmosphere in accordance with the requirement of tribal students. One of the essential requirements is a trained warden who has knowledge about tribal culture, affection for tribal children, a keen interest and dedication to her work of master's degree of social welfare. There is no doubt that without basic infrastructural facilities there can be no improvement in the standard of living of tribal students residing these hostels. The hostel atmosphere will help in the motivation and reduction in the dropout rate that leave education because of the unsuitable hostel atmosphere.

Jojo (2013) elucidates functioning of Ashram school scheme. He says the objective is far from being met and the lack of infrastructure as well as teaching capacity in these schools is hampering the progress of tribal children in many Ashram schools. This article attempts to document the functioning of Ashram schools and tries to assess the quality of education received by the ST children in central and eastern India. An attempt has been made to look at the infrastructure, staffing, amenities and the quality of curricular, co-curricular and extra-curricular activities. In its methodology, the article deals with explanatory research design; survey and evaluative design were allowed to access the functioning of Ashram Schools. Findings of the data collected from 13 AS reveals that lack of quality in education pose major challenges to the educational development of the tribal's.

Bhatty (1998) addresses the issues of economic constraints, schooling quality and parental motivation which area set of actors that influences the determining factors related to education within a household and invariably affecting the overall picture of educational deprivation at the national level. Author finds an exaggerated emphasis being placed on child labour and inadequate motivation among poor parents as the major obstacles to universalization of primary education. Rather, it is the direct costs of schooling, which impose substantial burden on families, and the low quality of schooling facilities, which reduce the child's interest in education, that primarily account for educational deprivation. In both these aspects – reducing private costs of schooling and improving schooling quality - the state has a crucial role to play.

Mungekar (2009) found out few startling facts about the tribal education in India and also recommended elementary education of good quality is imparted to all free of cost and the minimum population norm or criterion, wherever stipulated in any infrastructure scheme, should be relaxed in terms of tribal population.

Sahoo (1992) A critical study of Ashram Schools of Orissa found that merely opening of Ashram Schools on political or administrative pressure does not solve the problem. The aims and objective of setting up of such schools will be gradually ignored by teachers, administrators and planners. Without providing minimum educational facilities opening new Ashram Schools is likely to be dysfunctional because baring free lodging and boarding facilities these schools are like general schools.

Sridhar (2000) Tribal Education: A study of Ashram schools in Karnataka‖ found that Ashram Schools have been successful in retaining the respondents for longer periods in the school system. These schools were instrumental in bringing out qualitative, changes in their attitudes, aspirations, awareness and values.

Ramama (1990) evaluates the problems of education among the tribal communities of Andhra Pradesh with special reference to Ashram Schools. He says that developmental programme aimed for tribal communities would succeed only when their critical consciousness is awakened. Education is an essential input in achieving this goal. Further, it also found problems of absenteeism, wastage and stagnation. And it is observed that not all the tribal communities are utilizing this facility equally reasons behind this are shifting cultivation, and located on hills and interior of the forest and absence of physical facilities and non-local teachers.

Tandi (2021) discuss on elementary education and the system of education in India. Their work also explains different steps taken by the government to improve the quality of education which is inevitable for development of nation and outline the impact of various schemes on enrolment, infrastructure, teaching and learning level of children at elementary level of education. Likewise, it found that in-school community building can effectively promote academic motivation and engagement as well as achievement when coupled with an emphasis on academics. Because, community building also promotes social, emotional, and ethical growth and the prevention of problem behaviors, it may powerfully meet the needs of both students and society.

Centre for Budget and Policy Studies (CBPS) study titled Residential Schooling Strategies: Impact on Girls' Education and Empowerment (2015) points out that though several residential schooling strategies exist for girls in the publicly funded school system in India, there is no definite policy on residential schooling in general or for girls in particular. This study reviews literature coupled with validation visits to a few sites and consultations with key stakeholders.

A recent study conducted by Centre for Budget and Government Accountability and Child Rights and You points out that Maharashtra stands behind Bihar and Orissa in budgetary in allocation for education. The state budgetary allocation for education in 2015-16 was merely 2.3per cent, which even behind Bihar and Orissa. From this 1.9 per cent is allocated to *Ashram Schools*. Interestingly, 69 per cent of the AS fund allocation siphoned as teacher's salary and 8 per cent is earmarked for infrastructure development while Rs.40, 000 is spending on each student. (CBGA & CRY, 2016) As a result, generally, only 23 per cent of the earmarked fund is available for curricular and welfare of students. Here the government seems to be conveniently forgetting the rationale of TSP allocation.

Concluding Remark

The persistence of educational backwardness among Adivasis in India is particularly disappointing because, at the time of independence, the founders of modern India made a range of radical efforts to eliminate it. Being at the bottom of socio-economic ladder tribal communities in India are the groups that have been excluded disproportionately in relation to other social groups. As a socially disadvantaged ethnic minority, they are largely deprived of constitutional equality that often glosses over the prevailing societal inequalities which they are subjected of since ages. In this scenario, they are unable to participate and enjoy the substantive benefits of citizenship and become powerless in effectively articulating their demand for rights and crucial entitlements like employment, education, housing and other social opportunities (Tandi, 2019).

Though, successive governments in India are concerned with the crucial question of tribal development. It is usual for government to see education is the basic key for the socio-economic development of the tribal communities. As these communities in India have been on the receiving end of socio-economic and educational development, it is essential to address the lacunas exist within the policy deliberations. Their backwardness primarily causes out of primitive agricultural practices, lack of infrastructure facilities and geographical isolation. Since independence, special consideration was given for the planning of education by the government for tribal population. Educational schemes have been introduced by government aiming at addressing backwardness so that the tribal may develop their economic, social and educational status and they can be assimilated into the mainstream (Tandi and Sarma 2020).

On this backdrop, Ashram Schools represent an innovation and are different from the general type of school seen in rural India. Students are provided free boarding and other educational amenities. These schools are expected to impart quality education in areas which are remote and sparsely populated and were, on account of the geographical spread of the numerous hamlets, single teacher school cannot be established.

References

- Bhatty, Kiran (1998), Educational Deprivation in India: A Survey of Field Investigations Economic and Political Weekly, Vol. 33, No. 27 pp. 1731-1740
- Cambridge Dictionary. (2019), 'Tribe'. https://dictionary.cambridge.org/dictionary/english/tribe (5 January 2020)
- Centre for Budget and Policy Studies (CBPS) (2015), *Residential Schooling Strategies: Impact on Girls education and Empowerment*, Bangalore
- CBGA&CRY (2016). How Have States Designed Their School Education Budgets?‖, Centre for Budget and Governance Accountability (CBGA), New Delhi.
- Chakrabarti, Atulananda *(1958), Thoughts on Indian Education*, Manager of Publications, Government of India: New Delhi.
- Dubey S. M. (1974). A study of scheduled caste and scheduled tribe college students in Assam‖, Department of Sociology, Dibrugarh University
- Government of India, (2011). Census of India 2011, https://censusindia.gov.in/census.website/ (19/10/2022)

- Government of India, (2022). *Particularly Vulnerable Tribal Groups*, New Delhi: Ministry of Tribal Affairs. https://tribal.nic.in/ (19/10/2022)
- Google (2022) Tribe, https://www.google.com/h?q=Tribe&oq=Tribe&aqs=chrome..69i57j46i433i512j0i433i512j0i131i433i512j46i512j0i512j0i433i512j0i457i512j0i131i433i512j0i433i512.2751j0j15&sourceid=chrome&ie=UTF-8 (19/10/2022)
- Jojo Bipin, (2013), Decline of Ashram Schools in Central and Eastern India: Impact on Education of ST Children, Social Change, 43,3 (2013) 377-395
- Kelakar, Vijay (2013). Report on the High-Level Committee on Balanced Regional Development, Government of Maharashtra.
- Lal, B. Suresh. (2019), Tribal Development in India: Some Observations, Researchgate. https://www.researchgate.net/publication/334680540_Tribal_Development_in_India _Some_Observations
- Mungekar Bhalchandra (2009), Standards of Administration andGovernance in the Scheduled Areas, Third Report of Standing Committee on Inter Sectoral issues relating to Tribal Development, Ministry of Tribal Affairs, and New Delhi
- Pandey, M. R. (1981). Social Aspects of Academic Achievement and Aspirations of Scheduled Tribe Students, Ph.D. Soc., KV
- Ramana, G. V. (1990). *Problems of Education among the Tribal Communities of Andhra Pradesh: Case study of Ashram schools"* PhD Thesis, Sri Venkateswara University, Tirupati
- Sahoo Ramchandra (1992), A critical study of Ashram schools of Orissa, PhD thesis, Indian Institute of Education, Pune
- Sridhar N. (2000). *Tribal Education: A Study of Ashram Schools in Karnataka*‖ PhD Thesis, Sri Krishnadevaraya University, Anantapur
- Tata Institute of Social Science (TISS) (2015). Tribal Sub-Plan in Maharashtra: A Diagnostic Study, TISS, Mumbai.
- Tandi, S. (2019). Participation of Tribal Students In Higher Education: A Study of Odisha, IJRAR, International Journal of Research and Analytical Reviews (IJRAR), E-ISSN 2348-1269, P- ISSN 2349-5138, Volume.6, Issue 1, Page No pp.43-56, February-2019, Impact Factor-5.75 , Journal No-43602 Available at : **http://www.ijrar.org/IJRAR19J2731.pdf**
- Tandi, S. and Sarma, R. (2020). Impact of Higher Educational Institutions on the Tribal of Odisha: A Sociological Analysis, Parishodh Journal, Volume IX, Issue III,pp. Page No:5389-5402, ISSN NO:2347-6648, Impact Factor-6.3

- Tandi, S. (2021). Historicity and Status of Higher Education in India, Educational Quest: An Int. J. of Education and Applied Social Sciences: Vol. 12, No. 3, pp. 199-207, Online ISSN: 2230-7311, Print ISSN: 0976-7258, DOI: 10.30954/2230-7311.3.2021.4
- Tandi, S., and Tandi, S. (2019). Tribal Participation and Higher Education in Odisha, 2019, pp . 1-157, ISBN: 978-620-0-21985-5. LAP LAMBERT Academic Publishing, Editor- Liuba Esanu, International Book Market Service Ltd., OmniScriptun Publishing Group, 17 Meldrum Street, Beau Bassin 71504, Mauritius. Jul 2, 2019, 12:27 PM.
- TRRI, Pune Report No of 5. (2002), Politicians Controlling Aided Ashram Schools.

Health Care Practices among Tribals of South Odisha

Jalandhar Sahu

Guest Lecturer in Sociology
Vikarm Dev University, Jeypore, Koraput
Email: pin2sahu786@gmail.com

Abstract

The tribal people are facing number of problems related to health and sanitation. The tribal people live in a specific territory. Their culture, life style and economy differ from others. Their distinctive culture, resident's style of life and economy system is also responsible for the problem of health. Tribals live in the village surrounded by hills, forest, river side etc. And in this area, they lack communication facilities. Due to lack of communication facilities, they are not able to avail the benefits of the various programs related to general health, family welfare, communicable disease, child and reproductive health etc. The tribal people are living in such areas where one has to face a number of difficulties going and coming. Due to these difficulties government doctors, nurse and health servants are not interested to live in these tribal areas. They go there just to get their salary not and to serve the people. The system of supply of medicine at the health centre and sub centre also not up to mark. It takes much time in reaching to the patients. On many several occasion the medicine reaches the centre or patient after expire date. The tribal people are facing a number of health problems and diseases like malaria, TB, diarrhoea, leprosy, waterborne diseases etc. besides all this health problems or ill health of tribals it has been observed that there is great difficulty in persuading the tribal people to avail modern medical treatment because they have firm, rigid and well- developed system of primitive medicine or traditional medicine. They have hold firm belief that a disease is always caused by hostile spirits, ghost's or breach of some taboos. Henceforth, they seek remedies through magico-religious practices to propitiate the supernatural powers. The tribal house households also prefer herbal medicine, this paper is tried understand the health care Practice of tribal people particularly (Gadaba, Kandh and Paraja) of Koraput.

Key words- *Tribe, health, Ethnos Medicine,*

Introduction

The tribal people are facing number of problems related to health and sanitation. The tribal people live in a specific territory. Their culture, **life style** and economy differ from others. Their distinctive culture, resident's style of life and economy system is also responsible for the problem of health. Tribals live in the village surrounded by hills, forest, river side etc. And in this area, they lack communication facilities. Due to lack of communication facilities, they are not able to avail the benefits of the various programs related to general health, family welfare, communicable disease, child and reproductive health etc.

Understanding Health: The Tribal Perspective

The world Health Organization has defined health as "a state of complete physical, mental and social well-being and not merely the absence of disease and infirmity" (WHO.1971). However comprehensive this definition may be, it has rarely been put into practice. But the present study analysis to the understanding of tribals health which some extent different to WHO definition. There are 90 percent respondents' opinion is "I don't know". But some respondents are explaining the meaning of health and illness.

According to one respondent-"Health means physically healthy".

According to one other respondent says that "Health means living in a better place and eats good food".

According to another respondent explain that "Health means good body".

According to one more respondent says that "without disease is a good health".

According to one other respondent says that" Regularly eating medicine and the body when it sick that is health ".

The all definition is related to the meaning of good health. The maximum respondents do not know the meaning of health and some of them try to explain the meaning of health because they are the educated person in primary levels of education and they know the meaning of health. The tribal health in this villages, unfortunately was never taken seriously. Though some intensive field work has been done by social scientists but some of the studies treated the problems of tribal health in peripheral and casual manner. For meaningful understanding of the tribal health, it is important to understand the people themselves their indigenous medicines and understand how under the existing social, economic medicines and cultural setting these needs can be best met to the satisfaction of people themselves.

Major Health Problems of Tribal People

The concept of ill-health becomes a functional one and not clinical in the context of tribal health. This is precisely the reason that among many tribals; symptoms such as pains and aches, weakness, scabies, prolonged cough, mild fever, wounds, etc., are not taken seriously as symptoms of disease. Due to the multidimensional factors, this villager is facing many problems like poverty, illiteracy, difficult terrain, isolation, superstation and inadequate health facility. Several anthropogenic factors like deforestation, industrialization, displacement-rehabilitation and socio-cultural transformation process like diffusion and intrusion of the non-tribals to tribal habitats have created a complex change in the tribal life as a whole, and eventually influenced their health and nutritional status. On the other hand, due to geographical reasons, they inhabit very small villages scattered over a large stretch of mountainous terrains. Wide dispersal of smaller habitation with poorer communication facilities results in poor outreach of health care. The general health problems are malnutrition related diseases, parasitic diseases including malaria, diarrhoea, respiratory disorders, etc., and genetic disorders including sickle cell disease, thalassaemia, etc. The data on morbidity, mortality and other health indicators reveal that the health status of tribal population is very poor.

The tribal people classified the causes of illness into two broad categories.1-Supernatural and 2-Physical. The supernatural causes of diseases include (a) breach of taboo; (b)sorcery; (c)Sprit intrusion;(d)evil eye;(e) wrath of gods and goddess; and (f)ghost intrusion. The physical causes of illness recognized are (a)the effect of weather;(b)the effect of wrong food;(c) contact with certain living organisms; (d)blood getting impure;(e)accidents and natural calamities; and (f)unknown causes. These causes are very much affected to the tribal health. This tribal community are following a distinct way of life, entertain their own cultural values possess viable mechanism to adopt to their not so hospitable environment and have various techniques to cope with the diseases affecting them.

Health Care Practices of Tribals

It has been observed that there is great difficulty in persuading the tribal people to avail modern medical treatment because they have firm, rigid and well- developed system of primitive medicine or traditional medicine. They have hold firm belief that a disease is always caused by hostile spirits, ghost's or breach of some taboos. Henceforth, they seek remedies through magico-religious practices to propitiate the supernatural powers.

The tribal house households also prefer herbal medicine, Ayurvedic medicine and modern medicine depending upon desirability, availability, accessibility, affordability, and acceptability. More and more tribal groups are now coming into the fold of modern medical care. Pattern of Treatment of Disease It has been observed that there is great difficulty in persuading the tribal people to come to avail modern medical treatment because they have firm, rigid and well-developed system of primitive medicine. They hold firm belief that a disease is always caused by hostile spirits, ghost or breach of some taboos. Henceforth, they seek remedies through magic-religious practices to propitiate the supernatural powers. The cure or treatment of the disease is essentially sought through getting rid of the wrath of gods, evil spirits and observance of punishment in case of breach of a taboo. 'dishari' as he commonly known, serves as the mediator for diagnosing the diseases and plans the treatment. The 'Gunia' is supposed to have power to identify the angry gods and evil spirits. The identifications and treatment of sickness becomes a holy ceremony among all the Gadaba tribal group. Herbal medicines or indigenous medicines are their next preference for getting treatment, which is obtained, through the village people. It was observed that all the four tribal groups perpetuate the use of Tulsi leaves, turmeric powder in case of fevers, and invariably in case of injuries. There is enough evidence to suggest that the tribal population groups do use indigenous herbal concoctions to avoid pregnancies, treatment of infertility and some common ailments and some herbs used in the treatments of different diseases are presented in Table-

This paper does not mean that the tribal people do not avail the services of the modern medical care system. However, their attitude towards modern medical care is not encouraging. It has been observed that the decision to avail modern medical care is being influenced by many people that is the village headman, head of the hamlets/ households, village dishari. Their decision is also governed by the level of their education, their deep-rooted belief in magico. religious practices and also by their awareness and exposure to the outside world. Provision of proper health care facility is an important aspect of human resource development. Tribals have their traditional

Ethno medicine method of health system. The concept of health in these communities is associated with certain traditional belief system and ritual when a person accidentally suffers a disease, they seek the treatment only from a priest (*dishari*) or a magic man (gunia). It is believed that only *dishari* or Gunia save the patient from all sorts of troubles. If by chance the sick person is cared, due to the application of some herb by the *dishari*, the medicine man (*dishari*) gets all credit. Earlier for the treatment of all diseases or solving any health problem usually tribals took only the help of local quacks for every minor disease they used to go to *dishari* or gurumai. For serious disease they only prefer, modern medicine facility. However, now the tribal prefer some modern Medicine. First of all, the young ages peoples first prefer to the hospital then Ethno Medicine but the old age. People's first refer to the *dishari* medicine practices because they only believe the *dishari*. They cannot be forgetting the Ethno Medicine in any condition. Any how they check of their health by the *dishari*. Vary Interesting fact that they cannot be prefer any Homeopathy or Ayurvedic medicine. They only prefer both medicine that is Allopathic on Ethno Medicine. It is observed that tribal people's giving priority to indigenous health practices is more due to the profound association of tribal society with its cultural and religious systems. The first preference for availing modern facility is comparatively less due to lack of communication facility, and predominantly owing to their illiteracy as well as poor economic conditions.

'Health care' is one of the greater human rights and it is observed that apart from other inequalities, tribal (Gadabba, Kandh and Paraja) of the villages area deprived of basic health facilities. The main causes of low health status of Tribal of the study area are-

a. While a large number of primary health centres and sub-centres have been created as part of the government's Health for All programme, National Family Health survey (NFHS) 1and 2 reveal that health services either do not reach disadvantaged section or are not accessed by them.

b. The tribal population is adversely placed in term of access to health care and nutritional status due to low economic condition, social hierarchy and stratification. C

c. They cannot be adopting the modern practices in their health condition. Basically, they depend only the ethno practices. So that's the reason problems are arises in the tribal society.

Among these there are communities who still depend primarily on *Dishari* or *Gurumai* for their health treatment. The wide spread poverty, illiteracy, malnutrition, absence of safe drinking water and sanitary conditions, poor maternal and child health services, ineffective coverage of national health and nutritional services, etc. have been found as possible contributing factors of dismal health condition prevailing amongst the tribal communities of Odisha. Many of the infectious and parasitic diseases can be prevented with timely intervention and health awareness.

Steps should to be taken by Government

1. Continuous survey should be done by the Government from door to door degrading people's health and giving them proper suggestions and making them aware of proper diet. They should give proper knowledge about age of marriage. Family Planning operation and Health schemes for various Health Problems Free and timely medicines should avail from Government.

2. Primary and Secondary school should open in these villages to that children can get proper education.

3. Government should take necessary steps to improve the health condition of the villagers by establishing improve the Health Condition and free medical treatment should be given to them- classes on Health facility and schemes should teach on regular, basis to the real people in their local language.

4. Communication Facilities should improve in these villages- Road linkages must be to the main road so that doctors can easily reach to these villages at the time of emergencies.

5. Government should give the free medicine in hospital for the treatment of tribal community.

6. The Anganwadi Workers, the multipurpose Health workers, volunteer organizations, primary school teachers, *dishari* (The Traditional medicine, practitioner) etc. can play ritual role in the implementation of various health programmes. These workers should need proper motivation, practiced training.

9. The health nutrition should be encouraged through local produce and local recipes.

10. Tribal women in their advanced stage of pregnancy should be advised to reduce their   work land and take adequate- rest.

11. The habit of taking alcohol and drugs during pregnancy should be discouraged.

14. A mass awareness should most essential for tribal community.

15. The medical staff behaviour should be developed.

16. Ambulance should be adequately provided with necessary equipment and medical personnel.

Reference
- Das, P. K. & Misra, M. K. (1988): Some Medicinal plants among kondhas around Chandrapur (koraput), J. Econ. Tax. Bot., Vol. XII (1), pp: 103-109.
- Das, P. K. & Misra, M. K.(1987): Some Medicinal plants used by the tribals of Deomali and adjacent areas of Koraput district, Orissa., Indian J. Forestry; Vol. X(4), pp: 301- 303.
- Das, P. K. & Misra, M. K.(1988): Some Ethno Medicinal plants of Koraput district, Orissa., Ancient science of Life, Vol. VIII (1), pp: 60-67.
- Das, P. K.(1995): Some Medicinal plants used by the tribals of Koraput, Orissa., Ancient science of Life, Vol. XIV (3), pp: 191-196.
- Gupta, P. C. & Kumar, R. (1997): Medicinal plants in Saran district(Bihar): A case study, Int. J. Mendel, Vol. XIV (3 & 4), pp: 95- 96.
- Jain, S.K. (1970): Some magico-religious beliefs about Plants among adivasis of Orissa, Adivasis, Vol. XII(1-4),(April), pp: 38-44.
- Joshi, P.C. (1994): Tribal Medicine in Indian Context-I; Vanyajati, Vol. XLII, (July), pp:3-9.
- Kalla, A.K., Joshi, P.C. (2004): Tribal Health and Medicines;Cocept Publishing House, New Delhi.
- Kaul, M. K., Sharma, P. K. & Singh, V. (1991): Contribution to the ethnoboany of Padaris of Doda in Jammu & Kashmir state, India., Bull. Bot. Surv. India,Vol. 33 (1-4), pp: 267-271.
- Kshirsagar, S. R., Govit, N. C. & Parabia, M. (2003): Ethnobotanical and ethnomedicinal plants from Tribal Areas of South Gujarat, Gujarat state, India, Vanyajati. Vol. XLXI., pp: 24-28.
- Kumar, K. (1999): Observation on Some Phytodiversity Resources used as food and Medicine by Santhal and Paharia Community of Bihar, Vanyajati, Vol.XLVII, (oct.), pp:21-22.
- Mibang, T. and Choudhuri, S. K. (2003): Ethnomedicines of the Tribes of Arunachal Pradesh, Delhi, Himalayan Publisher.
- Mishra, N.B. & Joda, B. (2004): "Herbal use of Juangs", Vanyajati, Vol. XLXII, (Oct), pp:3-5.
- Mohanty, G. N. & Moharana, A. K. (2006): The Santal Therapy vis-a-Vvs Animal based Medicines, Adivasis, Vol.46 (1) June, pp: 1-10.
- Mohanti, K. K., Mohapatro, P. C. & Samal, J. (2006): Tribes of Koraput, Council of Analytical Tribal Studies(COATS), Koraput, Orissa.

- Mondal, N., Bhattacharya, A. and Mandal, S. (1997): Ethnobotanical Studies on some Aquatic Plants of the Lateritic Belt of West Bengal, Int. J. Mendel, Vol.14 (3 & 4), pp: 79-80.
- Nayak, S. P. and Misra, M. K. (1991): Dependence of Tribals on Forest Ecosystem : A Case Study Bhogibandha village in Orissa; J. of Hum. Ecol., Vol.2(2), pp:135-140.
- Patnaik, N., Bara, F. & Mall, A. (1986): Herbal Medicines of Dongaria, Adivasis, Vol.XXVI, No.4, pp:1-4.
- Pattnaik, D.K. (2005): Weekly Fair: A New Source for Ethnobotanical Studies: The Research, Vol.I, A Research Bulletin of DAV College, Koraput, Orissa.
- Rai, R. and Nath, V. (2005): Use of Medicinal Plants by Traditional Herbal Healers in Central India, Indian Forester, Vol.131, (3), pp: 463-468.
- Raja, M. (1987): Structures and Functions of Rural Markets in Tribal Bihar; in Maheswari Prasad (ed.), "Tribes their Environment and Culture", Delhi, Amar Prakashan, pp: 256-265.
- Bhattacharya, A.K. & Patra, K. (2004): Medicinal Plants for rural women and child health care- Issues, Options and Strategy. Indian Forester, Vol. 30, (4), pp: 385-397.
- Census of India (2001): Orissa Final population Totals, Bhubaneswar, Dir. of Census Operation, Orissa.
- Chhetri, D. R. (2007): Medicinal plants scenario in Darjeeling Himalayas: Conservation and cultivation as alternative crop, Indian Forester, Vol. 133 (5), pp: 665-678

Constitutional and Legal Safeguards for the Rights of Tribal Communities in India: A Critical Study

Sakshi Dixit

Research Scholar, Dept. of Sociology and Political Science
Dayalbagh Educational Institute, Agra
sakshidixit130834@dei.ac.in

Abstract:

Tribal communities in India constitute a significant portion of the country's diverse socio-cultural fabric, yet they remain one of the most marginalized groups. Recognizing their historical disadvantages and socio-economic vulnerabilities, the Constitution of India provides various safeguards to protect their rights. This paper aims to critically examines the constitutional provisions, legal frameworks, and policy measures designed to uphold and promote the rights of Scheduled Tribes in India. The study explores the political rights of tribals, including reservation in legislatures, the Panchayats Act, and the provisions of the Fifth and Sixth Schedules, which grant special governance autonomy to tribal regions. The paper also investigates the cultural rights of tribals, such as the protection of tribal languages, the promotion of indigenous traditions, and initiatives to safeguard their intangible heritage. Additionally, it assesses educational safeguards such as the Right to Education Act, 2009, Article 21A, and state-sponsored schemes like Eklavya Model Residential Schools aimed at improving literacy and learning outcomes among tribal students. Despite these protective measures, the implementation of legal safeguards faces numerous challenges, including political underrepresentation, displacement due to industrialization, cultural erosion due to globalization, and inadequate access to quality education. The paper highlights these challenges, while recommending policy reforms to strengthen the enforcement of tribal rights. This research underscores the need for a holistic approach to tribal development, integrating legal protections, community participation, and targeted policy interventions. Strengthening tribal governance, preserving indigenous knowledge, and enhancing educational opportunities are essential for ensuring the socio-economic upliftment of India's tribal communities. In this research paper descriptive and analytical research methodologies are used and the data is collected from secondary as well as primary sources, such as books, government documents, journals, research papers and articles etc. This research seeks to contribute to the broader discourse on tribal rights and governance, offering insights for policymakers, researchers, and stakeholders involved in tribal development. The scope of this research is limited to Indian tribal communities and focuses on analyzing legal and policy frameworks at the national and state levels.

Keywords: Constitutional Safeguards, Cultural Preservation, Education Policy, Political Representation, Scheduled Tribes, Tribal Rights etc.

Introduction:

Tribal communities, also known as Scheduled Tribes (STs) in India, are indigenous populations with distinct social, cultural, and linguistic identities. The Constitution of India recognizes these communities under Article 366(25), which defines Scheduled Tribes as groups identified by the President under Article 342 based on factors such as geographical isolation, distinctive culture, primitive traits, and economic backwardness (Government of India, 1950). According to the 2011 Census of India, tribal communities constitute 8.6% of the total population, amounting to over 104 million individuals, primarily residing in remote and forested regions across the country (Registrar General of India, 2011). The tribal population is concentrated in states like Madhya Pradesh, Chhattisgarh, Odisha, Jharkhand, Maharashtra, and Gujarat, with some states in the Northeast having a predominantly tribal demographic (Xaxa, 2014). Tribes such as the Gond, Bhil, Santhal, Munda, and Khasi have rich traditions, distinct languages, and indigenous knowledge systems that contribute significantly to India's cultural diversity (Sharma, 2020). Despite their unique cultural heritage, tribal communities remain one of the most marginalized groups in India. They face social exclusion, economic hardships, displacement due to industrialization, and limited access to education and political representation (Ministry of Tribal Affairs, 2021). Therefore, safeguarding their rights is essential to ensuring their equitable development while preserving their traditional way of life.

Need for Special Safeguards for Tribal Rights- Historically, tribal communities have been subjected to land alienation, exploitation, and forced assimilation due to the expansion of mainstream society (Nathan & Xaxa, 2012). The British colonial policies disrupted traditional tribal governance structures, leading to economic marginalization and loss of ancestral lands (Guha, 1999). Post-independence, the Indian Constitution recognized the need for special safeguards to protect the rights of tribal communities, ensuring their political, cultural, and educational empowerment (Verma, 2017). Key reasons for such safeguards include:

- Political marginalization: Limited representation in governance structures despite constitutional reservations.
- Cultural erosion: Loss of tribal languages, traditions, and indigenous knowledge due to modernization.
- Educational barriers: High illiteracy rates and lack of access to quality education in remote areas.
- Economic exploitation: Displacement due to mining, deforestation, and industrial projects.

To address these issues, the Indian government has enacted constitutional protections, legal frameworks, and affirmative action policies, such as the Fifth and Sixth Schedules, the Panchayats (Extension to Scheduled Areas) Act (PESA), and the Forest Rights Act (FRA) (Ministry of Tribal Affairs, 2022). However, despite these measures, challenges persist in implementing these provisions effectively.

Objectives and Scope of the Research: This research aims to analyze the constitutional and legal safeguards for the political, cultural, and educational rights of tribal communities in India. The specific objectives of the study include:

1. To examine the constitutional provisions and legal frameworks designed to protect tribal communities.
2. To analyze the implementation of policies related to tribal political representation, cultural preservation, and education.
3. To identify key challenges in ensuring the effective execution of these legal safeguards.

The scope of this research is limited to Indian tribal communities and focuses on analyzing legal and policy frameworks at the national and state levels.

Research Methodology: This study follows a qualitative research methodology, relying on:

- Secondary data analysis: Examination of government reports, legal

documents, policy briefs, and academic literature on tribal rights.
- Comparative analysis: Evaluating the effectiveness of policies across different states with significant tribal populations.
- Legal framework assessment: Reviewing constitutional provisions, Supreme Court judgments, and government initiatives for tribal welfare.

Constitutional and Legal Framework for Tribal Rights:

The Indian Constitution recognizes Scheduled Tribes (STs) as one of the most disadvantaged communities, requiring special safeguards to protect their political, cultural, and educational rights. Under Article 366(25), Scheduled Tribes are those communities designated by the President of India under Article 342 based on their distinctive culture, geographical isolation, economic backwardness, and social vulnerability (Government of India, 1950). The Indian Constitution includes affirmative action provisions aimed at securing social justice, political participation, and economic empowerment for STs. These provisions ensure reservation in legislatures (Articles 330 and 332), local governance (Articles 243D and 243T), and administrative autonomy in Scheduled Areas (Fifth and Sixth Schedules) (Xaxa, 2014). Additionally, the state has a constitutional duty under Article 46 to promote the welfare of STs through special policies (Sharma, 2020).

To translate constitutional mandates into action, India has enacted several **legislative measures** to safeguard tribal interests. Some of the most significant legal instruments include:
1. The Provisions of the Panchayats (Extension to the Scheduled Areas) Act (PESA), 1996: Grants tribal self-governance powers in Scheduled Areas.
2. The Scheduled Tribes and Other Traditional Forest Dwellers (Recognition of Forest Rights) Act (FRA), 2006: Recognizes tribal land rights and traditional forest-based livelihoods.
3. The Scheduled Castes and Scheduled Tribes (Prevention of Atrocities) Act, 1989: Protects STs from social discrimination and violence (Ministry of Tribal Affairs [MoTA], 2022).

These legal frameworks aim to **empower tribal communities, prevent exploitation, and preserve their cultural heritage.**

Political Rights of Tribals:
- Reservation of Seats in Parliament and State Legislatures: Article 330 of the Indian Constitution provides reservation of seats for Scheduled

Tribes in the Lok Sabha, while Article 332 mandates their representation in State Legislative Assemblies (Government of India, 1950). These provisions ensure that tribal voices are represented in national and state-level decision-making (Verma, 2017).

- Reservation in Panchayati Raj and Municipalities: With the 73rd and 74th Constitutional Amendments, Articles 243D and 243T were introduced to provide reservation for Scheduled Tribes in Panchayati Raj institutions and urban local bodies (Xaxa, 2014). This ensures tribal participation in local governance, decision-making, and resource management at the grassroots level.
- Special Provisions for Tribal Governance: The Fifth Schedule applies to tribal-dominated areas in mainland India, granting the Governor special powers to regulate land rights and administration (Sharma, 2020). The Sixth Schedule, applicable to tribal regions in the Northeast, establishes Autonomous District Councils (ADCs) with legislative and executive powers over local governance, thereby ensuring tribal autonomy (Singh, 2018).
- The Provisions of the Panchayats (Extension to the Scheduled Areas) Act (PESA), 1996: The PESA Act, 1996, extends the 73rd Constitutional Amendment to Scheduled Areas, granting tribal gram sabhas the authority to manage their own land, resources, and governance (Ministry of Panchayati Raj, 2021). PESA strengthens tribal self-rule by ensuring that community decisions regarding land acquisition and resource use are binding (Mehta, 2019).
- The Scheduled Tribes and Other Traditional Forest Dwellers (Recognition of Forest Rights) Act, 2006 (FRA): The Forest Rights Act (FRA), 2006, recognizes individual and community rights of tribals over forest land, enabling them to use and conserve forests based on traditional practices (Government of India, 2006). This law is crucial in protecting tribal livelihoods and preventing displacement due to industrial and conservation projects (Sharma, 2021).
- Role of Tribal Advisory Councils (TACs): The Tribal Advisory Councils (TACs), established under the Fifth Schedule, act as advisory bodies to state governments on matters related to tribal welfare. They play a critical role in policy implementation, addressing grievances, and safeguarding tribal interests (Ministry of Tribal Affairs, 2022).

Cultural Rights of Tribals: The Indian Constitution acknowledges the unique cultural identity of Scheduled Tribes (STs) and provides safeguards to protect their language, traditions, and heritage. These constitutional provisions are crucial for preserving tribal customs, rituals, and traditional knowledge (Xaxa, 2014).

- Protection of Cultural Identity and Language: Article 29(1) guarantees the right of any section of citizens with a distinct language, script, or culture to conserve it (Government of India, 1950). This provision is particularly significant for tribal groups, as it safeguards their linguistic and cultural heritage from external influences (Sharma, 2021).
- Promotion of Tribal Heritage and Culture: Article 46 directs the State to promote the educational and economic interests of Scheduled Tribes while protecting them from social injustices and exploitation (Verma, 2017). This provision enables special development programs aimed at promoting tribal crafts, performing arts, and indigenous knowledge.
- Recognition of Tribal Languages under the Eighth Schedule: The Eighth Schedule of the Indian Constitution recognizes 22 languages, including tribal languages such as Santhali, Bodo, and Manipuri (Government of India, 2003). This recognition helps in the preservation and promotion of tribal languages in education, administration, and media (Singh, 2018).
- Initiatives for Tribal Language Preservation: The Scheme for Protection and Preservation of Endangered Languages (SPPEL), launched by the Ministry of Human Resource Development (MHRD), aims to document and promote tribal languages (MoTA, 2022). Additionally, the Central Institute of Indian Languages (CIIL) conducts research on endangered tribal dialects (Sharma, 2021).
- Protection of Indigenous Knowledge and Folklore: Traditional tribal knowledge systems, including herbal medicine, agricultural practices, and oral histories, are being documented under the Tribal Research Institutes (TRIs) and the People's Biodiversity Register (PBR) (Verma, 2017). These initiatives help prevent the misappropriation of indigenous knowledge by external entities.
- Intellectual Property Rights (IPR) for Traditional Tribal Art, Music, and Crafts: The Geographical Indications (GI) Act, 1999, protects traditional tribal handicrafts such as Warli paintings (Maharashtra), Pattachitra (Odisha), and Toda embroidery (Tamil Nadu) (Ministry of Commerce, 2021). These protections ensure that tribal artisans receive fair economic benefits for their traditional craftsmanship (Singh, 2018).

Educational Rights of Tribals:
- Right to Education (RTE) and Its Impact on Tribal Education: Article

21A, introduced by the 86th Constitutional Amendment, mandates free and compulsory education for children aged 6-14 years (Government of India, 2002). This provision aims to bridge educational gaps for marginalized communities, including STs, by ensuring equal access to schooling (Sharma, 2020).

- Protection Against Discrimination in Education: Article 15(4) enables the State to make special provisions for socially and educationally backward classes, including Scheduled Tribes (Verma, 2017). Article 17 abolishes untouchability, ensuring that tribal students do not face social discrimination in educational institutions (Singh, 2018).
- Promotion of Mother-Tongue Education: Article 350A directs the government to provide primary education in the mother tongue of linguistic minorities, benefiting tribal students whose native languages are different from mainstream regional languages (Government of India, 1950).
- The Right to Education (RTE) Act, 2009: The RTE Act, 2009, operationalizes Article 21A, ensuring that tribal children have access to free and compulsory education (Government of India, 2009). The Act also mandates inclusive education policies, special training programs, and relaxation of admission norms for tribal students (Sharma, 2021).
- National Education Policy (NEP) 2020 and Its Implications for Tribal Education: The NEP 2020 focuses on multilingual education, curriculum flexibility, and vocational training to address tribal educational needs (Ministry of Education, 2020). Key provisions include:
- Promotion of tribal languages through bilingual teaching methods.
- Expansion of digital learning to improve access in remote tribal areas.
- Introduction of skill-based education to enhance employability among tribal youth (Verma, 2021).

Government Initiatives:

Eklavya Model Residential Schools (EMRS): Launched in 1997, EMRS provides quality education for ST children in remote tribal areas (Ministry of Tribal Affairs, 2022). The government aims to establish 740 EMRSs by 2025 to improve higher education access for tribal students (Xaxa, 2014).

Ashram Schools: These residential schools are established under state tribal welfare departments, focusing on holistic education while integrating tribal culture and traditions into the curriculum (Sharma, 2020).

Scholarships for Tribal Students: Several scholarship schemes are available for tribal students, including:

- Pre-Matric and Post-Matric Scholarships for ST students.
- Top Class Education Scheme for ST students pursuing higher education.
- National Overseas Scholarship for ST students seeking education abroad (Ministry of Education, 2022).

Challenges in the Implementation of Constitutional and Legal Safeguards: Despite the existence of constitutional provisions and legal safeguards, the political, cultural, and educational rights of Scheduled Tribes (STs) face significant challenges in implementation. Various factors, including, hinder the realization of these rights (Xaxa, 2014). bureaucratic inefficiencies, socio-economic disadvantages, and conflicts between traditional and modern governance models.

Political Challenges:
- Limited Political Representation Beyond Reserved Constituencies: While Articles 330 and 332 provide for reservation of seats for STs in Parliament and State Legislatures, their political representation remains limited to these constituencies (Verma, 2017). Tribal leaders often lack influence in mainstream political discourse, and their voices are underrepresented in key decision-making processes (Sharma, 2021).
- Bureaucratic Inefficiencies in Implementing Tribal Governance Policies: The implementation of policies like PESA (1996) and FRA (2006) is hindered by bureaucratic red tape, corruption, and a lack of administrative capacity (Ministry of Tribal Affairs, 2022). Many Panchayats in Scheduled Areas are either not fully functional or operate under state control, undermining the intent of decentralized tribal governance (Singh, 2018).
- Conflicts Between National Development Projects and Tribal Self-Governance: Large-scale infrastructure and industrial projects, such as mining, dams, and urban expansion, often result in the displacement of tribal communities without adequate rehabilitation (Sharma, 2020). These projects frequently override provisions of the Fifth and Sixth Schedules, leading to conflicts between tribal self-governance and state/national interests (Verma, 2017).

Cultural Challenges:
- Language Endangerment and Lack of Adequate Representation in Mainstream Media: Many tribal languages lack written scripts, making it difficult to preserve and promote them in formal education and media (Singh, 2018). While some tribal languages like Santhali and

Bodo are recognized under the Eighth Schedule, many others remain endangered due to a lack of state support (Sharma, 2021).

- Influence of Globalization Leading to Cultural Dilution: The increasing penetration of global culture, urbanization, and market-driven economies has led to the erosion of traditional tribal customs, beliefs, and social structures (Xaxa, 2014). Younger generations, in particular, are increasingly adopting dominant cultural norms, leading to a decline in traditional practices and rituals (Ministry of Tribal Affairs, 2022).
- Conflict Between Tribal Customary Laws and National Legal Frameworks: Many tribal communities follow customary laws governing aspects like marriage, inheritance, and land rights, which often conflict with national legal frameworks (Verma, 2017). For example, tribal matrilineal inheritance practices in Meghalaya differ from the Hindu Succession Act, creating legal ambiguities (Singh, 2018). Similarly, certain tribal conflict resolution mechanisms clash with formal judicial processes, leading to legal disputes (Sharma, 2020).

Educational Challenges-
- High Dropout Rates Due to Socio-Economic Barriers: Tribal children face multiple socio-economic barriers such as poverty, lack of parental education, and seasonal migration of families (Xaxa, 2014). The Annual Status of Education Report (ASER, 2021) indicates that dropout rates among ST students remain higher than the national average due to economic hardships and social exclusion (Ministry of Education, 2022).
- Medium of Instruction Issues: Tribal Language vs. Mainstream Languages: A major challenge in tribal education is the lack of mother-tongue-based instruction at the primary level (Singh, 2018). While Article 350A mandates primary education in students' mother tongues, most schools follow state languages or English, making it difficult for tribal students to comprehend lessons and leading to lower retention rates (Sharma, 2020).
- Lack of Adequate Educational Infrastructure in Remote Tribal Areas: Many tribal areas suffer from a lack of proper schools, trained teachers, and educational resources (Ministry of Tribal Affairs, 2022). Programs like Eklavya Model Residential Schools (EMRS) aim to bridge this gap, but implementation issues and financial constraints continue to hinder their success (Verma, 2017).

Suggestions- While India has comprehensive constitutional and legal safeguards to protect the political, cultural, and educational rights of tribal communities, gaps in implementation and institutional inefficiencies continue to hinder progress. The following suggestions aim to enhance policy effectiveness and ensure inclusive development for Scheduled Tribes (STs).

1. Strengthening Policy Implementation Through Better Governance: A major challenge in tribal welfare is the ineffective execution of policies such as PESA (1996) and FRA (2006) due to bureaucratic delays, corruption, and political interference (Ministry of Tribal Affairs, 2022). To address this:

- Establish independent monitoring bodies to oversee the implementation of tribal welfare programs at national and state levels (Xaxa, 2014).
- Digitize land records and tribal entitlements to ensure greater transparency and accountability in the enforcement of forest rights and land protection laws (Sharma, 2021).
- Strengthen Gram Sabhas in Scheduled Areas, empowering them to exercise their constitutional autonomy under PESA, 1996 (Singh, 2018).

2. Enhancing Tribal Participation in Political Decision-Making: Despite constitutional reservations (Articles 330 & 332), tribal representation in mainstream political decision-making remains limited (Verma, 2017). To promote greater political inclusion:

- Encourage leadership training programs to equip tribal youth with the skills needed to participate in local governance and national policymaking (Sharma, 2020).
- Ensure greater representation of tribal communities in executive positions, including the bureaucracy, judiciary, and law enforcement agencies (Singh, 2018).
- Strengthen the role of Tribal Advisory Councils (TACs) to provide policy recommendations on tribal development issues (Ministry of Tribal Affairs, 2022).

3. Promoting Mother-Tongue Education and Digital Learning for Tribal Students: Language barriers remain a key factor in the educational marginalization of tribal students. Despite Article 350A's mandate to promote mother-tongue education, many tribal children are forced to learn in state languages, leading to higher dropout rates (Singh, 2018). To improve educational outcomes:

- Expand mother-tongue-based multilingual education (MLE) and integrate tribal languages into school curricula (Sharma, 2020).
- Develop digital learning platforms that provide interactive, culturally relevant educational content for tribal students in regional languages (Ministry of Education, 2022).

- Increase investment in tribal residential schools, such as Eklavya Model Residential Schools (EMRS), ensuring adequate infrastructure, trained teachers, and curriculum inclusivity (Verma, 2017).
4. Strengthening Legal Frameworks for Cultural Preservation and IPR Protection: Tribal art, music, and indigenous knowledge systems are often exploited without fair compensation, highlighting the need for stronger legal protections (Sharma, 2021). Steps to protect tribal cultural heritage include:
- Establishing a national framework for Indigenous Intellectual Property Rights (IPR) to prevent commercial exploitation of tribal art, folklore, and traditional knowledge (Singh, 2018).
- Ensuring legal recognition for traditional healing practices and medicinal **knowledge** under the Biodiversity Act, 2002 (Ministry of Tribal Affairs, 2022).
- Promoting government-backed financial incentives for tribal artisans and cultural entrepreneurs, ensuring direct market access without intermediary exploitation (Xaxa, 2014).
5. Expanding Community-Led Initiatives for Cultural and Educational Empowerment: Empowering tribal communities through grassroots initiatives can foster self-reliance and cultural preservation. Some key strategies include:
- Encouraging community-driven education models, such as tribal-run schools and informal learning centers, that integrate indigenous knowledge with formal education (Verma, 2017).
- Supporting tribal self-help groups (SHGs) and cooperatives to promote economic sustainability and social development (Sharma, 2020).
- Leveraging technology to connect tribal communities with national and global markets, enhancing their economic opportunities and visibility (Ministry of Tribal Affairs, 2022).

Conclusion- India's tribal communities, constituting approximately 8.6% of the total population (Census of India, 2011), have long struggled for political, cultural, and educational rights. The Indian Constitution provides several safeguards, including political reservations (Articles 330, 332, 243D, and 243T), cultural protections (Articles 29 and 46), and educational rights (Articles 21A, 15, 17, and 350A). Additionally, legal frameworks such as PESA (1996), FRA (2006), and the RTE Act (2009) aim to empower tribal communities. Despite these constitutional and legal provisions, challenges persist. Political representation remains limited beyond reserved constituencies, and bureaucratic inefficiencies hinder policy implementation (Ministry of Tribal

Affairs, 2022). Culturally, tribal languages face endangerment, globalization threatens indigenous heritage, and customary laws often conflict with national legal frameworks. Educational barriers, such as high dropout rates, inadequate infrastructure, and language mismatches in curricula, further marginalize tribal students. The Need for a Holistic and Inclusive Approach to Tribal Development: Addressing these challenges requires a multi-dimensional approach that integrates policy reforms, grassroots initiatives, and technological innovations. A holistic development model must combine government policies with active participation from tribal communities, civil society organizations, and private stakeholders to create sustainable and inclusive growth.

References-

- Census of India. (2011). *Demographic profile of Scheduled Tribes in India.* Ministry of Home Affairs, Government of India.
- Government of India. (1950). *The Constitution of India.* Ministry of Law and Justice.
- Government of India. (2002). *The 86th Constitutional Amendment Act.* Ministry of Law and Justice.
- Government of India. (2003). *Eighth Schedule of the Constitution.* Ministry of Home Affairs.
- Government of India. (2006). *The Scheduled Tribes and Other Traditional Forest Dwellers (Recognition of Forest Rights) Act, 2006.* Ministry of Tribal Affairs.
- Government of India. (2009). *The Right to Education (RTE) Act, 2009.* Ministry of Education.
- Ministry of Commerce. (2021). *Geographical Indications of India: Handbook on Traditional Art and Craft.*
- Ministry of Education. (2020). *National Education Policy 2020: Transforming Education in India.*
- Ministry of Education. (2022). *Annual Status of Education Report (ASER), 2021.* Government of India.
- Ministry of Panchayati Raj. (2021). *Implementation of PESA Act in Scheduled Areas.* Government of India.
- Ministry of Tribal Affairs. (2021). *Annual Report 2020-21.* Government of India.
- Ministry of Tribal Affairs. (2022). *Annual Report on Tribal Welfare 2021-22.* Government of India.

- Ministry of Tribal Affairs. (2022). *Policies and schemes for tribal welfare.* Government of India.
- Ministry of Tribal Affairs. (2022). *Annual Report on Tribal Welfare 2021-22.* Government of India.
- Registrar General of India. (2011). *Census of India 2011: Scheduled Tribes in India.* Government of India.
- Guha, R. (1999). *Savaging the civilized: Verrier Elwin, his tribals, and India.* Oxford University Press.
- Mehta, P. (2019). *Decentralization and tribal governance: An analysis of PESA implementation.* Economic and Political Weekly, **54**(12), 45-58.
- Nathan, D., & Xaxa, V. (2012). *Social exclusion and adivasi communities in India.* Oxford University Press.
- Sharma, R. (2020). *Indigenous knowledge systems and their role in sustainable development.* Economic and Political Weekly, **55**(10), 45-52.
- Sharma, R. (2021). *Forest Rights Act: Challenges in implementation and the way forward.* Social Change Review, **15**(3), 78-94.
- Singh, A. (2018). *Autonomy and self-governance under the Sixth Schedule of the Indian Constitution.* Journal of Public Administration, **63**(1), 32-47.
- Sharma, R. (2020). *Educational barriers for Scheduled Tribes in India: Policies and challenges.* Indian Journal of Social Policy, **9**(2), 85-100.
- Sharma, R. (2021). *Preserving indigenous knowledge: Legal and policy perspectives in India.* Social Change Review, **16**(1), 45-65.
- Singh, A. (2018). *Language preservation and educational inclusion for Scheduled Tribes in India.* Journal of Public Policy, **62**(1), 112-130.
- Verma, M. (2017). *Tribal rights in India: An analysis of constitutional and legal safeguards.* Indian Journal of Law and Society, **6**(2), 85-102.
- Verma, M. (2017). *Cultural and educational rights of Scheduled Tribes in India: A constitutional perspective.* Indian Journal of Law and Society, 7(1), 120-140.
- Verma, M. (2021). *Policy implementation challenges in tribal education under NEP 2020.* Indian Journal of Education Policy, 10(3), 55-75.
- Xaxa, V. (2014). *Report on the socio-economic status of tribal communities in India.* Ministry of Tribal Affairs, Government of India.

Paharia: A Lesser-Known Tribe of Odisha

Lohitakshya Joshi

Folklorist and Translator
Joshis', Ward No 10, Khariar
lohitakshyajoshi9@gmail.com

Abstract

Odisha is home to many tribal groups. Especially the south-western parts of Odisha have more tribal concentration compared to other parts of the state. Many of these tribes are the aborigines of the region and come under the primitive tribe category. "For thousands of years, primitive tribes persisted in forests and hills without having more than casual contacts with the population of the open plains and the centers of civilization" (Christoph:1977). This peaceful coexistence was possible because there was no pressure of the population and the tribes could live isolated in the hills and jungles in close proximity with nature. They didn't feel threatened by the mainstream civilizational forces in terms of rail, road, industries etc. The normal perception is that the upper caste people maintain a high standard of culture and practices and the tribals live with their age-old practices which we call superstition and banal. So, we level the stereotypical tag of backwardness on them. But paradoxically speaking, when observed closely, we see a very progressive attitude in their rituals and practices. Some of the practices as Christoph Von Furer-Haimendorf argues in the above-referred essay are "absence of caste- distinctions, equality of the sexes, preference for adult marriage, the liberty of divorcees and widows to remarry, and the independence of the nuclear family from any control on the part of a joint family" (Christoph:1977). At this backdrop the present paper seeks to negotiate one such tribe in western Odisha called the Paharia or Kamar.
Keywords: *Paharia, Tribes, kamar, Bamboo work,*

Introduction

The Paharia or Kamar, though have all the tribal characteristics, they are not yet included in the scheduled tribe list in Odisha. This peculiarity will be dealt in details in the later part of this paper. But before that let us know who are the tribes and what is the most agreed-upon definition of a tribe. While trying to define 'tribe', we come across the dichotomy between the general conditions and the specific conditions. This is because often the specific historical conditions do not conform to the general or ideal dynamics. Andre Beteille therefore makes a very simple and agreeable definition of tribe thus, "A tribe is in an ideal state, a self-contained unit. It constitutes a society in itself" (Beteille:1977).

S.C. Dube in his book *The Kamar* (1951), which is considered as the seminal work on this tribe, describes all aspects of the community. He visited the Paharia villages of the five South-eastern districts known as Chhatisgarh. Then Kharia Zamindari which is the present Nuapada district was part of the Central Province. This entire tract mentioned above is now a separate state named Chhattisgarh. The Paharias and some other tribal groups such as Gond, Soura, Bhunjia etc. prefer to live in this area due to its thick forest and comparative seclusion from the forces of more advanced civilization. In the present Nuapada district the Paharias are found mostly in the Sunabeda plateau of Komna Block and Kathfar-Patdarah plateau of Boden Block. This entire area is on the extreme western line of the district forming a borderline with Chhattisgarh state. The area used to be considered inaccessible until the recent years. Since the Paharia people depend largely on forest resources they prefer to stay in this region. Apart from the plateau area they also live in the hill slopes and even in some plain villages of Sinapali Block. In Odisha according to some unofficial sources the Paharias live in about seven districts. We also get an insight into the nature of the Paharias in Nuapada district from an insider of the community thus, "…. We have been living in Kathfar since 14 to 15 generations now. Thus, our village will be 1000 years old. As it is situated on the plateau it has not developed" (Panigrahi:2024).

There is no exact official data on the recent Paharia population in Odisha or Nuapada district. If we look at the Kamar population of Raipur district under the Central Province according to 1911 and 1931 Census it was 7185 and 9244 respectively. This means it showed an increasing trend then. But if we look at the population figure of the Paharias in Nuapada district now the situation is different. According to an NGO named Lokadrusti study in 2007 carried out in all the five blocks of Nuapada district the total household is 1278 with a total population of 4284. According to a report of another survey conducted by the NGOs Sajag and Sahabhagi Vikash Abhiyan, the population of the Paharias in Nuapada district remained almost stable between 2001-

2007. This is in clear contrast to the Census data of 1911 and 1931 of Raipur district as has been mentioned earlier. The reason ascribed to this downward trend is high infant mortality rate which was reported to be a warranting 128 per thousand during this period. The survey expresses deep concerns that, "the population of Kamar/Paharia is constantly declining and unless some special measures are taken up, they may get wiped out very soon" (Swain &Majhi:2001).

The Paharias usually prefer to live in isolated areas in single-tribe villages. They do not want to stay in multi-community villages with other castles and tribes. Hence, they build up their own settlements. The Paharia village does not consist of more than a very limited number of households which are connected by the ties of blood or marriage. Earlier they were very strict about their seclusion from other tribes and castes. They would not even stay a night in any village other than the exclusive Paharia settlement. If by chance they could not come back to their own village or any nearby Paharia settlement they would go out of the village and prefer to stay the night under a tree rather than live in a non-Paharia village. They would also not allow anyone other than the Paharias to construct a house in their village. Thus, they were very orthodox about their single-tribe small village structure. Given the choice despite a number of compulsions and the rapid process of acculturation they prefer to live in a single-tribe village even today. "They prefer to live in exclusively separate single-tribe village. But now a days they are living in villages of other tribes and castes. Still, they do not mix with them easily and construct their houses outside the village boundary. The concept of private property among the Paharia is very weak. They abandon their huts and even villages at the slightest provocation" (Deo & Joshi:2001). The above revelation has come through a study conducted by an NGO called Lokadrusti which was later published as a book. From the door-to-door study of 79 Paharia villages of Nuapada district covering a population of 4284 in 1278 households it is seen that the average village size is very small which is characteristic of the Paharias. The average number of households in a village is a little more than 19 only. This study also reveals that today the Paharias have begun to live in multi-community villages along with Bhunjias, Gonds and other tribal groups. Though they remain socially distinctive, they influence one another and develop forms of mutual adjustment. They even accept food and water from Gond, Bhunjia, Kultha and Mali. The first two are tribes whereas the last two are SEBC. Despite this inter community interaction the Paharias try to maintain their separate identity.

Kamars are known as Paharias in Nuapada district. In the past also they used to be known as Paharia in the erstwhile Khariar Zamindari which is now Nuapada district, and Bindranawagarh Zamindari which is now the adjoining parts of Chhattisgarh. S.C. Dube believes that the term Paharia might have come from the word 'Paharpatiya', literally meaning dwellers of the hills. Another popular belief is that the term Paharia is derived from the word 'Pahar' meaning mountain. So those people living in the pahar are known as Paharias and given the nature of habitation as has been discussed above, the term is aptly used for this community. This has been discussed in detail in the UNDP project report entitled "Paharias: The Struggle of a Tribe for Existence", carried out in 24 sample villages out of the 79 project villages in 2008. This report also makes an important reflection with reference to Verrier Elwin's work *Tribal Myths of Orissa* (1954/2006) where in it is argued that as they were "formerly known as Paharia, as they lived in the hills, but that ever since they took up bamboo work, they have been called Kamar" (Choudhary:2008). So, from this we also get an important clue to the very livelihood of the Paharias which we normally believe is originally bamboo work. This will be discussed in detail in the later part of this paper. The report further discusses on the term Paharia referring to Dr. Fanindam Deo, a famous historian and co-author of the book on Paharia referred earlier in this paper. Dr. Deo believes that the term Paharia is drawn from the term 'pahara' meaning keeping guard and this refers to the people who lived in and protected the hills and forest. From all these references we can safely construe an argument that these people were originally known as Paharia and the term came to be associated with them at a later stage.

On the other hand, the term Kamar according to ethnographic literature designates a professional caste on the basis of iron work. Even today the Kamar or the Lohoras, as they are known in Nuapada district and the whole of western Odisha, are professional ironsmiths on hereditary basis. But the Paharias/Kamars of this region and Chhattisgarh are in no way associated with with iron work. The Paharias are considered as the aborigines of this region and there is no literature to suggest that they are the offshoot of the Kamars who have migrated from other parts of the state or the country. It is important to note that their iron implements are not made by themselves, but are made by the Kamars or Lohoras of the locality. So, we can assert the fact that the Kamars/Paharias are not the Kamars/Lohoras and that they are a separate tribe. The Paharia mythology also do not have any such references to their association with iron work. S.C. Dube confirms this aspect:

There is nothing to prove the existence of any affinity between the Kamars of Chhattisgarh and the tribes or the castes of the same name in the other parts of the country. The Kamar tradition does not give us any clue regarding the original home and the earlier migrations of the tribe. The mythology of the Kamars does not indicate any ancient association of the tribe with iron or smithery. Today all the iron weapons, instruments and implements of the Kamars are made by the Lohars, the professional Hindu blacksmiths, living in the villages. The traditional occupation of the Kamars, according to one of their famous legends, are all connected with the axe, bow and arrow, I.e., *dahi* and *beora* cultivation, collection of forest produces and hunting (Dube:2004).

So, it is clear that the paharias are in no way related to the Lohoras in the region or the Kamars in the other parts of the state. But on the other hand, the Paharias/Kamars of south-western Odisha and Chhattisgarh which is known as the region of Paharia concentration, are related to each other including marriage relations. So, it is wrong to club them with the Kamar community in its literal sense. That precisely is the confusion which led this otherwise aboriginal tribal group being deprived of their tribal rights and identity in Odisha government records since the formation of a separate state of Odisha. Though they are considered by the other tribal communities as older and truly autochthonous they are still not recognized as tribe by the government. This is the biggest irony they live with till today. Russel and Hiralal in their book *The Tribes and Castes of the Central provinces of India,* Vol. III classifies the Kamars as a Dravidian tribe and an offshoot of the Gonds. But in the later period this view was not accepted because it was not substantiated with sufficient reason.

Today the Paharias are associated with bamboo work which is believed to be the mainstay of their economy and a hereditary source of their livelihood. But studies reveal that the Paharias were originally a hunter-gatherer group. They lived on forest produces and hunting. Gradually they adopted shifting cultivation for their sustenance. In the past they lived partly on their primitive agriculture and partly on hunting, fishing and food gathering from forest. But gradually due to the factors such as squeeing of their forest rights, process of rapid acculturation, they had to adapt to newer ways and practices. Dube in 1940s rightly calls it a transition of the Paharia economy, "The economy of Kamars today is in transition. As a result of the impact of alien cultures and their complicated economic systems, the virtual self-sufficiency of the tribal economy of the Kamars has broken down. They have been forced to adapt themselves to new economic standards and techniques" (Dube:2004). Due to this their preferred isolation was disturbed and they were forced to come out of their seclusion. They had no way but to seek new avenues of livelihood. In this state of transition, they adopted bamboo basket making which gradually came to be identified with their life and livelihood. So, the conversion from hunter-gatherer tribe to a bamboo basket making economy, the choice was not simple and they were in a way forced to this adaptation. In course of time due to this switch over they began to build their settlements near the bamboo forests. Today they depend primarily on bamboo work. Men, women and children, old and young alike, participate in this work. But the irony is that their products do not reach the market directly. This is again due to their habitation which is far away from the urban weekly market. So, they rely on the middlemen who come periodically, buy from them at cheaper price and in turn sell in the market at much higher price. Thus, the Paharias are subjected to distress sale.

We do not get any written history regarding the origin of the tribes. In this regard, therefore, folklore serves an important purpose of highlighting this aspect to some extent. Compared to other tribes and castes the folklore of the Paharias is poor in respect of myths, legends etc. Also, from these oral sources and the practicing traditions, rituals and various social institutions of the Paharias we come to know about them. Often, we treat this as mere superstition with our own judgement notwithstanding the fact that they have a different worldview, a culture of value and significance in the context of their own community and individual life. We fail to acknowledge the fact that their culture is dynamic, their traditions are vibrant and their festivals are the reflections of their faith and beliefs. That is why we often talk of mainstreaming them, civilizing them. "Often, we see these practices superficially and dismiss them as mere superstition, but a closer scrutiny and understanding show that there are actually necessary dualities in keeping with the people's fundamental concept of balance with their own ethos and milieu. Further critical engagements reveal the strength and relevance of their belief system" (Joshi:2021). In this context this paper seeks to negotiate with the marriage as an institution among the Paharia community.

Clan plays an important role like many other tribes and castes. The Paharias do not marry within their own *Gotra*. Marriage outside their community is also strictly forbidden. They are also very strict about their marriage relations like who cannot marry whom and it is interesting to note that unlike other castes both male and female are equally regulated which relation they can marry and which they cannot. So, no gender bias is seen in this regulation. S.C. Dube talked about seven *Gotras* in his book referred earlier in this paper. They are i. Jagat, ii. Netam (Maitam), iii. Markam, iv. Sori, v, Kunjam, vi. Marai and vii. Chedaiha. People of these Gotras can marry among themselves but cannot marry within their own *Gotra*. The Paharia marriage may be classified into five categories on the basis of its procedure. They are i. Bihaw or Lagin or regular marriage, ii. Run-away marriage, iii. Paithu or marriage by intrusion, iv. Serving for a wife and v. Widow-remarriage. But in the recent context and that of Nuapada district Paharia marriage is of four types namely i. Udhulia marriage, ii. Ghicha marriage, iii. Penruka or water-pouring marriage and iv. Milamisa marriage.

Udhulia (elopement) marriage is like the runaway marriage where in the boy and the girl like each other and when their parents and society come on their way they have no option but to run away from the village. They live in some other village or in the forest for some months and ultimately come back to their village. They are mostly accepted by the society then.

Ghicha marriage or marriage by intrusion is a little different. Here unlike the previous form of marriage, mutual consent is not the precondition. But close scrutiny reveals that the girl has silent consent and approval to the marriage. But on the surface level it seems that the boy holds the hands of the girl he likes and the parents are left with no option but to give the girl in marriage to the boy.

Penruka or water pouring marriage means when the girl is brought to the house of the boy with the consent of her parents. It may happen at a tender age also, but marriage is not formalized unless the girl reaches the marriageable age. Such formalization may happen even after the couple attains their parenthood also. But they continue to live as husband and wife even before the formalization ritual.

Milamisa or marriage by acquaintance means the boy and girl live in relationship like couple but marriage is not solemnized. This is an ancient form of marriage which has now become obsolete. In addition to all these forms of marriage the most prevalent one among them is the regular marriage. It begins with the *mahala* or engagement. As has been mentioned earlier in this paper marriage among the Paharias takes place when they become adult. From the firsthand experience of a Paharia boy named Sukal Sai Paharia of Kathfar-Patdarah plateau which is now a book entitled *Sukal's Diary* (2024) we come to know in detail about a Paharia marriage.

When a Paharia boy attains the age of 22-23 the family elders seek his opinion on marriage. If he has liking for someone, he says it and it progresses. Else the family members decide the marriage. But normally initiative is taken by the bridegroom side. It is very categorically mentioned by S.C. Dube thus, "The talks of marriage are opened by the boy's people, who send their *mahalias* with the proposal to the house of the proposed bride. The *Mahalia* is either a brother, near relative or friend of the bridegroom's father, and is selected for the job because of his intelligence and that in handling situation, and capacity for negotiating well" (Dube:2004). The *mahalias* do not tell the purpose directly to the bride side. They resort to different twist in the conversation before telling them the purpose of their visit. Then both the parties ascertain the character of the bride and the groom. If they are satisfied the *Jhankar* or the village religious head offers the cock brought by the boy's parents to the deities in the witness of the Sun and the Moon as a mark of confirmation and respect to the deities. Then they drink liquor brought by the boy's side. They then finalize the date and time of the marriage. The marriage is then solemnized according to the Paharia tradition.

What is interesting here to note that child marriage is not found among the Paharias. There is also no system of bride price. Whatever the bridegroom side brings is as part of tradition and not on demand. They bring cock, rice, coconut etc. which are used in the marriage ritual. They maintain their sanctity in marriage and uphold the fact that their daughters are not to be sold. They have equal respect for man and woman. Also, in Paharia social system cases of divorce are not found. They rather have the provision of widow remarriage which speaks of the advanced attitude of the community. All the widow as a rule marry again. She usually waits for a year after the death of her husband. After that she becomes the wife of the younger brother of her deceased husband. In case there are more than one younger brother for marriage the ultimate choice remains with the widow. Moreover, in case she has a different choice other than the prescribed norm of the younger brother of the deceased husband, her wish is again respected. But in that case the man she wishes to marry has to come forward to make an open and formal proposal. In some cases, if the widow does not wish to marry her husband's brother, she may elope with the man of her choice. This is also an accepted norm within the Paharia social framework.

Another interesting aspect in the Paharia marriage system is monogamy. They are mostly against polygynous marriage because they believe it ruins the family peace. For them more wife in the family means loss of peace. They understand the sanctity of a marriage and therefore any formal procedure of divorce is unknown in the Paharia vocabulary. But it does not mean that the wife does not have a choice to leave her drunkard husband who beats her. In such cases the Paharia society allows the wife to run away and find another husband of her choice who she thinks will keep her peacefully. This is a socially approved system which is symptomatic of their advanced worldview.

It is true that the Paharia tradition, livelihood options and social structures are in constant flux like other tribes and castes though the pace is slower compared to others. But despite this they still are very orthodox and try to maintain their originality and securing which they believe is the key to the beauty and sanctity of their identity.

References:

- Christoph Von Furer-Haimendorf, (1977) "Tribal Problems in India", *Tribe, Caste and Religion in India,* Ed. Romesh Thapar, Macmillan India, Delhi, pp.1
- Beteille A, (1977) "The Definition of Tribe", *Tribe, Caste and Religion in India,* Ed. Romesh Thapar (Delhi: Macmillan India,) p.8
- Panigrahi, A.M, Trans. Lohitakshya Joshi, 2024, *Sukal's Diary,* Pen in Books, Bhubaneswar, pp.107.
- Swain R& Majhi G, 2001, "Plight of the Kamar Tribals of Orissa", SAJAG and SVA Report, pp.4.
- Deo F & Joshi L, 2004, *Lesser-Known Tribes of Orissa,* Lokadrusti, Khariar, pp. 7.
- Choudhary K & Others, 2008, "Paharias: The Struggle of a Tribe for Recognition, UNDP Report, pp.9.
- Dube S.C., 2004, *The Kamar,* Oxford University Press, New Delhi, pp.5.
- Joshi L, 2021, "The Kitchen-shed Concept of the Chuktia Bhunjia", *Essays on Culture: New Perspectives,* Authors Press, New Delhi, pp. 21.

The Promise of Development, Displacement and Violation of the Tribal Rights in Koraput District, Odisha.

Mr. Kanhu Charan Barada

Lecturer in Political Science, Govt. Women's College,
Jeypore (Koraput), Email: kanhubarada94@gmail.com

ABSTRACT:

The concept of development is a historical legacy. The word development is commonly understood in terms of economic growth or change or literally means improvement of the economic status of the society and the standards of quality lives of people. The idea of development pertains to a specific form of economic advancement and social and political structures. Thus, development is globally defined in terms of industrial and technological growth. Development is just another form of social change; it cannot be understood in isolation. The analysis of development actions and of popular reactions to these actions should not be isolated from the study of local dynamics, industrial development, challenges before advance of modern technology in the tribal belt like Koraput. Development seeks the welfare of others. In the name of development most of development agencies systematically exploit people and the local environment in a crucial way. Development-induced displacement or loss of land results in the marginalisation and impoverishment of the people particularly of the schedule tribe of Koraput. The pursuit of development adversely affected the marginalized sections causing deprivation, displacement and devastation, and drastically altered the relationship of the tribes with the natural environment and the natural resources. The present paper is an attempt to analyse various implications of displacement on social-economic and cultural aspect of the dispossessed tribals by major industries like NALCO, HAL and highlight issues and Consequences of Development, displacement, and violation the Tribal Rights in the Koraput district of Odisha.

Keywords: Development-induced displacement, Tribal rights, Koraput district, Odisha, Human rights, Marginalization, Economic development, NALCO, HAL, etc.

Introduction:

The process of economic, social, political, cultural, and technological progress or improvement of the standard of living is generally referred to as development. During its 4th December 1986 session, the General Assembly of the United Nations adopted the doctrine of 'Right to Development'. There is a strong emphasis placed on the right to self-determination and sovereignty and it asserts that all civil, political, economic, social and cultural rights are equally important and should all be promoted and protected equally.

There has been systematic exploitation of people and the environment as a result of development projects. The result has been the strengthening of power structures that ensure that benefits flow from the periphery to the centre. The mechanized nature of these projects prevents displaced people/ project affected people (DPs/PAPs) from getting on-project jobs or becoming part of the official employment statistics. If we include the DPs/PAPs as unemployed then the number of unemployed in India would be greatly increased. Development-induced displacement or loss of land results in the marginalisation and impoverishment of the DPs/PAPs, particularly of the weaker sections.

Development projects which displace people from their Own habitat have only benefited the powerful, the high Castes, and the urban population. These categories enjoy Project benefits like irrigation, employment, electricity, and other infra-structural gains, and so are unable to Understand the sufferings and the marginalisation of the Displaced population. Therefore, it is necessary to initiate Dialogue between these two groups-the losers (the original owners) and the gainers.

The Driving Force of Development Policy:
1. Self-Reliance
2. Inward looking development strategy
3. Focus on Socialist model of development
4. Economic Planning
5. Growth of Private Capitalists
6. Introduction of Foreign Exchange Regulation Act (FERA) 1973 and Monopolies and Restrictive Trade Practices (MRTP) Act 1970

7. Economic reforms system (Financial sectors)
8. New World order of Globalisation
9. Privatization on Public Sector Units
10. Enhancing efficiency (latest technological developments in the global frontier)

Review of Literature:
1. 1. **Aswal B.S., (2012),** 'Tribal and Human Rights' has defined the Tribal Development and European Union Regional Integration and its implication on Human Right. The researcher has studied the entire concept as to rights of person's tribal people. He also observed the situation of tribal women, children, prisoners and tribal people refuses right.
2. 2. **Agarwal A.N, (2013),** 'Tribals of Odisha' shows the pattern of socio-economic conditions of tribals in Odisha with respect to three indicators that is, health, education and economy. He gave emphasis on education as an important component of human development which indicates a person's productivity and income earning potential by imparting basic as well as specialized skills. Economic growth is a necessary condition for human development and it is one of the major components to satisfy the basic needs of life.
3. 3. **Chakrabarti Dr. Shambhu Prasad, (2018),** 'Tribal Rights in India' has explained the conceptual and historical perspective of tribal rights in India. His article was eloquent to reflect constitutional interpretations relating to the rights of tribal people. He also referred a number of problems the tribal faces from non-tribal. He also emphasized the importance of collective approach of sociological, political and anthropological for the tribal study.

Objectives of the Study:
The Present study focuses on the following objectives -
1. To Study the Socio- economic Development Plan and Programmes in Koraput.
2. To explore the various emerging Contemporary issues and Challenges faces by Tribal peoples of Koraput.
3. To highlights the Constitutional Safeguard and suggestions for the development of Tribal Peoples.

Research Questions:

1. Tribal rights are not implemented properly in the of Koraput.
2. The state machinery has failed to safeguard the interests of tribal communities and their rights has become jeopardy.

Research Methodology:

The study is based on secondary sources of data and information. The focus of the study is mainly on Tribal rights in India. The research methodology adopted for the purpose of research includes both empirical and doctrinal methods. The main sources of secondary data include books, journals, websites, periodicals, News- papers, report of tribal development etc. The study was conducted with searching and studying Secondary literature and collected different interviews were made by various reputed researcher and journals with scheduled tribe people living in the region.

Area of the Study:

Researcher has selected Koraput district of Odisha as pilot study. The district is tribal dominated districts of Odisha. The important source of Income of tribal people is cultivation and cattle raring and mostly Tribals are still not getting proper assistance form the Government as well as corporate companies after the displacement.

Study and Evaluate of Tribal Rights:

1. **Tribal Land Rights Acts, 1976:**
   The Tribal Land Rights Act, 1976, protects tribal people's rights over their land, preventing non-tribals from buying or taking over their land, ensuring their livelihood and cultural preservation.

2. **Tribal Forest Rights Act, 2006:**
   The Forest Rights Act, 2006, recognizes tribal communities' rights to forest land, resources, and livelihoods, correcting historical injustices and promoting sustainable forest management and conservation.

3. **Forest Dwellers Act, 2006:**
   The Forest Dwellers Act, 2006, recognizes and vests individual forest-dwellers with forest rights, including land, minor forest produce, and habitat. It aims to correct historical injustices, promote sustainable forest management, and ensure livelihood security for forest-dependent communities.

4. **Land Acquisition Act, 2013**
   The legislation allows for the purchase of land for the benefit of the

tribe in addition to requiring the tribal agreement and rehabilitating and resettling displaced individuals.

5. **Tribal Mining Right:**

   Tribal Mining Rights refer to the rights of tribal communities to control and benefit from mining activities on their familial lands, ensuring their consent, participation, and fair share of benefits.

6. **Tribal Property Rights:**

   Tribal Property Rights refer to the rights of tribal communities to own, control, and inherit land, forests, and other natural resources, free from encroachment and exploitation, and in accordance with their customary laws and traditions.

7. **Human Rights:**

   Human Rights are defined under Protection of Human Rights Act, 1993 under as it's Section 2(d) as the rights relating to life, liberty, equality and dignity of the individual guaranteed by the Constitution or embodied in the International Covenants and enforceable by courts in India. International Human rights law lays down the obligations on Governments to act in certain ways or to refrain from certain acts, in order to promote and protect human rights and fundamental freedom of individuals or groups.

8. **SC/ST Prevention of Atrocities Act, 1989:**

   Scheduled Castes and Tribes are protected from discrimination and violence by the SC/ST Prevention of Atrocities Act, 1989. It criminalizes atrocities such as forced labour and land grabbing. The law ensures strict punishments, special courts, and victim protection. It is crucial in safeguarding tribal rights, especially against displacement and exploitation in Odisha.

Welfare Measures are included :-

- Corporate Social Responsibility (CSR) by NALCO and HAL etc.
- Integrated Health Management System (Mobile Health Services for Peripheral Village)
- Skill Development Programme (Make in India,PMKVY,PM Internship,PM-USHA)
- Samagra Shiksha and Right to Education
- District Human Rights Protection Cell
- The Indian government's focused efforts towards tribal development date back to the implementation of the Tribal Sub-Plan (TSP) in 1974-75,
- Launch of Dharti Aaba Janjatiya Gram Utkarsh Abhiyan

- Eklavya Model Residential Schools (EMRS)
- Pradhan Mantri Janjati Adivasi Nyaya Maha Abhiyan (PM-JANMAN)
- The Pradhan Mantri Adi Adarsh Gram Yojana (PMAAGY)
- Development Action Plan for Scheduled Tribes (DAPST)

Issues and Challenges Faced by Tribal communities in Koraput District
1. Displacement problem of NALCO (Damanjodi)

The problems of the people of Odisha who have been displaced by the projects of National Aluminium Company Limited (NALCO) are being periodically reviewed by the Rehabilitation and Periphery Development Advisory Committees (RPDAC) constituted by Government of Odisha. In Mahanadi Coalfields Ltd. (MCL), compensation against acquisition of land, trees/ crops and structures is assessed as per Right to Fair Compensation and Transparency in Land Acquisition, Rehabilitation and Resettlement Act, 2013 (RFCTLARR Act, 2013) and being paid to the villagers after vesting of land with MCL under The Coal Bearing Areas (Acquisition and Development) Act 1957 (CBA (A&D) Act, 1957).

A total number of 635 persons were displaced by project activities in NALCO. Out of which, 600 persons were displaced in Damanjodi, Koraput District and 35 persons were displaced at Angul District. Out of 600 Land displaced persons (LDP) at Damanjodi, 599 LDPs/ their nominees were employed in NALCO. Regarding balance one case, decision is awaited from District Authority due to non-finalization of the nominee because of their family dispute. Out of 35 LDPs at Angul, 34 LDPs/their nominees were employed at NALCO while one LDP had preferred for one-time cash assistant in lieu of employment. In MCL about 16,297 persons have been identified to be displaced, out of which 11,837 have already been provided resettlement benefits. But till date out of 11,837 families, only 8,248 families have shifted from their respective villages. Out of 11,837 families, 3,455 families have been provided with resettlement plot at Resettlement and Rehabilitation site and 8,382 families have been provided with Cash in lieu of plot till date. Resettlement benefits for balance families are under process. The resettlement benefits are provided as per Rehabilitation and Resettlement (R&R) Policy of Government of Odisha.

2. Issues of Dasmantpur Block of Koraput district (2021)

A village in Odisha's Dengajaniguda, Dasmantpur Block of Koraput district is opposing aluminium maker Nalco's plan to build a new red mud pond, alleging the toxic waste would render their fields unsuitable for agriculture while causing diseases.

More than 600 tribals, Dalits and members of Other Backward Castes (OBCs) in Dengajaniguda village under Dasamantpur block of Koraput district have been preventing the revenue officials from identifying land near their village for construction of Nalco's second red mud pond. Red mud, also known as bauxite residue, is an industrial waste generated during the processing of bauxite into alumina (the Bayer process) and is composed of various oxide compounds, including iron oxides which give it the red colour. The disposal and utilisation of red mud have been traditionally hindered due to its extreme alkalinity.

Villagers led by **Bansi Bisoyi** said the existing red mud pond of the alumina refinery, situated about two kms from the village, has already led to several health problems. "Our tubewells spew red water and it is leading to several skin problems among villagers. The doctors are not able to detect the ailments. Water seeping from the first red mud pond has destroyed our farmland, natural streams, nullahs and has affected many people. We are forced to collect water from nearby streams

Another villager **Tuni Muduli** of this area alleged leaching of chemicals from the existing red mud pond has rendered farmlands unsuitable for cultivation. **Pinki Bisoyi,** another villager, said they have not gained anything from Nalco's alumina refinery, which came up in 80's in Damanjodi. "As there is no high school, our children are unable to study beyond class 5. There is no employment for our youths," she alleged.

3.   **Displacement Problem in Sunabeda areas of Koraput.**

In the year 1960, The Government of Odisha had handed over a total of 12,000 acres of land to the Hindustan Aeronautics Limited (HAL) at Sunabeda, Koraput. Total of 10 villages were affected namely, Kaki, Chakarliput, Thalaput, Kadigam, Charangul, Khalpadi, Chulapari, Rajpalama, Bodigam, Chikapar wherein a total of 435 families were displaced and only 138 familes have been rehabilitated. While HAL has been established on 3121.15 acres of land, it has handed over nearly 6,000 acres to various Central institutes, including the Central University of Odisha and the Cobra Batallion, and a private english medium school. Now HAL, has unused 2918.53 acres of land in its hand. The displaced adivasi's under the banner of HAL Displaced Persons Association have been making repeated demands to the district administration and HAL authorities for the overall development of all the affected villages, employment to at least one person of each displaced household, education facilities in peripheral villages and the return of unused land acquired by HAL.

The worse problem is that still, it noted the lack of livelihood opportunities, educational facilities and easy access to basic amenities like drinking water. In May 2021, acting on a petition filed by advocate **Radhakanta Tripathy**, the National Human Rights Commission directed the Chief Secretary of Odisha to investigate the grievances of individuals displaced and affected by several projects in the Koraput district, including HAL. Mr. Tripathy in his petition requested the NHRC to verify the MoUs signed by HAL and NALCO with the Government of Odisha and determine the real implementation status of Record of Rights, (RoR), rehabilitation and livelihood among others.

4. **KOTIA issue of Koraput emerging the identity Crisis:**

Twenty-one villages in Koraput district in Odisha, more commonly known as the Kotia group of villages, have been caught in an identity crisis since the 1950s. Both Odisha and Andhra Pradesh claim jurisdiction over them, as they are situated along the inter-state border, although the villages are part of the Kotia panchayat in Koraputs Pottangi constituency. After Odisha was formed in 1936, the state government wrote to the then government of Madras Presidency to take steps for delineation of the interstate boundary with Andhra Pradesh. H.S. Gilby, the then assistant director of Survey and Land Records, was appointed to demarcate the boundary in 1942 According to his report, the 21 villages fell within the boundary of Andhra Pradesh. The dispute started in March 1955 when some subordinate government officers from Andhra Pradesh tried to collect rent from the village residents, following the formation of the state in 1953. Y.V. Chavan, the then home minister of India, tried to bring the chief ministers of both the states together to resolve the dispute in a meeting in September 1968. Chavan noted that based on Gilbys report of 1942, which Odisha had accepted, it was difficult to support the states claim over the disputed villages. The Odisha government filed a case in the Supreme Court in 1968. In the original suit, 73 villages were specified to be disputed, but, subsequently, the number was reduced to 21 in 1980. The disputed villages are Doliamba, Madakaru, Kotiya, Digurasembi, Equrasembi, Gangaibhadra, Dhulipadar, Sidivalasa, Arjuvalasa, Panika, Narlavalsa, Tadivalsa, Ranasingi, Simageda, Mahipani, Pattuchenaru, Pagulchenaru, Solapguda, Harmadangi, Kanadora and Barnaguda.

The recent change of new govts in Odisha and Andhra Pradesh has put people living in the contentious Kotia panchayat under Pottangi assembly segment of Koraput Lok Sabha is worry about the Special Status to Kotia.

For years, people living in the 21 of the 28 villages in Kotia panchayat have enjoyed the fruits of both Odisha and Andhra Pradesh. The 5,502 eligible voters, including 2,913 women, residing in the 21 contested villages have participated in the elections in both states. This has resulted in villagers holding dual voter IDs, Aadhaar and ration cards and benefiting from the social schemes of both states.

5.   **Violation of Human Rights in Koraput**

In 2022 the National Human Rights Commission (NHRC) sought an action taken report from the Odisha DGP within four weeks over two encounter killings in Koraput district on November 10. Police sources said Jaya Kumar Nag of Baragaon in Nabarangpur district and Dhana Kamara of Sariguda in Malkangiri district were killed during an exchange of fire between police forces and suspected Maoists in a forest in Boipariguda area of Koraput on the night of November 10. The Human Rights commission passed the order on Thursday, acting on a petition filed by rights activist and lawyer, Radhakanta Tripathy.

The protesters said Dhana was not a Maoist, while the kin of Nag, the other person killed that night, claimed he was a daily wager. They demanded compensation to the next of kin of the deceased and action against the police officers. The petition to the NHRC stated that the encounter killings of both Dhana and Nag were fake. "They did not have any link with Maoists. The facts and circumstances of the cases clearly indicate a painful and alarming situation in the state. The two men were poor daily wagers," Tripathy said. "The encounter death amounts to a terrible violation of human rights in the state particularly in Koraput district.

6.   **Proposed bauxite mining at Balda, Nandapur**

Balda is a Village in Nandapur Tehsil in Koraput District of Odisha State, India. It is located 46 KM towards South from District headquarters Koraput. 2 KM from Nandapur. 453 KM from State capital Bhubaneswar. According to the 2011 Census Balda Village Total population is 1385 and number of houses are 264. Female Population is 67.9%. Village literacy rate is 62.3% and the Female Literacy rate is 41.4%.

In present times on 6th March ,2025 the district administration of Koraput Odisha State Pollution Control Board (OSPCB) officials held a public hearing on Environment clearance for proposed Blada Bauxite Mining project under Nandapur block.

The main demands of the Villagers focused on:

➢   Safe Drinking Water
➢   Establishment of Educational Institutions
➢   Health Care Services and Sustainable livelihoods
➢   Employment for the local Youths
➢   Spiritual and Protection of Cultural life style

➤ Environmental Protection Mechanism

1. **Constitutional Safeguard and Provisions for the Welfare of Tribal Communities.**

    Tribal communities in India are granted special protection under the Constitution to preserve their rights, customs, and political structures. Here are the key provisions:

    - Article 244: Oversees the management of Scheduled Areas through the Fifth and Sixth Schedules.
    - Fifth Schedule: Provides self-governance to Scheduled Areas and Tribes in most of India, excluding the northeastern states.
    - Sixth Schedule: Grants autonomy to tribal areas in northeastern states through Autonomous District Councils, allowing for self-governance and decision-making.
    - Article 275(1): Provides financial grants to states for tribal welfare programs.
    - Articles 330 and 332: Reserves seats for Scheduled Tribes (STs) in state legislatures and parliament.
    - Article 46: Protects STs from societal injustice, promotes their economic and educational interests, and advances their welfare.
    - Article 15(4) and 16 (4): Reservation of seats in educational institutions and government jobs for scheduled castes and schedules tribe to help them overcome historical disadvantages and improve their socio-economic status.

2. **Policies and Programs for Tribal Development**

    The Indian government has launched several programs and policies to promote tribal welfare and development. Some of these initiatives include:

    - Tribal Sub-Plan (TSP): Ensures funding for tribal development across various sectors.
    - Integrated Tribal Development Project (ITDP): Supports livelihoods and infrastructure in tribal-dominated areas.
    - Eklavya Model Residential Schools (EMRS): Aims to improve education for indigenous children.
    - Vanbandhu Kalyan Yojana: Focuses on economic empowerment and overall tribal welfare.
    - PM-JANMAN- during the financial year 2023-24 Hon'ble PM launched Pradhan Mantri yojana, Adivasi Nyaya Maha Abhiyan for socio-economic development of 75 PVTG communities residing in 18 states and one UT.

Conclusion and Suggestions

The present paper has identified the following key factors which are important to be addressed by the Central and State Government and industry authorities as well as the district administration for a 'win-win' situation for the displaced as well as the to solve the territorial disputes, violations of Human Rights and so on.

- Compensation for the encroached land in scheduled area and a methodology for setting the issue
- The land losers not getting displaced are claiming for job in the company. Criteria to be developed with sound logic for employment to the affected persons.
- Employment guarantee for the second generation claimed by the displaced families as an unsolved issue and find appropriate substitute or alternative.
- Restoration of Common Property Resources and their accessibility.
- Proper steps should be taken to protect their economy and cultural heritage in rehabilitation colonies.
- Involvement of Local people in the decision-making process is highly essential for the inclusive development of the area.
- Citizen – Government and Public authorities should maintain the cordial relations which boost the overall growth of the region.
- Iligal encounter to the innocent person must be Judicial investigation.
- Promises Policy and projects are to be implemented soon.
- Education is the key issue in the region so government should plan to establish the Higher Education institutions for the betterment of people.
- Redressal Grievances Mechanism must be ensured by the district administration.
- Youth are the backbone of our country, in this regards more skill development, employment assurance and employment generation programmes must be regulated in rural areas of Koraput district.
- To Promote and protect the rights of the individuals, Human Rights Protection cell and Human Rights Watch centre should be set up in the disadvantage's region of Koraput.
- Traditional knowledge system, agricultural Practices must be encouraged for which the indigenous peoples, Marginalised section interest and overall, the interest of peoples of Koraput can be fulfilled.

Way forward:

- Introduction of comprehensive compensation package to the land displaced peoples.
- Payament should be made for the taking the tribal land.
- Better educational facilities with adequate quality education must be ensured.
- Access to quality healthcare facility both primary health care service, maternal and child health care services and provide the essential medicines to the tribal peoples.
- To promote sustainable livelihoods for the tribals, access to credit, common market service and provide training in modern agricultural practices.
- Government should be keen interested to involve the tribal peoples in the decision-making process and the rights of tribal to their land should be properly recognise and legally protected.

REFERENCES:

- Panda, S. M. (2013). Development-Induced Displacement: Impact on Adivasi Women of Odisha. *Social Change*, 43(4), 533-550. https://www.jstor.org/stable/26165001
- Chakrabarti Shambhu Prasad, (2018), "Tribal Rights in India", Patridge Publishing, Singapore.
- Chakrabarti Shambhu Prasad, (2018), "Tribal Rights in India", Patridge Publishing, Singapor.
- Aswal B.S. (2012) 'Tribal and Human Rights', Cyber Tech Publication, New Delhi.
- Agarwal A.N. (2013) 'Tribals of Odisha', Gyan Publishing House, New Delhi.
- Sahu, Santosh Kumar. (2017) 'Development Process and Social Movements in Contemporary India',Kalyani Publishers.
- Srinivas, B K & Nayak, Jayant Kumar 'Development, Dispossession and Impoverishment in National Aluminium Company (Nalco) Displaced Villages: A Study in Koraput,Research Journal of Humanities and Social Sciences. 9(2): April-June, 2018.
- Sabar, B. (2010). Development induced Displacement and Human Rights Violation in Orissa: An Anthropological Insight. *Social Action, 60*.
- Sahu, M. (2016). Development and population displacement in Odisha: A human rights perspective. *Journal of Politics and Governance, 5*(3), 25-33.

- Tripathy, S. N. (2020). Problems of displacement and deprivation of tribes due to mining industrialisation in Eastern India (Orissa). In *Development, Environment and Migration* (pp. 57-73). Routledge India.
- Xaxa, J. (2013). Development: A Curse to the Displaced People: A Study in Odisha. *Research Journal of Humanities and Social Sciences*, 4(1), 39-43.
- Sabar, B. (2010). Development induced Displacement and Human Rights Violation in Orissa: An Anthropological Insight. *Social Action*, 60.
- Pattnaik, B. K. (2013). Tribal resistance movements and the politics of development-induced displacement in contemporary Orissa. *Social Change*, 43(1), 53-78.
- Behera, A., & Nathan, H. S. K. (2024). *Negotiating Development at the Margins: Natural Resources, Conflicts and People's Movements in Odisha*. Routledge India.
- Samal, J. S. (2025). Mining-induced displacement and tribal resistance: The case of Odisha, India. *Energy Research & Social Science*, 121, 103950.
- Ojha, D. K. (2012). Impact of displacement and rehabilitation on the social structure of the Paraja tribe of Odisha. *Afro Asian Journal of Anthropology and Social Policy*, 3(2), 62-70.
- Koraput.odisha.gov.in
- Landconflictwatch.org
- Hindustantimes.com
- https://timesofindia-indiatimes
- https://www-newindianexpress

Orality and Performativity in Marriage Rituals: A Multispecies Study Among the Ho Community of Jharkhand

Neha Kumari

Research Scholar, Department of Anthropology and Tribal Studies, Central University of Jharkhand, Email id-kneha6170@gmail.com

Ritesh Chaturvedi

Research Scholar, Department of Anthropology and Tribal Studies, Central University of Jharkhand

Dr. Rajanikant Pandey

Assistant Professor, Department of Anthropology and Tribal Studies, Central University of Jharkhand

Abstract:

The chapter explores the Ho janjatiya beliefs about marriage, known as *Aere*, which emphasises the activities of animals and plants as indicators of good and bad omens. These omens are detected through non-human species' behaviour, particularly animals and plants. To mitigate or eliminate negative omens, the Ho people create idols representing various types of plants and animals. These idols are used during rituals to ward off to eliminate bad omens in the future. Rather than focusing solely on non-human species, the Ho recognize their significance and inclusion in human life. The Ho of Jharkhand take these events very seriously in their marriage rituals, and this comprehensive study of multispecies demonstrates the importance of incorporating non-human species in human life.

Keywords: Aere Bonga, Ho janjatiya, marriage rituals, non-human species

Introduction:

Oral tradition is an intangible communication form that represents shared beliefs through community ideals and material forms like dance and music (Kumar & Nayak, 2021). Whereas performance is a term commonly used in anthropology and folklore to describe various cultural aspects such as folk dance, theatre, and songs. Oral tradition and performance are daily manifestations of intangible cultural heritage, highlighting the richness of culture through the interaction of men in expressive ways (Abrahams, 1972). The concept of multispecies interactions in marriage rituals highlights the interconnectedness of human and non-human participants in cultural practices (Darlami Magar, 2024). In the Ho community, marriage ceremonies often involve the participation of animals, plants, and other natural elements, which are considered essential to the ritual. These interactions reflect the community's deep bond with the natural world and their belief in the spiritual significance of relationships between different species. Including animals and plants in marriage, rituals enhance the ceremonial experience and reinforces the community's ecological awareness. The Ho's follow the oral traditions of plants and animals, examining the methods used to frame their orality. The Ho community is the fourth largest tribal group in Jharkhand and primarily resides in forested areas like West Singhum, East Singbhum, and Saraikela Kharsawa districts, influenced by surrounding forests and various species, including plants and animals. The interconnection of these species affects their economy, culture, spirituality, and lifestyle. Ho's marriage rituals include non-human species, emphasizing the importance of human life and other creatures in multispecies studies. This perspective highlights the agency of more-than-human entities in the context of multispecies and post-humanism (Kaarlenkaski, 2020). The culture of the Ho people emphasizes the significance of animals and plants in their lives, showcasing the diversity of species through their oral traditions and examining the methods used to describe these aspects. The *Aere* in marriage rituals highlight the concepts of orality and performativity with multispecies studies.

Objectives:

This study aims to highlight the significant role of plants and animals in marriage rituals i.e. *Aere*, which are the most prominent aspects of the entire ceremony.

Research Methodology:

This study relies entirely on primary data, with fieldwork conducted in Barandiya village, located in West Singbhum, Ho janjatiya village.

Aere: The Marriage Rituals

In Ho cultures, *Aere* is one of the most important practices observed in marriage rites. The word *Aere* simply refers to the different omens and foreboding signs, which came across at weddings. The Aere process begins during a family visit to set a wedding date. Observations of the Aere start at this time and continue until a day or two after the marriage. This phenomenon is also frequently noted during the engagement (bala). The diverse indications provided by plants and animals offer valuable insights into both positive and negative aspects of this indication. Both of the families meticulously recorded every incident that occurred during the wedding event. *Aere* is considered a spirit (*bonga*) and worships to reduce the negative *Aere* in it. When a bad *Aere* occurs before a marriage, the *Aere bonga* is worshipped before the ceremony, and when it occurs on the wedding day, it is worshipped immediately after the ceremony. Both parties observe plant and animal behaviours, record incidents, and hold consultations. Village priest (*deuri* or *pandaiit*) demonstrates inauspicious *Aere*, while representatives from both parties observe and record these incidents. The *pandaiit* observes and records incidents along the road, carefully listening to both families. After careful consideration, they perform the *Aere Bonga* ritual a few days before the wedding to reduce negative omens and the bad *Aere*. In the village, the people believe that if the *pandaiit* assesses the omen as minor and assures that there will be no further issues in the marriage, the wedding ceremony can proceed without reciting the auspicious prayer. If the *pandaiit* says that a bad incident occurs in the marriage, then the marriage continues by worshipping the *Aere Bonga*. The *Aere* incident is a mandatory ritual in both love and arranged marriages, previously it was only observed in arranged marriages.

Nature's Signals: Indications of Aere through Plant and Animal Behaviors

Dog (Seta)

Dogs are considered unlucky when they dig in the ground, move their legs and bark. People believe that if the *Aere bonga* is not worship, it will result in death of anyone after marriage. A dog carrying a bone on its way to a relative's home seen as a sign of good things to come, and the person who sees the dog is likely to enjoy good food that day.

Pig (Sukri) and crow (ka:h)

The *Aere* story describes a pig rolling in mud and a crow pecking on its head, a recurring event believed to indicate that if this incident occurs during a wedding, the woman may face poverty in her future life. This concept is based on a *pandaiit* interpretation of the *Aere*.

Swallow bird (Dhaanchud)

People believe swallow birds, similar to koyal, called *Dhaanchud*, are unlucky if they move from right to left and back to right when making a sound. This sign suggests that marriages are short-lived and may eventually break down for any reason.

Ox (Uri):

Oxen behaviour during marriage ceremonies as quarrels is considered a bad sign, as they form a herd and move their feet back and forth, which could indicate a high likelihood of someone's death after marriage in the area. Second, an inauspicious *Aere* occurs when two oxen plough while one is standing and the other is sitting, indicating a bad omen for the girl and the boy. If the other ox does not get up, it signifies a lack of work, and if the boy goes to see, it signifies a decrease in work. This omen is likely to be visible after marriage.

Snake (Bing)

The rat snake (*Rul bing*) is a rare sight during the day, and its appearance during marriage is considered a bad omen. After seeing it once, it disappears, and people never see it again. This belief is based on that viewing the snake can cause white spots and leprosy in both families.

Myna (Rami)

The Myna (*Rami*) is seen in quarrelling it indicates a life after the marriage spent in quarrels and fights. However, if *Maina* forms a group with love, Ho believes that sweetness will remain for life longs.

Crow (Ka:h) and hen (Sim)

People in the courtyard witnessed a hen grazing with chicks, and a black crow ran away, picking up the chicks in the shell. The incident was observed as a child separated from its mother and predicted future absence. As a result, people worshipped *Aere bonga*, a crow and hen, as it symbolized a future separation from the mother.

Goat (Merom):

A goat feeding milk to her children is considered a good omen, but if any other sign is seen, it is inauspicious. For example, if a goat climbs a roof during marriage and struggles to feed his kids, it means the woman may face difficulties in feeding her children.

Burial Stone (Sasan diri):
The breaking of a burial stone's *sasan* is considered a bad omen, as it signifies a separation between two brothers on the second day of marriage. This can lead to mutual division in the house and sometimes separation between husband and wife. Breaking *sasan* is a significant occurrence, and some even cancel marriages after showing it to the *Pandaiit*.

Plant:
Trees and plants also detect the *Aere*. While going on the way, a tree breaks due to a storm without wind, then it is an inauspicious sign, it indicates the death of someone in the house. Otherwise, there is a possibility of breaking the relationship after marriage.

Good omen:
Good omens include actions such as fetching water, plucking flowers, going for worship, feeding a cow, carrying water for washing, and seeing a black ant (*mui ko*) going to a herd. Because of these omens, there is mutual harmony in the family, no financial crisis and no health-related problems occur in life after marriage.

Performative Aspects of Aere Bonga
Ho's primary focus is on reducing the worship of bad omens, which is considered crucial for overall well-being. The location of *Aere Bonga* worship was shared by both of the families. The ritualist's performance can occur before or after the wedding. The boy's family often brings a goat for worship, while the girl's family provides a chicken, and there are compulsions to sacrifice the cock and goat. The villagers claim that each *Aere* has a unique demand for specific sacrifices of animals and ritual items. The bad omen can be worshipped with a cock (*sim*), goat (*boda*), sheep (*mindi*) depending on how much these *Aere* are effective, indicating the type of omen. If a bad omen is small, then one may worship only with a cock (*sim*), but if it's considered to be big, then one may sacrifice a goat or a sheep. Sometimes bad *Aere is not removed after worshipping or sacrifices then the Pandaiit* states that the *Aere* is not removed, so both families have to wait till the *Aere* is removed. In such situations, they frequently cancel their marriage. The male members of the families are only allowed to participate in the worship of *Aere Bonga*, along

with *pandaiit* who perform the rituals. The primary focus of this worship is to create idols of animals which are observed during the *Aere*, along with other animal idols are being made even if they are not visible during the *Aere*.

During the day of worship, animal sculptures are crafted to represent creatures associated with *Aere*. These include shrews (chundi), chameleons (donda), lizards (jonjoi), snakes (bing), and other animals. Additionally, animals observed in Aere such as oxen (uri), cows (gundi uri), dogs (seta), cats (bilai), goats (merom), chickens (sim), mynas (rami), and more are also depicted. These animal idols are meticulously created using clay and straw. To worship *Aere* it is necessary to bring branches of trees like Banyan (*bai daru*), Sal (*sarjom*), Tiril (*kendu*), and Peepal (*hisa*), along with an earthen pot, arrow (*saar*), bow (*asar*), steel or aluminium pot (*loki*), and rice beer (*diyan*). The ritualist performance extended for a considerable duration on that particular day. The tree branches brought for worship are arranged in sequence at the worship place, all cut to the same size. The *Pandaiit* then places the crafted animal idols in a line. Following this, the *Pandaiit* creates twelve boxes, each containing rice flour and coal ash (hasangar) in the center. These twelve boxes, filled with animal idols, rice flour, and coal ash, are carefully stored in a line, ensuring their preservation and protection.

Pandaiit added brick powder to twelve boxes and performed animal sacrifices, particularly for goats, cocks, and sheep. Before the sacrifice, *Pandaiit* feeds rice grains to the animals, ensuring they consume them for the ritual to be complete. During these performances, people from both sides of the village sit in opposite directions. The *Pandaiit* predicts *Aere* Bonga's marriage during the sacrifice based on the lack of consensus in the village, with no one seated in the same direction. If the animal quickly eats the rice grain, it signifies *Aere Bonga's* agreement to the marriage. Conversely, if the animal delays eating, it signifies disagreement. Should the bonga's fault be severe, *Aere* may deny the marriage, prompting the *Pandaiit* to pray to the village deity, Desawali. If Desawali agrees, the animal eats the rice, completing the sacrificial process. Throughout, *Pandaiit* uses words to encourage the animal as it eats.

The next step involves crafting animal statues from clay and straw, to which the *Pandaiit* applies vermilion tilak, creating idols of all animals observed during the *Aere*. The application of vermilion tilak symbolizes their return to their homeland. Villagers bid farewell to *Aere Bonga*, with cocks and goats receiving blood as part of the farewell. Subsequently, both parties engage in a ritual dialogue, claiming, "You should take your girls back, and I will take my boys because you do not have a good home and family. Our boy or girl is good; we will find another family and not marry here." This ritual exchange helps reduce evil and is not intended to break the marriage but is a ceremonial part of the ritual.

Following this, people hold branches from banyan, sal, kendu, and tiril trees, pulling them until they break. This act also helps reduce defects. Finally, both parties exchange their aluminium pots (loki) and share rice beer, further removing defects in the Aere. After cooking and eating the sacrificed meat together, they exchange greetings (johar) and return to their respective villages.

Conclusion

The Aere Bonga ritual among the Ho community of Jharkhand offers a unique window into the complex relationships between humans, animals, and the natural world. Through the performative aspects of Aere Bonga, the Ho community seeks to rectify defects and ensure a harmonious marriage. The ritual's emphasis on multispecies interactions, orality, and performativity highlights the importance of considering the agency of non-human entities in shaping cultural practices. The Aere Bonga ritual also underscores the significance of indigenous knowledge systems and traditional practices in maintaining ecological balance and promoting social harmony. As we navigate the complexities of the Anthropocene, the Ho community's Aere Bonga ritual offers valuable insights into the importance of recognizing and respecting the interconnectedness of all living beings. Ultimately, this study demonstrates the need for a more subtle understanding of the intersections between human and non-human worlds, and how these communities continue to innovate and adapt in the face of environmental and social change.

References

- Abrahams, R. D. (1972). Folklore and Literature as Performance. Journal of the Folklore Institute, 9(2/3), 75–94. https://doi.org/10.2307/3814159
- Darlami Magar, C. B. (2024). Performative Quality in the Ritual of Matchmaking in Serena Nanda's Essay 'Arranging a Marriage in India'. Voice: A Biannual & Bilingual Journal, 16(2), 114–127. https://doi.org/10.3126/voice.v16i2.72781
- Kaarlenkaski, T., & Steel, T. (2020). Posthumanism and Multispecies Ethnology. Ethnologia Fennica, 47(2), 1–4. https://doi.org/10.23991/ef.v47i2.100197
- Kumar, M., Nayak, A., & Swain, P. K. (2024). CULTURES OF ORALITY AND PERFORMATIVITY IN THE PERFORMING ART TRADITION OF PURULIA CHHAU. ShodhKosh: Journal of Visual and Performing Arts, 5(1), 124–136. https://doi.org/10.29121/shodhkosh.v5.i1.2024.750

Traditional Agricultural Practices: An insight from the Paraja Tribe of Koraput

Swapnasarita Sethy

Ph.D. Research Scholar, Gangadhar Meher University, Sambalpur, Odisha
Email ID-swapnasaritasethy1996@gmail.com

Abstract

Paraja is one of the largest tribes in the state of Odisha with 3,74,628 population. They are divided into four types such as Bada Paraja, Pengo Paraja, Jodia Paraja and Selia Paraja. Generally, the first two groups include the Bada Paraja and other two groups the Sana Paraja groups. Cultivation is one of the primary occupations of the Paraja tribe, along with the collection of forest products, hunting, fishing, domesticated animal and wage labour for sustaining their lifestyles. The present paper is based on an empirical study carried out in Balda village of Koraput district, Odisha to highlight traditional cultivation practices with associated ritual practices. Most of the Paraja tribes depend on both shifting and settled Cultivation by using traditional technology. The major crops raised by the Paraja are paddy *(dhana)*, bitter gourd *(karela)*, pumpkin *(kumuda)*, white gourd *(chharakumuda)*, cucumber *(kakudi)*, bean (semi), yam *(nangala kanda)*, chilli *(mircha)*, semolina *(Suan)*, flax *(Alsi)*, potato *(Alu)*, sweet potato *(Kanda)*, tomato, maize *(Janha)*, ground nuts *(Badam)*, and ragi *(Mandia)*etc. In this paper researcher mainly focus on the agricultural practices of Paraja tribe as well as the rituals associated with agricultural practices.

Keywords: Paraja tribe, Cultivation, *Paraba*, Cropping Pattern, *Nagala and Juadi*

Introduction

The various tribal communities residing in Odisha have significantly contributed to the state's cultural heritage through their diverse cultural practices, Parajas one of the major tribes of Odisha. According to 2011 Census the population of the Parajas is 374,628 and the literacy rate is 34.92% in which 46.4% of males and 24.44% of females' literacy rate. The Paraja are primarily found in Koraput, Nabarangpur, Malkangiri, Rayagada, and Kalahandi of Odisha. Majority of the Parajas of the Koraput district are inhabited in Semiliguda, Sunabeda, Pattangi, Lamptaput, Laxmipur, Kundra, Boipariguda, and Jaypore blocks. The ward Paraja literally means the common people, who are citizens under King or Raja. In Koraput district Parajas live with Gadaba, Kondha, Rana, and Domb people (Patra,2017). Balda is a small village coming under Rajpalma gram panchayat, Sunabeda Block of Koraput district. In the studied village Paraja tribes depends on both shifting and settled Cultivation by using traditional technology along with the collection of forest products, hunting, fishing, domesticating animal and wage labour for sustaining their livelihood (Pattnayak, 2020:). They cultivated food crops in their agricultural field as well as kitchen garden and domesticated cattle, goat, pigs, and chicken for both consume and selling purpose in local market. Shifting cultivation carried on hilly land (*Donger Jami*), and settled cultivation caried on valley land (*Beda Jami*) and plain land (*Pada Jami*). These cultivation practices have been intertwined with their social and cultural practices.

The major crops raised by the Paraja are paddy (*dhana*), bitter ground (*karela*), pumpkin (*kumuda*), white ground (*chharakumuda*), cucumber (*kakudi*), bean (*semi*), yam (*nangala kanda*), chilli (*mircha*), semolina (*suan*), flax (*alsi*), potato (*alu*), sweet potato (*kanda*), tomato, maize (*janha*), ground nuts (*badam*), turmeric (*haldi*) ginger (*ada*)and ragi (*mandia*). They also observed cultivation associated ritual like Chaiti Paraba, Bihana Anukula puja, Asadha Paraba, Bandapana Paraba, Hundi paraba, Katara puja, Nuakhai puja and Manashika Puja etc. which reflecting their deep connection with nature, spirit, and community.

Objectives of the study

To study the traditional paddy cultivation practices among Paraja tribe of Koraput District

To explore various ritual which associated with cultivation practices.

Methods of data collection

The paper is based on cultivation practices with associated ritual significance among the Paraja tribe of Odisha. The study was conducted in Balda village falls under Rajpalma panchayat, Sunabeda tehsil of Koraput district, Odisha. The present study is qualitative and empirical in nature. It comprises both primary as well as secondary data. For primary data were collected by using unique anthropological tool such as observation method, interview method, case study method and focus group discussions etc. The secondary data is collected from existing literature like books, journals, government survey report and e-sources.

The Study Area

Balda village is located in Rajpalma panchayat, Sunabeda tehsil, of the Koraput district, Odisha. It is situated 10km away from Sunabeda Block and 28km away from district headquarter Koraput, geographical area is 926 hectares and village code- 429977(censusindiagov.in., 2015). Balda village is established nearly 60 years ago, about its origin there story i.e. the people of that village lived another place and that is old Balda, but due to flood in Kolab River they shifted to this place. Their main language is *Desia* but few natives communicate in Odia and Hindi with others. The Balda village is under Rajpalma panchayat, which contents 10 village i.e. Rajpalma, Kuturput, Doraput, Routput, Podapalma, Budaput, Sisaguda, Chalkaliput, Nuaguda, NAD Colony. Total household of village is 96 and population is 346 in which male is 178 and female is 168. Among them 76 household belong to Paraja tribes (Pattnayak, 2020). Cultivation is regarded as the main livelihood of the Parajas which share cultural beliefs and taboos the whole community, reinforcing social ties and shared heritage.

Findings of the study

The entire data was collected from the Parajas households in study area who are engaged farming in various types of agricultural land.

Types of cultivation among Paraja tribe

Mainly Paraja tribe of Koraput engaged in both shifting and settled cultivation. In the studied village of Balda, cultivation carried on three types of the land Such as plain land (*Pada Jami*), valley land (*Bedha Jami*) and terrace or hilly land (*Donger Jami*). Two types of soil found their village generally red soil both in hilly and valley land, and Black and red combined soil in plain land.

Shifting cultivation among Paraja Tribe

Shifting cultivation is a primitive form of agriculture that requires a lot of manual labour and does not require significant financial investments. (Mohapatra,2002:107). The Paraja are mainly hill framers, relying on both settled and shifting cultivation for their livelihood. They use basic farming tools such as wooden plough, yoke, hoes, sickle, and axes for their agricultural activities. Throughout all stages of farming, there is a strong sense of mutual cooperation and coordination among the community members (Krishna Kumar, et.al, 2023). Shifting cultivation is also known as *Donger Chas* among Paraja Tribe, typically carried out in the following steps first choosing a forest area and clearing the plants, usually in December and January, burning the cleared plants during February and March, showing and planting seeds in April and May then harvesting all crops in October to December. The same cultivated land continuing cultivation for a few years, abandoning the cultivated land and moving to a new forest area and later returning to the original site to resume shifting cultivation (Biswal and Sudeep Ku.,2013). Various types of crops grown in the hilly land (*Donger Jami*) such as ragi, horse gram, black gram, semolina, flax, yellow pigeon peas and maize are following multi cropping pattern expect paddy etc.

Settled Cultivation among Paraja Tribe

Settled cultivation is the same piece of land for longer periods, using more structured methods of farming. This type of agriculture typically involves the use of tools and techniques that improve soil fertility and increase crop yields over time, such as irrigation, crop rotation, and the use of organic or synthetic fertilizers. The Paraja tribe permanent connection to the cultivated land including valley land (*Beda Jami*) and plain land (*Pada Jami*) towards more sustainable agricultural practices. According to the Paraja Cultivator both valley land and plain land requires access to resources like more water, capital, modern technology and fertilizers for cultivation last 5-10 years. Paddy is cultivated only valley land and, ragi, horse gram, black gram, semolina, ginger, turmeric, potato, sweet potato, groundnut, maize etc. are cultivated in plain land and various types of vegetables grown in their kitchen garden only for consumption purpose.

Agricultural Callender of cultivated crops in study area

Name of the crops	Month of Sowing seed	Month of Harvesting	Purpose of cultivation	Selling price of crops
Dhan	Landi Mas	Pusha Mas	Consume and sell	19
Shua	Ashadha Mas	Pusha Mas	Consume and sell	35
Mandia	Ashadha Mas	Pusha Mas	Consume and sell	30
Alasi	Ashadha Mas	Pusha Mas	Consume and sell	70
Kolata	Ashadha Mas	Pusha Mas	Consume and sell	90

Ada	Landi mas	Magha Mas	Consume and sell	90
Alu	Bandapana mas	Diali Mas	Consume and sell	20
Biri	Ashadha	Pusha Mas	Consume and sell	80
Kandula	Landi mas	Pusha Mas	Consume and sell	50
Haladi	Landi mas	Magha Mas	Consume and sell	50
China Badam	Landi mas	Pusha Mas	Consume and sell	30
Vegetables Tamato, Marcha, Kobi, baigana, beans,	Landi mas/ Ashadha Mas	Bandapana mas	Consume	
Janha	Landi Mas	Magha Mas	Consume and sell	5

Cropping Seasons of the Paraja Tribe

The Paraja tribe experiences two main cropping seasons: the Kharif and Rabi seasons. The Kharif season, known as *Barsadinia chasa*, begins in June and lasts until December. During this time, villagers focus on various agricultural activities, growing crops such as paddy, semolina, flax, potato, sweet potato, tomato, maize, ground nuts, turmeric, ginger and ragi and variety of vegetables. The Rabi season, or *Kharadinia chasa*, runs from January to May. In this season, some villagers primarily engage in planting vegetables, including bitter gourd, beans, chilies, pumpkins, and tomatoes etc in their kitchen garden.

Cropping pattern of the Paraja Tribe

In this village, three patterns of cropping cultivation are observed: mono- cropping (*Gotepati*), double- cropping (*Duipati*), and multi- cropping (*Bahupati*). Mainly mono cropping occurred in valley land, as well as double cropping and multi cropping found in both hilly and plain land. Mono- cropping refers to the cultivation of only one crop in a field. In this village, crops such as paddy, linseed, and groundnuts fall under this category. Double cropping involves growing two different crops on the same field at the same time. In this village, examples include combination like ragi and black gram, semolina and black gram, maize and potato, and ginger and pumpkin etc. Multi cropping means growing a variety of crops and vegetables on the same field, with harvesting occurring at different times. In this village, mainly hilly land (*Donger Jami*) and plain land (*Pada Jami*) of kitchen garden area is using for mix of crops like tomatoes, chilies, maize, pumpkins and beans, as well as combinations like turmeric, ginger, sweet potato and cucumber, pumpkins, bitter gourd, white gourd all growing together in one field.

Agricultural used implements in the studied area

Villagers used different implements like wooden plough, yoke, pick axe, hoe, harrow for preparation of land. To used bullock and wooden plough to ploughing the land, then weeding by hoe or hand, then Rotavator the soil by using pickaxe, after first rains show used harrow for breaking soil crust and also for uprooting weeds in cultivation field and prepared the land. Very few people are using tractors for preparation of land. The village people more depended to rain for their cultivation. In summer season few people used water pump nearest river irrigate for cultivated field. They used indigenous ways to seed selection, seed sowing, used fertilization and after mature the crops then harvesting.

Agricultural used implements in the studied area

Sl. No	Implement name (English)	Local Name	Activities
1	Wooden plough and Yoke	*Nagala and Juadi*	Plough the land
2	Harrow	*Mai*	Breaking soil and plaining land
3	Hoe	*Kodaki*	Digging and weeding
4	Sickle	*Ila*	Cutting crops
5	Big Sickle	*Akudi*	Threshing the straw from grain
6	Axe	*Tangia*	Digging the crops
7	Pick axe	*Gainti*	Digging and Rotavator
8	Winnower	*Kula*	Clean the crops and separate the grain from husk
9	Sieve	*Chalani*	Clean the Crops and separation of different types of grains for elimination of alien material.

10	Bamboo basket	1. *Tipini* 2. *Dudi* 3. *Kalaki*	1. Carrying farm products 2. Storage grain time 3. Storage grain long time

Traditional Method of Paddy cultivation
Paddy cultivation:

The agriculture system of the studied area mainly is based on rainfall in the Kharif season. The villagers cultivated two types paddy such as *Danger paddy and Beda paddy*. They used healthy seed mostly preserved one year before in their indigenous ways. The Danger Paddy cultivation started in the month of May; the farmer ploughing the lands with a pair of bullocks or buffalos by wooden plough. The farmers are sown the seed in the field directly rather than transplanting the seedlings, after the first rainfall occurred month of June, they do not care more to the cultivated land only prefer manual weeding and use the fertilizer like dung compost for more production. Then after the paddy mature, they are harvesting paddy.

Beda Paddy cultivation starts in month of May; the field is prepared by ploughing in traditional way using a pair of bullocks. The sowing of paddy seeds direct by hand after rainfall in the studied area. Then the paddy plants grown takes 35 to 40 days for average size 3.3 inches, then the respective plants pulling by hand in cultivated land and transplanting into puddled and levelled fields under flood like conditions of another land in the month of August. The land can get the water from August to October by the rain. The fertilizers like Urea, Gromor, Potash and dung of domesticating animals are applying to the land for more production. After the maturation of the paddy, they harvest. Then drying crops in sunlight for storage next season seed and consumption. In the village peoples are cultivated many types of paddies like *Mesha Dhan, Gatia Dhan, Saru Dhan, Karkali Dhan and Keuta Dhan etc.*

Special Festival observed during cultivation

Most of Paraja tribe beliefs that gods and goddesses are protecting the crops from insects, disease and their favour increases the harvest crops. They are performed various ritual from land preparation to harvest ground in different stages of agricultural practices. The agriculture associated ritual linked with productivity and fertility cult like Chaiti Paraba, Bihana Anukula puja, Asadha Paraba, Bandapana Paraba, Nuakhai Parab, Hundi Paraba, Katara puja, and Push Paraba (Dandapat,2021).

Chaiti Parab: This festival observed in month of April (*Chaiti Mas*). After rising the moon which known as *Chaiti Janha* about 8 to 15 days Paraja tribe celebrated Chaiti Parab. The whole day is spent bin feasting, nightlong dancing and singing together. Men and boys go into the forest for Communal hunting (*Benta Jatra*). With depletion of forest and restrictions imposed on it, the scope of hunting has declined in course of time (Patra, 2011:48). They worship *Hundi Debta* in *Nishani Munda* with sacrifice the bird and animal during communal hunting (*Benta Jatra*). The village *Dishari* worship various types of seeds like paddy, ragi, black gram, semolina, flax, ground nuts and various vegetable seeds for good harvesting coming cultivation season. They eat Mango after the worship completed.

Bihana Anukula Puja: This festival observed in last week of month June (*Landi Mas*) to show the first rain fall in the studied area. The village *Dishari* first showing the seed in the near cultivation land of the village in early morning to sacrifices a hen or egg for fertile of land for good harvesting. Then Individual households offer worship sacrifice coconuts, egg or fowl for fertile soil and showing seed in their cultivation land the good time suggest by village *Dishuri*.

Ashadha Parab: this worship observed in the month of July (*Ashadha Mas*) occurred in the village in the instruction of village *Dishari* after the first rainfall in the village. For good Rain fall offer worship *Indra Debata* sacrifice a cow in the entry point of village roadside area by the male member of the community.

Bandapana Parab: this festival worship month of August (*Bandapana Mas*) individual worshipping household deity *Budharaja* for good harvest crops and put the *Kendu, Chatreng,* and *Valia Dala* in the cultivated land for good harvesting. Then eat new harvesting green vegetables and leaf in their kitchen garden or cultivated land.

Nuakhai Parab: this festival observed in the month of October (*Osha Mas)* the close kinship families cooked new crops before harvesting, then offer the food village deity and household deity before eating the birds or anyone. Then take the food as prasad the whole kinship member. Then the cutting and harvesting the crops started in the studied area.

Hundi Parab: this festival observed in month of October (*Dasara Mas*). This festival is very interesting the adolescences boys' and girls' theft vegetables in cultivated land of the villager without any hesitation, then they collected rice in every villager's house and arrange a feast used the theft vegetables and sacrifices of fowl, goat or ship to be evidence of *Hundi Debata* near *Nissani Munda* for strong bonding the friendship among them and dancing and singing in the late night.

Katara Puja: this worship observed mostly between November-January (*Diali Mas- Push Mas*) after harvesting the crops in the crop gathering area in the near cultivated area which known as *Katar*. It is individual worship sacrifice either fowl, goat, pig or sheep, prepare non-vegetarian food and offer to the deities of cultivated land during *Katara puja* and then the farmer bring the crops to the home.

Push Parab: this festival observed in the full moon day of January (*Push Mas*) which known as *Push Parab* in the studied village. Food prepared with mixed new harvest crops offer to family god and goddess, then offer to the domesticated cows and buffalos for health well-being of cattle and well-being of the family member. The family prepared cake (pitha) and various types of delicious food for family member.

Conclusion

The Paraja tribe are mainly hill farmers and the backbone of their subsistence economy is shifting and settled cropping. They are mainly cultivated for self-consumption food. The income of the household comes from agriculture, forest collections, poultry, and wage labour. Primitive farming methods, exploitation by middlemen, poor land quality, and lack of irrigation facilities leading to low harvests among the Paraja tribe. Festival celebration has cultural significance based on their agricultural activities and their deities.

Acknowledgements

I would like to express my sincere gratitude to all those who have supported and guided me throughout the process of writing this paper. First and foremost, I extend my deepest thanks to my teachers Dr. B.K. Srinivas, Dr. Meera Swain and Dr. Minaketan Bag, for their encouragement and assistance during the writing process. Finally, I would like to acknowledge my friends and respondents of the studied village for their constant support and understanding, which kept me motivated during the entire Paper writing. Thank you all for your invaluable contributions.

Paraja Cultivator   Ploughing the land by Bullock and Buffalo

Paddy Seedling   Paddy Transplanting

Paddy cutting   Paddy drying in sunlight

| Paddy storing in the Dudi | Ritual place of the Village: Nishan Munda |

Data Collection from Farmer

References

- Patra, D. (2011). The cultural history of the tribals of the Koraput region. *Orissa Review*, 46-49.
- Patra, D., (2017). The Parajas: A Socio-Cultural Study. Odisha Review, Pp-75-76. (https://magazines.odisha.gov.in/Orissareview/2017/Jan/engpdf/75-76.pdf)
- ©2025VillageInfo.in (https://villageinfo.in/odisha/koraput/sunabeda/balda.html#google_vignette)
- Dandapat, S. (2021). Traditional Ecological knowledge and continuation of Swidden Cultivation: A case study of the Dongria Kondh of Niyamgiri Hills, Odisha. *Man In India*, 101(3-4), 159-173.
- Mahapatra, L. K. (2002). Problems and Welfare of Orissa Tribes. *Tribal and Indigenous People of India: Problems and Prospects*, 99-127.
- Pattanaik, J. (2020). Livelihood and Natural Resources: A Socio-Cultural Study of the Paraja Tribe of Koraput District, Odisha, India.
- Gupta,(2021). Paraja: A critical analysis of exploitation & loss of culture. *International Journal of Current Research*, Vol. 13, Issue, 04, pp.17054-17057
- Biswal, D. K., & Kumar, S. (2013). Shifting cultivation and policies of sustainable development: A meaningless obsession. *Journal of Economic and Social Development*, 9(1), 132-138.
- Babu, N., Shukla, A. K., Tripathi, P. C., & Prusty, M. (2015). Traditional cultivation practices of turmeric in tribal belt of Odisha. *Journal of Engineering Computers & Applied Sciences*, 4(2), 52-57.

- Behera, H. C. (2021). Traditional agriculture, culture and the indigenous knowledge (IK) among the Kondhs in Odisha, India. *Journal of Huma Ecology, 73*(1-3), 44-55.
- Adhikary, P. P., Madhu, M., Dash, C. J., Sahoo, D. C., Jakhar, P., Naik, B. S., ... & Dash, B. (2015). Prioritization of traditional tribal field crops based on RWUE in Koraput district of Odisha.
- Satapathy, M. K., & Bisoi, S. S. (2021). Indigenous Knowledge and Practices on Conservation of Natural Resources by Tribal Communities of Koraput District, Odisha, India. *Environment and Ecology, 39*(1A), 216-229.
- Ojha, D. K. (2012). Impact of displacement and rehabilitation on the social structure of the Paraja tribe of Odisha. *Afro Asian Journal of Anthropology and Social Policy, 3*(2), 62-70.
- Garada, S. (2012). Socio-Cultural Background of Tribal Culture in Odisha. *A J. Arts Humanit. Manag*, 59-75.
- Kumar, K., Marinescu, A., & Nayak, S. (2023). SOCIETY, CULTURE AND NATURAL SURROUNDINGS. INDIGENOUS KNOWLEDGE AND PRACTICES OF THE DONGRIA, DHURUVA AND POROJA TRIBES OF RAYAGADA AND KORAPUT DISTRICTS, ODISHA, INDIA. *Revista Romana de Sociologie*.
- Pal, A. Socio-Cultural Practices of Paroja Tribal Women in The Post-Colonial Era–A Case Study of Koraput District, Odisha.
- Ota, A. B., & Mohanty, S. C. (2020). Paraja. Castes & Scheduled Tribes.

Biodiversity, Tribal Knowledge and Life in India

Resmita shaw

Department of Sociology, Ranchi Central University

Tanmay Biswas

Department of Philosophy, Raiganj University
Email: tanmaybiswas25@gmail.com

Abstract: -

Tribes are known for their close proximity with the nature all over the world. They use natural resources as part of their survival while protecting these as part of their duties and obligations. Thus, the concept of nature-man–spirit is very ancient as both biological diversity and cultural diversity are directly related to the origin of many tribes in India who personify their origin from some plants and trees protecting them as sacred grooves. The present paper seeks a critical note on the relationship of biodiversity, traditional knowledge and rights of tribes in India.

Keywords: indigenous people; forest; tribes; rights; act; development; protection

Introduction:-

Man is social by nature. Both social and natural environments are responsible for the continuum of human population. Thus, plant and tress have special place in the life and living of human beings and in case of tribals these have emotional bonding as most of tribals are having their inhabitations in and around natural surroundings©. Various labels have been assigned to name inhabitants in forest when comparison is made between tribal and non-tribal. They are also known as Adivasi (adi means first, original and vasi means dweller, inhabitant). They have been also given self-identity with the modern concept of indigenous people. Debate over a definition of indigenous peoples has often focused on African and Asian indigenous peoples. In the Asian context, the term "indigenous peoples" is generally understood to refer to distinct cultural groups, such as "Adivasis", "tribal peoples", "hill tribes" or "scheduled tribes", while some indigenous peoples in Africa are referred to as "pastoralists", "vulnerable groups" or "hunter-gatherers" (Office of the United Nations High Commissioner for Human Rights [OHCHR], 2013, p.7). According to the World Bank, operational directive 4.20, 1991: Indigenous peoples can be identified in particular geographical areas by the presence in varying degrees of the following characteristics: (a) close attachment to ancestral territories and to the natural resources in these areas; (b) self-identification and identification by others as members of a distinct cultural group; (c) an Indigenous language, often different from the national language; (d) presence of customary social and political institutions; and (e) primarily subsistence-oriented production(The World Bank Operational Manual, 1991, p.1).The International Labour Organization's (ILO) Convention concerning Indigenous and Tribal Peoples in Independent Countries (No.169) distinguishes between tribal and indigenous peoples as follows, highlighting also the importance of self-identification (OHCHR, 2013, p.2): 1. (a) Tribal peoples in independent countries whose social, cultural and economic conditions distinguish them from other sections of the national community, and whose status is regulated wholly or partially by their own customs or traditions or by special laws or regulations; (b) Peoples in independent countries who are regarded as indigenous on account of their descent from the populations which inhabited the country, or a geographical region to which the country belongs, at the time of conquest or colonization or the establishment of present State boundaries and who, irrespective of their legal status, retain some or all of their own social, economic, cultural and political institutions.2. Self-identification as indigenous or tribal shall be regarded as a fundamental criterion for determining the groups to which the provisions of this Convention apply. Plants and trees have greater importance in the life of tribals not only for economic purposes but also from the point of their social and cultural importance in preserving the age-old tradition of tribal people in the area. Hoffmann (1950) mentions 71 different wild plants used by the Munda's as potherbs 26 of whose tubers, corns and roots are used as vegetables, 15 trees and shrubs where young leaves are used as potherbs, 10 others whose young leaves are eaten raw and of 25 wild trees and plants whose leaves are used as vegetables (p.179). The knowledge, innovations and practices of indigenous peoples and local communities are manifestations of their cultures. Protecting a people© culture means maintaining those conditions that allow a culture to thrive and develop further (Dutfield, 1999, p.514).The importance of trees in the life of man is critically analyzed by ASTRA IDL Ltd., the makers of MUCOSOL, which rightly says: "A tree that lives for 50 years generates Rs 5.3 lakh worth of oxygen, recycles Rs 6.4 lakh worth of soil fertility, facilitates Rs. 6.4 lakh worth of soil erosion control, creates Rs 10.5 lakh worth of air pollution control and provides Rs 5.3 lakh worth of shelter for insects, birds, and animals. Besides, it provides flowers and fruits. Our net loss is worth more than Rs 33 lakh when one tree falls or is felled©© (Goyal, p.8). According to the North American indigenous peoples© organization, the Four Directions Council (1996), „[i]ndigenous peoples possess their own locally-specific systems of jurisprudence with respect to the classification of different types of knowledge, proper procedures for acquiring and sharing knowledge, and the rights and responsibilities which attach to possessing knowledge, all of which are embedded uniquely in each culture and its language© (Dutfield, 1999, p.508)

Biological diversity and Cultural diversity

There exists a close proximity between the biological diversity and cultural diversity. Biodiversity encompasses the variety of all life form on the earth. India is one of the 17 mega-biodiverse countries in the world and has 45,000 identified plant species, including 15,000 flowering plants and 81,000 faunal species. Though it has only 2.5% of the land and less than 2% of the world's forest area but it supports more than 7% of the global recorded species (Chaudhry, Dollo, Bagra & Yakang, 2011, p.339). Mohan (2007) has aptly remarked on the notion of biodiversity in the following words (p.22): Biodiversity, for a lack of a better description, represents a congruent human-environment interface. Given the complexity of the planet and its inhabitants, one must eschew a one-dimensional approach to aspects and issues that warrant perpetual dialogue and discourse. Since natural environs and layers of ecosystem transcend artificial national boundaries, conflict over land, water, minerals and other precious resources have bedeviled civilization ever since civil society came in existence. Article 26 of the United Nations Draft Declaration on the Rights of Indigenous People, 1994, has clearly mentioned that „indigenous peoples have the right to own, develop, control and use the lands and territories, including the total environment of the lands, air, waters, coastal seas, sea-ice, flora and fauna and other resources which they have traditionally owned or otherwise occupied or used. This includes the right to the full recognition of their laws, traditions and customs, land tenure systems and institutions for the development and management of resources, and the right to effective measures by States to prevent any interference with, alienation of or encroachment upon these rights (United Nations High Commissioner for Human Rights [UNHCHR]). Article 27 further notes in this regard that „indigenous peoples have the right to the restitution of the lands, territories and resources which they have traditionally owned or otherwise occupied or used or damage without their free and informed consent. Where this is not possible, they have the right to just and fair compensation. Unless otherwise freely agreed upon by the peoples concerned, compensation shall take the form of lands, territories and resources equal in quality, size and legal status (ibid).Related to natural objects where ancient texts basically the Vedas narrate that human body is made up of five components (panchabhutas) i.e., sun, soil, air, water and space. Since time immemorial tribal people are trying to preserve nature as it provides food, cloth, and shelter for their existence in this world. The cultural complexes like tradition, belief, practices and celebration of various festivals and rites are directly involved with the environmental conservation. Anthropologist Herskovits (1948) says that culture is the man- made part of environment where human beings inculcate their ethos and eidos and pass these to their future generation (p.17).In fact, tracing of right to environment was done by recourse to Articles 48A and 51-A of the Constitution of India, which are essentially post- modernist policies for eco-friendly development and citizens participation for conservation of natural resources. When the genesis of right to environment has such complex background; solid application of convergence amidst environmental, developmental and consensual or concerted act becomes an imperative (Bhat, 2009, p. 812). To protect, preserve and to evolve the sustainable use of natural resources, the Parliament of India passed the Biological Diversity Act in the year 2002.Section 2 (b) of the Biological Diversity Act, 2002 of India defines biological diversity as: The variability among living organisms from all sources and the ecological complexes of which they are part of, and includes diversity within species or between species and of ecosystems. Section 2 (c) further notes that the biological resources mean plants, animals and microorganisms or parts thereof, their genetic material and by-products (excluding value added products) with actual or potential use or value, but does not include human genetic material.

According to the All-India Ethno-Biology Survey conducted by the Ministry of Environment and Forests, Government of India, there are more than 7,500 species of plants that are being used by 4,635 ethnic communities for human and veterinary health care across the country. Men have been using different parts of various plants as drugs since ancient times which not only promote good health but also help in maintaining a balanced environment (Goyal, p.1). Various researches have shown the dependence of tribals and other forest dwellers on herbs and animals. Fernandes, Menon & Viegas (1988) remarked that traditionally tribals had kept a balance between human needs and ecological imperatives and preserved forests as a resource for posterity (p.224). They had what can be claimed a constructive dependence on forests and other natural resources. As a result of the vicious circle initiated by industrial clear felling or displacement projects, there has been a transition to destructive dependence on the same resources.

Traditional knowledge and Tribes in India

Tribal people not only in India but also in other parts of the world have been known for their unique cultural identities since time immemorial. They are very close to nature and natural objects like trees and plants which have not only economic importance for them but also have cultural importance. Various trees and plants have religious as well as health importance among the whole tribal India. So far, the preservation of these is concerned, tribal people are keener to save biological resources than anything else as them

survival and life activities directly depend on them. However, it has been said that tribal people are exploiting the nature by following the age-old tradition of shifting cultivation basically in north-eastern regions of the country. The traditional knowledge (TK) of most of tribal people is on the verge of decline or we can say that the most of the benefits of traditional knowledge are being taken by the outsiders and tribals are getting very less so far, the economic importance is concerned. The social structure that creates, use, preserve, and pass down TK between generations and the customary laws and protocols that govern these processes, are deeply rooted in their traditional location and community setting, and indeed may be conceived as integral to the land and environment itself (Taubman & Leistner, 2008, p.60). TK can be characterized as: The content or substance of knowledge resulting from intellectual activity in a traditional context, and includes the know-how, skills, innovations, practice and learning that form part of traditional knowledge systems, and knowledge embodying traditional lifestyles of indigenous and local communities, or contained in codified knowledge systems passed between generations. It is not limited to any specific technical field, and may include agricultural, environmental and medicinal knowledge, and knowledge associated with genetic resources (ibid).Studies conducted by Roy (1915, 1917, 1925), Vidyarthi (1963), Rai (1966) and Rath and Behera (1985) significantly contribute the understanding of symbiotic relationship between the tribal people and the biological resources of the country. The ancient literature of India and world on medicine suggests that the primitive people of antiquity have been using several kinds of medicinal plants for combating diseases. The ancient Indians used the „snake root plant‟ (Rauvolfia serpentina) about 3000 years ago to treat several diseases from mental disorders to insomnia and snake bite. They also used the poppy juice (Papaver somniferum) to relieve pain and anxiety (Gene Campaign, 2000).A single plant has many utilities. The same plant may be used for different disorders: for example, Calotropis gigantea is used as a vermicide and for chest pain, Centella asiatica used for gynecological problems and for jaundice, Dodonaea viscosa used for headache, stomach pain and piles, Wrightia tinctoria for treating mumps and as lactagogue. In certain cases, a combination of different plants is used in the treatment for e.g. Albizia lebbeck together with Cassia fistula and Euphorbia hirta is used for urinary disorder. Capparis zeylanica with Pongamia pinnata, Cissus quandrangularis and Toddalia asiatica are used for venereal disease (Ravishankar, 2003).Prakash (2005) has noted that among the tribal communities of Andhra Pradesh, trees and plants designated as part of sacred grove are forbidden for normal human interference as it is an abode of the spirits/deities (p.61). Ratha (2006) describes that in worshiping the bel (Aegle marmelos) and aswath (Ficus religiosa), the Paudi Bhuyan of Orissa share the great tradition of the country (p.4). The simili (Combax ceiba) tree personifies Goddess Durga and it is worshipped during Dasahara festival. Kusum (Haldina cordifolia syn. Adina cordifolia) is regarded as the abode of Goddess Basari. The sal (Shorea robusta) personifies the presiding deity of the village. Huge sal trees occupy central positions of most villages symbolizing man-plant coexistence. The tardy situation of development is that more than half of the construction workers in the country are tribals and reason is very clear that the process of displacement and deforestation in the name of development is behind this. The studies by Rothermund (1978), Mahapatra (1992), Vyasulu (1984) and Mohanty (1997) in different parts of the country state that benefits of Minor Forest Produce (MFP) are largely going in the hands of non-tribals and tribals are getting less. Vyasulu (1984) has vividly mentioned the poor state of affairs as far as the rights of tribals are concerned in their own produce (p.65). He notes that in the case of salseed (Shorea robusta) the tribals receive only five percent of the value of their product (per kilogram of seed, the collector received Rs.1, the contractor Rs.12, and the multinational Rs. 20). It is further noted that per every rupee spent in tribal areas for development and welfare, at least four (and possibly more) rupees worth of resources are taken out. Mohanty (2005, p.41, as cited in Mahapatra, 1992) details: Even when National Parks, Tiger Reserves, Bird Sanctuaries, Lion and Elephant Safaris and other such game sanctuaries are carved out invariably in the heartland of forested tribal areas, the humane consideration and arguments in favour of the rights of these wild animals...are never challenged. But, paradoxically, the same humane considerations and arguments in favour of...scheduled tribes, are usually not given any weight.

Indigenous people have various modes of livelihood. Besides agriculture, they also engage themselves in hunting of wild animals and gathering of roots of edible plants as their source of livelihood. Although hunting of animals may endanger the environment and thus may result in disharmony of maintaining biodiversity, the traditional communities are aware of this and they themselves trace alternative methods of survival as well as hunting. This is very much true in the case of some tribal communities in our country. The Onges, who love to hunt wild pigs (Sus scrofa andamanensis) had developed a technique to ensure that pigs were not over-hunted in any particular location. Every time an Onge killed a pig, he half broke a branch of the largest tree in the area. This branch then hung half broken from the tree and was a signal to all other Onges that a pig had been killed there recently. No one else would then hunt a pig in that locality, but move to some other locality. After a sufficient period of time had passed, the branch would totally dry up and fall off, once again opening the area for hunting (Sahai, 2013, p.167). The tribals have emotional attachment with their land. The observation of Honorable Supreme Court is worth mentioning here as under: Agriculture is the only source of livelihood for scheduled tribes, apart from collection and sale of minor forest produce to supplement their income. Land is their most important natural and valuable asset and imperishable endowment from which the tribals derive their sustenance social status, economic and social equality and permanent place of abode and work and living. It is a security and source of economic empowerment. Therefore, the tribes too have great emotional attachment of their lands. The land, on which they live and till, assures them equality of status and dignity of person and means to economic and social justice and is a potent weapon of economic empowerment in a social democracy (Samantha v. State of A.P.[1997]8 SCC 191). Keeping in view all the above aspects, the international community unanimously took the initiative to protect the TK not only as knowledge per se but also a source of livelihood and life of tribals living across the globe. Some of the important developments are as under.

International law developments on traditional knowledge

Many countries are signatories to different international conventions and treaties for the protection of the rights of indigenous peoples. Such conventions and treaties give legal rights and remedies only when provisions in the conventions are enacted into national legislation. Some of the international conventions, treaties and programs for indigenous peoples are briefly given below. The legislative journey related to protection of traditional knowledge and rights of indigenous people is not much old. Various countries follow their own pattern in this regard.The importance of traditional knowledge and use of biological diversity at the international levelhas been recognized by the Convention on Biological Diversity ([CBD], 1992). This is important from the perspective of indigenous people and local communities, which is main feature of CBD. The objectives of Article 1 of the CBD are the conservation of biological diversity, sustainable use of its components and fair and equitable sharing of the benefits arising out of the utilization of the genetic resources by appropriate transfer of technologies, taking into account all rights over those resources and to technologies, and by appropriate funding (CBD, 1992). The CBD is based on reciprocity and the convention recognizes biological resources to be used by other countries that do not harbor the genetic resources with consent from the countries. It also widens horizons for additional support from developed countries to resource existing in developing countries. The convention recognizes rights of the countries. Article 8(j) states that: Subject to national legislation respect, preserve and maintain knowledge, innovations and practices of indigenous and local communities embodying traditional lifestyles relevant for the conservation and sustainable use of biological diversity and promote their wider application with the approval and involvement of the holders of such knowledge, innovation and practices and encourage the equitable sharing to the benefits arising from the utilization of such knowledge, innovations and practices (Shrestha, Shrestha, Rai, Sada & Shrestha, 2008).The other relevant provisions of CBD, 1992 are: Article 10 (c): Protect and encourage customary use of biological resources in accordance with traditional cultural practices that are compatible with conservation and sustainable use requirements, Article 10 (d): Support local population to develop and implement remedial action plan in degraded areas where biological diversity has been reduced, Article 15 (1): Authority to determine access rests with national government, and Article 15 (2): Each contracting party shall facilitate access to genetic resources for environmentally sound uses by other Contracting parties and not to impose restrictions that run counter to the objectives of this Convention (CBD, 1992).

International Labour Organization

Convention 169 (1989) International Labour Organization (ILO) Convention 169 on Indigenous and Tribal Peoples is one of the key instruments in the body of international law relating to indigenous peoples. Adopted in 1989, the Convention has been ratified by only 18 countries (as of January, 2007) of which 13 are in Latin America, (Argentina, Bolivia, Brazil, Colombia, Costa Rica, Dominica, Ecuador, Honduras, Guatemala, Mexico, Paraguay, Peru, and Venezuela). The other countries that have ratified the Convention to date are Denmark, Fiji, Norway, the Netherlands, and Spain (IFC, 2007, p.2). Education, employment, customary law, child labor, and forced labor, etc. are the major concerns of the Convention.

Traditional knowledge under Indian

laws. The Biological Diversity Act, 2002 has major dimensions on the protection of tribal knowledge. The Act mainly deals with access to genetic resources by foreign companies, individuals or organizations. The National Biodiversity Authority (NBA) was set up under Section 8 of the Act to deal with requests for access to genetic resources by foreigners, and to manage requests to transfer the results of any related research out of India and to determine benefit sharing arising from the commercialization (Venkataraman & Latha, 2008, p. 332). The salient features of the Act are to:
  (a) regulate access to biological resources of the country with the purpose of securing equitable share in benefits arising out of the use of biological resources; and knowledge relating to biological resources.
  (b) conserve and sustainable use of the biological diversity;
  (c) respect and protect knowledge of local communities related to biodiversity;
  (d) secure sharing of benefits with local people as conservers of biological resources and holders of knowledge and information relating to the use of biological resources(ibid).

The Biological Diversity Act (BDA), 2002 as a Central Law lays emphasis on the establishment of State Biodiversity Board under Section 22 (1) at State levels as well as Biodiversity Management Committees (BMCs) under Section 41 (1) at local levels by respective State Governments. The

Section 41 (1) reads as under: Every local body shall constitute a Biodiversity Management Committee within its area for the purpose of promoting conservation, sustainable use and documentation of biological diversity including preservation of habitats, conservation of land races, folk varieties and cultivars, domesticated stocks and breeds of animals and microorganisms and chronicling of knowledge relating to biological diversity (BDA, 2002). Thus, the BMC has to play vital role in the conservation and preservation of biodiversity. The Section 41 (2) of the Act has clearly mentioned this in the following words:

The National Biodiversity Authority and the State Biodiversity Boards shall consult the Biodiversity Management Committees while taking any decision relating to the use of biological resources and knowledge associated with such resources occurring within the territorial jurisdiction of the Biodiversity Management Committee (ibid).

Concluding remarks

The preceding paragraphs highlight the interface of biodiversity, traditional knowledge and the tribes in India. The pace of development is supposed to always go with the tune of people for whom it is needed. In the rapid growing change of environment, the rights of every person must be protected. The progress of any society depends on the shoulders of each and every person without interfering in the social and cultural boundaries to one another. Here it becomes pertinent that all sorts of efforts are needed to protect the rights of tribals as we have seen that the rapid impact of the process of globalization and changing environmental conditions is leading the extinctions of certain tribal groups in the country who are failing to adjust with new changes related to their survival. Here the case of tribals living in Andaman and Nicobar Islands of India become more crucial whose population is declining day by day. In the era of globalization and free market, the emerging concept of Corporate Social Responsibility may become a powerful tool to protect, preserve and promote TK The Corporate houses may come forward as part of their responsibility in this regard both in terms of cash and kind. Cash rewards may be made as an acknowledgement to the elderly tribal people who are the repository of TK and in kind by providing monetary support to organize training workshops for the tribal youth along with certain job-oriented incentives. Efforts are needed from all corners of the society especially the policy makers, NGOs. Civil Society Organizations, community members and all nature lovers to adopt appropriate measures for the betterment of tribal people and their culture, preservation of traditional knowledge and to serve the purpose of humanity. Mohan (2007) emphasizes that: A genuine respect for diversity, biodiversity and discourse will serve as a guiding principle for national policies that will preserve and conserve life sustaining resources in the mutual interest of nature and human society. Policies and programs thusly formulated will ushers in an era of "bio globalism" that I believe is conducive to social democracies that promote freedom and justice (p.25). Thus, the documentation of traditional knowledge and role of biodiversity in protecting the rights of tribal people in the country become essential. The Government of India is taking due care in this regard. The letter dated on 17th February 2015 written by Dr. Hrusikesh

Panda, Secretary, Government of India, Ministry of Tribal Affairs to concerned departments of all States/Union Territories, is worth mentioning here as concluding remarks: There are many medicinal practices for tribals, which may have been documented in Ayurveda, but may not be in practice much. It is more likely also that there could be many medicines and practices which have not been documented at all, particularly, for tribals living in remote areas who have been able to resist many diseases and have remained healthy. Some work has been done by some Tribal Research Institutes(TRI), Indian Council of Medical Research (ICMR), Botanical Survey of India, Anthropological Survey of India and Ayurvedic Institutions. However, we need to document these practices not only as very useful medical practices, but also for the sake of biodiversity and also preservation of our rich heritage.

References

- Bhat Ishwara, P. (2009). Law & social transformation. Lucknow: Eastern Book Company.
- Chaudhry, P., Dollo, M., Bagra, K., Yakang, B. (2011). Traditional biodiversity conservation and natural resource management system of some tribes of Arunachal Pradesh, India. Interdisciplinary Environmental Review, 12(4), 338– 348.http://dx.doi.org/10.1504/IER.2011.043342
- Chhibber, B. (2008). Indian cultural heritage and environmental conservation through traditional knowledge, Mainstream, vol. XLVI, No 25, viewed February 13th, 2016, <http://www.mainstreamweekly.net/article746.html>
- Convention on Biological Diversity (1992) Article 1. Objectives, viewed October 18th, 2016. <https://www.cbd.int/convention/articles/default.shtml?a=cbd-01>
- Convention on Biological Diversity (1992) Article 10. Sustainable use of

components of biological diversity, viewed October 18th, 2016.<https://www.cbd.int/convention/articles/default.shtml?a=cbd-10>

- Convention on Biological Diversity (1992) Article 15. Access to genetic resources, viewed October 18, 2016.<https://www.cbd.int/convention/articles/default.shtml?a=cbd-15>

- Graham, D., (1999). Rights resources and responses, in Cultural and spiritual values biodiversity, United Nations Environment

- Programme (UNEP), Kenya, viewed, December 25th, 2015<http://www.unep.org/pdf/Cultural_Spiritual_thebible.pdf>

- Fernandes, W., Menon, G., & Viegas, P. (1988). Forests, Environment, and Tribal Economy: Deforestation, Impoverishment, and Marginalisation in Orissa. New Delhi: Indian Social Institute.

- Gene Campaign (2000). Indigenous knowledge in the Jhabua district of Madhya Pradesh, viewedFebruary9th,2016<http://genecampaign.org/wpcontent/uploads/2014/07/Indigenous_Knowledg e_in_the_Jhabua_District_of_Madhya_Prdesh.pdf>

The Historical and cultural significance of Dhemsa dance: A critical analysis of Koraput district of Odisha

Lili Bariha

Ph.D. Research Scholar in History
KISS Deemed to be University, Bhubaneswar
E-Mail – barihalili1234@gmail.com

Abstract

This article also appears to provide a critical insight into the cultural and historical background of Dhemsa dance that is one of the livelier folk and aboriginal bedtime and tribal dance of Eastern India and more particularly of the district of Koraput of Odisha. In a systematic manner that links the origin and decoders of Dhemsa, the research shows the ways in which it is a living archive of the memory and historical identities of the Chhau community. The study interrogatively examines the phenomenology, semiotics, and ethnographic purposes of this dance form to understand the diverse utility of this form among the tribal populace.

This paper uses quantitative data collected from participant observations, interviews, and document analyses along with the support of other disciplines. The study emphasizes the need to accord Dhemsa strategic significance as a tool for preserving cross generational cultural produce, promoting tribal identity, and enhancing social inclusion of tribes. Moreover, the article analyses in a critical manner how Dhemsa becomes a tool of subversion by working the socio-cultural opposition against modem and socio-political orien- tation, which seeks to marginalise these communities.

Key word: Dhemsa dance, tribal culture, folk traditions, Odisha, cultural preservation, indigenous rituals.

Introduction

Dhemsa is one of the famous folk-dance forms accomplished by the Adivasi local people who are exported in tribal areas of Koraput district of Odisha. It is most acute in the states of Orissa, Jarkhand, Chhattisgarh and West Bengal. As a true experience of the folk culture the dance is rooted in the religious and agricultural customs of these peoples. In the past, the Dhemsa was a dance that was performed during rites of passage ceremonies but also for fun and it has an enduring contribution the retention and upkeep of the tribal standards in the community (Rath, 2018). This research aims to provides a systematic way of uncovering the historical and cultural relevance and importance of Dhemsa through the lens of anthropology, sociology and cultural analysis. Thus, presenting the analysis of the dance sources, its rituals and symbolism, and the relation to the socially constructed contemporary meaning, the study contributes to the critical comprehension of the dance's role in the tribal context (Mishra, 2020).

Historical context

The Dhemsa dance is an energetic dance form performed by the tribals of Koraput of Odisha which has its origin in the socio-cultural dimensions of tribal life. It is mostly identified with the tribes of the area, like Kondh, Paraja, Gadaba and Bhotra (Mohanty, 2019). Historical background of Dhemsa could be researched through tales of folk lore, histories of tribes and many anthropological studies that indicate that Dhemsa had existed from ancient ages.

Agricultural Connection: The origin of Dhemsa is associated with the agricultural cycle and it was initially performed by the community. It is danced to pay respect to the Earth and natural products especially after the farming year or when farmers are through with the harvest.

Ritualistic Beginnings: The tetons claim that Dhemsa was danced in honor of tribal gods or spirits. This tradition was momentarily performed for the congregation to feel a connection with the super-natural power of prayer and prosperity. These performance dances were common during festivals or ceremonials, thus meaning it had its origin in spirit related issues (Sarangi, S., Das, S., & Jena, M. K, 2018).

Cultural Exchange and Evolution: Intertribal contact within the region may have shaped the evolution of Dhemsa because different tribes inhabited the locality. Exchange in people and goods that involved the tribes of Koraput and other area led to change in music, steps as well as its culture (Tripathy, 2020).

Objectives

1. To conduct research with historical background of how the Dhemsa dance has evolved over the years.
2. In order to know the cultural and ritualistic aspect and importance of the Dhemsa dance.

Methodology

The current research uses an ethnographic research methodology and includes the collection of surveys, interviews, and historical and cultural document analysis. Ethnographic observations were made at different Dhemsa performances during cultural fairs, harvest festivals and social functions among the tribes of Koraput district in Odisha. Ethnographic interviews with the participants of dance events performing on behalf of tribes, community representatives, and cultural scholars were conducted to assess the position of the dance in contemporary culture. Types of secondary sources include secondary historical sources, ethnography, and article on tribal folk lore and dance in Koraput district.

Historical origin and and evaluation of Dhemsa dance

As for Dhemsa dance it has the connection with agricultural and spiritual aspects of life of the tribal people in Eastern India. Originally, the dance was done in connection with festivities such as harvest, feeding, worshiping the gods, and other occasions that are rite of passages for example weddings and other forms of puberty rites. Such performances were first staged in natural theatres and they were associated with nature rituals, their motif being connected with the Erechtheism and the agricultural calendar – sowing, bearing fruit, and reaping.

Another historical topic of study concerning Dhemsa is its importance to bringing communities together. According to available records and traditions depicting early performances of the dance, everybody in the community would dance including women and children. The dance also got more structured at specific aspects of festival time and the actual choreography patterns involved were more complex.

Ethnographic data provides evidence that the Dhemsa dance was historically a celebratory ritual, which under normal circumstances was practiced to invite the blessings of deities for prosperous harvests, hale and hearty cattle, and shield against disasters. The hegira of the dance to nature and agricultural worship rites, can therefore be viewed as a neo-animistic where the powers of nature were considered to be sacred, and with the ritual dance, devised ways and means of calling on the powers within deities that were inherent within these elements (Panda, 2019).

Cultural and Ritualistic significance

The following article discusses one form of traditional Manipuri dance known as Dhemsa dance and explores more than just a beautiful form of entertainment. To the indigenous calendar the dance represents as a continuity of their customs, and also becomes an outlet for spiritual communications. It is normally done circular because as everyone knows life is circular and(cosmology of tribal life death) death too is part of life circle. The performers, sometimes dressed in body paints, feathers, bead or bells, that depict natural features move their bodies in a manner that reflects respect and ancestor worship **(Rao, 2017).**

Traditionally, Dhemsa finds itself involved actively in the lifecycle events. During the harvest festivals, the dance act aims at giving thanks after reaping while during other rites of passage dances become channels of invoking blessings especially fertility, health, and success. The music which goes along with the dance is made from familiar instruments like dhol (a drum), mandar, nagara and so on makes it all completely divine making participants to be fully immersed in a spiritual level.

That Dhemsa is a ritualistic form of dance is clearly brought out in the repetitive motifs of the performance. The uniformity of motion where a dancer moves in harmony with other dancers identifies our community contribution. This collective performance also makes cohesive groups and increases the general feeling of belonging in the society.

Musical and aesthetic dimensions

The stylistic features which characterise Sena dance are very importance in comprehending Dhemsa dance's cultural significance. The music being complex in rhythm, the drummers play the central role of regulating the pace of the dance. Different types of instruments, for example the dhol and nagara are associated with certain beats and these beats are associated with certain things such as the earth, wind and water amongst others. The musical features of Dhemsa are very closely associated with life cycles and cycles of seasons, cropping and social activities.

Dhemsa like any other dance form involves the footwork and hand movement in conjunction with the approved movements also the movements differ from one region to the other. The formation is a line of dancers and or a circle with the movements further embodying the values of the community and its connection to cyclic force of nature **(Choudhury, 2019)**. Sensual and creativeness of the content are parallel to socio-cultural values of the tribe, as the elements find connection with the rhythm of existence and divinity of collective participation.

The clothing departed that used while performing is also of immense cultural relevance. Contemporary dances are characterised by costumes which are usually made of cotton and native fabric materials, and colourful in nature with symbolic images and picture of tribal art. Feathers and bells used in the costume also aim at the exploration of the interrelation between people and the nature **(Das, 2018)**.

Contemporary relevance and social impact

Nowadays, Dhemsa has become more famous among people living in modern India because of progressing understanding of the role of original folklore in Indian tribes' identity. But as the form progressed through modernism and commercialization of cultural performances there has been a big issue on the conservation of authenticity. With the constant expansion of the Long Sword dance from a community tradition to urban areas and cultural festivals, the original intent of using the dance for the purpose of rites of passage may be replaced by a desire to perform **(Senapati, 2022)**.

At the same time, the Dhemsa dance has evolved as a tool of counter-cultures in its social context . With displacement, fear of losing land rights and socio-political marginalization as illnesses entrepreneurial performances offered by Dhemsa have been embracing the tribal identity. It has also been featured through protest and activism, as a means to address people to the plight of indigenous people. In such performances, what Dhemsa represents remains the spirit of tribal people, their rootedness and their defiance at the process of cultural integration.

But the general beautifying of Dhemsa in the context of the contemporary culture has its advantages and limitations. Despite commercialization, which lowers its ceremonial and cultural aspects, some of the native groups and cultural associations are today trying to preserve and popularize the type of dance as the true product of indigenous culture. Thus, the future problem or issue remains the conflict between the maintenance of cultural elements and trends of sociocultural change.

Findings and discussion

Findings: The result shows that Dhemsa dance is an indispensable part of socio-cultural and spiritual aspect of tribal population of Koraput. Key findings include:

1. It plays the most important responsibility of fostering unity in the community as well as preserving culture.
2. The continued use across the decades of many of its aspects in tribal festival and cycle events such as birth and marriage.
3. The downsides of globalisation, commercialization and impacts that emanate from urban centres.
4. A changing social connotation of the feather together with its use among indigenous people to fight for their rights.

Discussion: Retention of Dhemsa when people and markets try to undermine the traditional culture is an indication of flexibility offered by those traditions in the tribal realm. That is why there is a great need for the teams' cooperation to study and rally genuine forms of the folk art. Some of its features and its adaptation into a suite for urban consumption causes one to question if it is cultural appreciation or mimicry. Various measures should be taken to make certain that the owners and developers of Dhemsa particularly the Amisio and the Sukuma communities continue to dictate how Dhemsa is portrayed and that increases the chances of a yield.

Conclusion

The Dhemsa dance, in that sense is not merely a folk-dance form, but is a depiction of the tribal civilization, its existence and its faith. Largely associated with pre-colonial horticultural practices of minority tribes, Dhemsa is chiefly used in social relations, as well as in festal occasions to do with cycles of life. In the present era it serves not only as a cultural emblem, but also as means of indigenous defiance of pressures towards assimilation into the mass-tribe in today's complex world system.

Further research should be devoted to the analysis of the interconnection between the standard theatrical performances and their modern equivalents, and the role of commercialization and globalization as the main factors which threaten the genuineness of this phenomenon. Dhemsa definitely is an important aspect of the tribal culture, and its preservation must be undertaking earnestly so as to preserve the indigenous art forms of today's world **(Behera, 2022).**

References

- **Bhaumik, S.** (2005). *Folk Dances of Eastern India: A Study of Tribal Traditions.* Kolkata: Tribal Cultural Institute.

- **Chaudhuri, P.** (2010). *Rituals and Music of the Adivasis*. New Delhi: Oxford University Press.
- **Das, A. K.** (2017). *Performing Arts of Odisha: An Ethnographic Study*. Bhubaneswar: Utkal University Press.
- **Sahoo, S.** (2018). *Tribal Identity and Cultural Expression: Dhemsa in Odisha*. *Journal of Tribal Studies, 21*(3), 45-62.
- **Tripathy, M.** (2016). *The Folk Traditions of Chhattisgarh: A Case Study of Dhemsa Dance. Journal of South Asian Studies, 40*(2), 127-142.
- Elwin,Verrier.(1990). The Tribal World of Verrier Elwin. Oxford university press
- Patnaik,N.(2002). Folklore of tribal communities, Gian Pub, House publisher
- Dube, S.C. (2005), INDIAN SOCIETY, National book trust publisher

Bhunjia The Premitative Tribe Of India

Tikeshwar Rana

Lecture in History, Model Degree, Nuapada, Odisha, India
tikerana89@gmail.com

Abstract:

Odisha is known as the soul of India. Odisha is the wonderland and native place of 62 scheduled castes communities and 13 ethno-culturally vulnerable groups or PVTGs. Among them, Bhunjia society is mainly known as a primitive vulnerable tribal group of Odisha. They are mainly resided in the Sunabeda plateau in Odisha and Chhattisgarh and mostly found in Nuapada district of Odisha. Bhunjia societies worship many gods and goddesses, but mainly they worship 'Sunadei,' who is the supreme deity of this tribe. The festival of Sunadei is held in the month of September-October for 15 days. During this 15-day long period, they keep a burning lamp at the shrine of 'Sunadei,' and large numbers of people come to see the burning lamp brought to the abode of the linga (symbol of Lord Shiv) under an old Banyan tree and celebrate the festival. The societies believe that pregnancy is the rebirth of their ancestors. They are divided into two sections – Chuktia Bhunjia and Chinda Bhunjia. They speak a mixed dialect of Baiga and Chhattisgarhi. The Bhunjia societies are independent and socially, politically, and traditionally have their own village. In 2009, the Annual Adivasi Exhibition at Bhubaneswar held by SCSTRIT, showed the tribal culture of Bhunjia communities and also the Bhunjia society welcomed the Chief Minister of Odisha to see their livelihood, traditions, cultural artifacts, rituals, and many traditional things in this exhibition. They are primarily dependent on agriculture, food gathering, and hunting etc. Marriage is known as 'Bihaghar' in their local languages. The Bhunjia society's women only wear saris without any undergarment; both males and females are non-vegetarian, but they eat meat, consume egg and fish, and vegetarian foods in their festivals in the villages.

Keywords: Bihaghar, Baiga, Chuktia, Chinda Bhunjia, Sunadei.

Introduction:

The 'Bhunjia' means the person who lives on the soil. The word is derived from the word 'bhum' which means the earth and 'jia' means depend on. 75% population of Bhunjia societies lives in Nuapada district, so Nuapada is also called the homeland of Bhunjia tribes. The Chuktia Bhunjia tribes live in Sunabeda plateau, while Chinda Bhunjia is found in plains areas with their tribal and non-tribal groups. The Chuktia tribes do not wear shoes to give respect to Mother Earth. According to the census 1981, the population of Bhunjia was 7000, and now it is approximately 10000.

Nuapada district is situated in the western part of Odisha with beautiful waterfalls, plateau, and agricultural communities from the historical period. According to Russell, "the term Bhunjia indicates to living on the soil," and it is also said that in earlier times, the Bhunjia were known as Matia. Russell and RV Hiralal have described that Bhunjia had originated from the union between Gonds and Halvas, in "The Tribes and Castes of Central Province of India."

Now it is also seen that 'Bhunjia' are living in various parts of the world. There are many government institutions which help and impact the life of Bhunjia with important development in their society. The institutions are Forest Ranger's Office, Co-operative Stores, and Rural Upliftment Programme of OXFAM, to make their life easy to survive with governmental and natural supports. Bhunjia do not have their own language and they do not possess to speak mother tongue; in Odisha, they speak the dialect form of a mixture of Odiya and Chhattisgarhi languages.

Objectives of the Study Are:

According to many sources of information about Bhunjia societies and their cultural festivals, programmes etc., there are important objectives which show the development sequences of this tribe are given below:

1) Cultural festivals and their patterns are a vast field to study about Chuktia Bhunjia societies, which are collected through many religious, social institutes.
2) To provide information about 'Bhunjia society' to know their culture and religious and indigenous practices, also the aims of this article paper.
3) Understanding the challenges of Bhunjia tribes in their habitations are also the objective of this article paper.

4) Understanding the lifecycle and development programme in their economic fields and festivals are also the major things to study.
5) There are many government schemes and state programmes which help to reduce substantial poverty and illiteracy rate of tribal populations.

Agricultural Religious Festivals of Bhunjia Tribes:

Bhunjia tribes are worshipping many Hindu gods and goddesses and celebrating various types of religious festivals throughout the year. They are mainly celebrating agriculture festivals and many other festivals, but Sunadei Jatra is the important cultural festival of this tribe, held in the month of September-October and sacrifices for their supreme deity who provides food, shelter, and protection for their tribe.

Chaitra:

Chaitra is the agriculture festival of Chuktia Bhunjia society during the month of April-May. The tribal peoples offer goat and hen, rice, coconut to their deity to protect them from various kinds of pandemics, drought, and for the happiness of society.

Charu Jatra:

The Charu Jatra is celebrated to desire more crops and paddies and for protection of their food, paddies. They worship "Dharni Mata" and celebrate the ritual by sacrificing goat and breaking the coconut.

Charu Jatra has three steps to celebrating: (1) in the period of sowing paddy, (2) during harvesting, (3) storing the crops bundles in their threshing room and also worships in the farm.

Hariyali:

Hariyali is the agricultural festival which is celebrated every year, and each house of villages celebrates this ritual after finishing of transplantation work in the farms. They prayed their deities for providing greenery environment and happiness of peoples; they sacrifice hen, sundried rice, goat to their deity.

Chauldhua:

The term "Chauldhua" means washing the new crops and paddies before eating. The Bhunjia tribes celebrate this tradition in their homes and worship ancestors with sacrificing goat and hen etc. After this ritual, they can cook food.

Bihanchina:

It is organizing in the month of Chaitra on the 10th day. During this agricultural festival, the paddies and crops are kept from people for sowing. The priest sacrifices hen, pigeons and goats, worshipped the paddies in this tribal ritual.

Nuakhai:

Nuakhai is the important agricultural festival of Bhunjia tribes. They worship their deity Sunadei and ancestors at their homes to housing the paddies, and welcoming the new rice of the season. It is celebrated in the month of Bhado (August – September).

Ushavana Festival:

Ushavana festival is celebrated by the Chuktia Bhunjia during the month of March – April. This is the festival of Mahul (Madhuca indica) flowers. The villagers go to the forest for collections of Mahua flower and before it, the village council decided the date of collection, and every house has to contribute some money or other thing to buy required materials for their goddess Ushavana. They pray Ushavana deity for having a good collection of Mahua flowers.

Seasonal Collection of Minor Forest Product:

SEASON	COLLECTION
Summer (March-May)	Mahua flower, seed, chhar, kendu, sal leaf, mango, jam, neem seed, tamarind, kusum seed, kaju flower, khajur
Rainy (June-October)	Various kind of wild vegetables such as mushroom, vansh, kanki, boda, titethi, varasia and some greens like punjala, noni, kona, charmet etc
Winter (November-February)	Creepers (peng, young bamboo shoot, dhai), koilk, amla batodi kosa, kunduru, kudel, phul, kanta, sukla kanaga, doto kendu, pipel, kudal, purmula

In this tribe, the people are mainly dependent on forest products, agriculture, flower collections from forest and food like amla, kendu leaf and they mainly produced cultivated paddy, mustard, biri, turmeric etc. After collecting these things, they have to face for selling these products. Collections and gathering food are divided into five major groups:

SL	Types of collection	Remarks
1	Plucking (Todum)	Different varieties of flowers, fruits, green leaves etc.
2	Picking (Antrun)	Different kinds of fruits, mushroom, leaves and some specific flowers etc.
3	Cutting (Katun)	Firewood, timber, rope, bamboo, broom, grass, lac, twigs etc.
4	Digging (Khanun)	Tubers, roots, soils etc.
5	Killing (Marun)	Fish, animals, birds, insect etc.

Religious Life of Bhunjia Tribe:

The Bhunjia tribe lives in dense forest of Nuapada district. They are mainly believed in Sunadei deity as the supreme deity of this tribe. Some myths say that once upon a time Bhima was ploughing the Sunadei plateau for cultivation work. After that, the Sunadei deity also ploughed Mangurbeda, Kelbeda, Uhusrabeda, Bhilabeda, Gatibeda, Korrabeda, Saharasbeda. At this time, at a place with the touch of his plough, blood came out from the earth, and then he dug the earth and took out the Sunadei deity and built a temple in that place for goddess Sunadei and there is a banyan tree near the temple.

The Bhunjia tribe is divided into Barag with their designation and these are originated by Sunadei deity and it is also said that Sunadei is the eldest daughter of Niranjan and mother Adimata. She has one brother Budharaja and 12 sisters. First, the priest as Pujhari has only the right to worship the deity. The second category is known as Chhatriya and his work is to hold the umbrella in the time of worshiping. And third is known as Katariya, his work is to sacrifice the animals, hen for goddess Sunadei who protects the villagers from pandemics, disease and drought etc. and Dihari is another category who is a messenger between peoples and deity. With this entire category, the Sunadei Jatra is celebrating for 15 days long and a musical band party comes from Dom caste for the happiness and spreading the message of Sunadei deity to all people.

Besides it, they have to sacrifice and offer some sundried rice, goat, hen, coconut to their deity but there are certain rules for sacrificing are given below:

1) The animal should not be suffered from any disease and only male Bhunjia can sacrifice for Sunadei deity.
2) The female animals and birds should not be able to giving birth a baby. That can be sacrifices for deities.
3) The animals for sacrificing should be males and females.
4) The female deities of Bhunjia society only accept the female animal, bird for sacrifices.
5) Animal's legs should not be broken and also ears not be punched for sacrificing.
6) God of Bhunjia tribe is only accepting male animals with cock for sacrifices.

Supreme Deity Sunadei

Name of the village	Presiding deities	Gender	Abode
Koked	Mania Budha	Male	Under a Sargi tree
Gadbhatta	Mania Budha	Male	Under a Sargi tree
Sunabeda	Sunadei	Female	In a constructed house
Junapani	Mandal Deota	Male	Under a Simili tree
Senbahali	Mandal Deota	Male	Under a Simili tree
Chhinmundi	Thakur Deota	Male	Under a Sunari tree
Jamgaon	Budha Mai	Female	Under a Mahua tree
Salepada	Thakur Deota	Male	Under a Sunari tree
Kutrubeda	Methak Dei	Female	In agriculture field

Lifecycle Rituals of Bhunjia Tribe:

Life cycle rituals are the part of human life; in this long time period, humans are observed and experiencing various types of knowledge, importance of life, festivals, functions, agriculture, and they change their life style with time. In Bhunjia tribe, there are also many rituals from birth to end of life they follow these rituals respectively as their ancestors have taught them.

Birth:

The Bhunjia society women are giving birth to their child at home, not in hospitals. At that time, the older, experienced women of society come in their house and take care of the pregnant lady. The women cut the umbilical cord of the child after birth. No one is allowed to be present at that time, especially men, instead of older women. This is also the part of this ritual. After giving birth, the mother and father can cook in the kitchen shed for six days, after that the kitchen shed are destroyed according to this ritual and for 3 months the mother is not allowed to cook in the kitchen shed, and Bhunjia society women only wear saris. The naming ceremony is also done at that time.

Kand Biha:

Kand Biha is basically known as "marriage with an arrow." The Kand Biha is happening after the initiation ritual of Bhunjia society's girl between 7 to 8 years old age group. A girl does not take food from outside of home and also cannot touch a male person even their father and brother also. These are some restrictions of Kand Biha but adolescent age group has to follow more rules and rituals. The girls of Bhunjia society are come in marriageable in the age of 10-14 years old. During this time a girl has to stay for 7 days in the confined room and are not allowed to touch and see the outsider person, especially males, in this time. In this time a girl is known as polluted, so when she goes to his maternal uncle's house for purification on the 7th day, his uncle gives him turmeric mixed water with ring, then she drinks it, after this ceremony the girl becomes purify. After attaining first puberty, the girl cannot talk with male person and are not allowed to go alone outside the home. And also she could not enter in kitchen shed for 3 months in first puberty time. These are the rituals for only adolescent age group girls.

Bhunjia Marriage:

Marriage is known as essential for every person in every tribe. Cross-cousin marriage is very popular among Bhunjia societies. In their local languages, marriage is called "Bihaghar." They believe that marriage brings up the source of happiness, social pleasure, stability of economic fields, cooperation, creation of child etc. The Bhunjia tribe is divided into 2 exogamous moieties, Makram and Netam, as it is an endogamous tribe. In this tribe, marriage is arranged by parents of any bride or groom. There is a tradition that before marriage, the bride's family has to discuss and consult with his uncle (mother's brother) and the role of maternal uncle in Bhunjia society is on a high position in marriage. Marriage could not be arranged without the permission of the maternal uncle.

In some cases, polygamous marriage is also allowed in this society.

If the first wife is died for any reason, a man can marry other women for continuing their life. Sister exchange marriage, widow marriage, levirate marriage are prevalent in this society. Some Bhunjia society believes that marriage is essential for the need of sexual relationship and to give birth to a child. These are known as the main purpose of marriage of Bhunjia society.

Types of Marriage in Bhunjia Society:

There are many marriage forms allowed in Bhunjia society. The marriageable age group among Bhunjia society is around 14 to 20 years old.

Child Marriage:

The child marriage was allowed in this society from earlier times but in these modern times, many tribes are not allowed for child marriage and now it is known as "Thari Biha." In this ceremony, the child as groom and bride had to exchange on plates.

Amba Biha:

Amba Biha is also known as marriage with a mango tree. The couple or boy or girl who is not married or delaying in his/her marriage or who has done love marriage, they have to marriage with mango tree before marriage. This is a tribal ritual for purification of couple or boy from his heart, body and mind, after this ritual they can able to come in their society and pray to their ancestor.

Kand Biha:

This is known as "marriage with an arrow" and this happens before the puberty comes in Bhunjia societies girls in the age 7 to 8 years old. After this ritual, girls cannot take boiled food from outside areas.

Bandani or Remarriage:

Remarriage is also allowing in these tribes but there are some rules to remarriage. If the woman is widow or men is widower or for any reason, they could not continue their marriage life then a man can marry to other woman and this marriage ceremony held on the village invoking God and goddess for their better marriage life.

Arranged Marriage:

This is held by two families in the village. This type of marriage is so expensive and arranged by negotiation and usually starts from the groom's side. The parent of the bride has to go to maternal uncle's house for permission of marriage of his daughter. During this time bride parent has to wait and after permission of his maternal uncle, the marriage is allowed between those families. Cross-cousin marriage is also arranged by parents in the village.

There Are Some Rules for Marriage:
1) Makram and Netam moiety are allows to marriage.
2) Same clan marriage is not allowed in this society. If someone does this, the society had punished them; they could not enter in their tribe and could not participate in festivals, also do not take fire, water and other thing of village for 12 years. If they want to come in their society so they had to compensation of money and sacrifices goat, hen or other animals for purification of their soul and bodies.
3) Due to the fraternal relationship among Pujhari, Disori, Bhawargadias, so they cannot marriage.
4) Bada Majhi had the highest position in society. If any family members are marriage to their same clan. Then the clan members and societies punished them.
5) Deodaria, Bhoye, Barik, Sosengia, Disoridalei, Bhawargadia could not take food from Bada Majhi.
6) In the time of birth and death of clan members, only the clan family member can observe purity and pollutions.
7) After death of Netam clan family and there is no one to heir of their property in that time so in these cases, Barge, Chhatria, Bhoye will be heir of their property without permissions.
8) As Netam, Makram moiety had also followed these rituals and Kokdia Majhi, Kuarkari Majhi, Malik, Jhankar, Pujhari will have to heir to their family 'property.
9) In Bhunjia's marriage ('Bihaghar'), the role of maternal uncle (Mama) is important and before marriage the parents of bride have to go their maternal uncle house for taking permission of marriage.
10) In this society, Bhunjia are allowed to polygamy marriage, when his wife could not able to birth or if his wife is died then a man can marry to another woman in society. They praying God and goddess and sacrifices hen, cock, goat, bird for better marriage life.

References:
- CHANDRA, R. (1997). Contact and Culture Change among the Bhil. The Eastern Anthropologist.

- D. Majhi. (1999). Traditional Political Organisation among the Bhunjia of Sunabeda Plateau of Nuapada District. Bhubaneswar: P.G. Dept. of Anthropology, Utkal University.
- Dalton, G. (1971). In Essay on Tribal and Peasant Economics (pp. 348-62). Economic Anthropology and Development, Basic Books, Inc. Publishers.
- Dalton, G. (1971). Traditional Tribal and Peasant Economics: An Introductory Survey of Economic Anthropology, A McCaleb Module in Anthropology from the Series Addison.
- Wesday Modular Publications.
- F. Deo. (1995). Tribes of Nuapada District. Nuapada.
- K. S. Dubey. (1960). Possible Origin of Bhunjia and their Ethnic Reletionship. The Eastern Anthropologist.
- K. S. Dubey. (1960). Possible Origin of Bhunjia and their Ethnic Reletionship. The Eastern Anthropologist.
- Laik, S. (1999). Development Programmes among the Bhunjias of Sunabeda Valley Nuapada District. Bhubaneswar: P.G. Dept of Anthropology, Utkal University.
- N. K. (1993). Kinship, Politics and Laws in Naga Society. Calcutta: Anthropological Survey of India.
- N. Patnaik, P. (1984). in their book "Life in Sonabeda Plateau.
- N. Patnaik, P. a. (1984). Life in Sonabeda Plateau: Anthropology of the Bhunjias of Kalahandi.
- Bhubaneswar: SCSTRTI.
- Prof. Dr. A. B. Ota, Shri T. Sahoo. (2010). Chuktia Bhunjia. Bhubaneswar-751003: ST & SC Research and Training Institute (SCSTRTI).
- T. K. Mishra. (1998). Users Become Managers: Indigenous Knowledge and Modern Forestry.
- Economic and Political Weekly.

Geetkudia: The Tunes From The Hilltop
(Environmental Consciousness In Tribal-Songs Of Odisha)

Parameswar Mund
Hill town, Bhawanipatna, Kalahandi, Odisha
Email: parameswarmund@gmail.com

Abstract:

Gitakudia: The Tunes from the Hilltop presents a poignant exploration of the vibrant yet endangered oral traditions of the tribal communities from the undivided Koraput and Kalahandi districts of Odisha, India. Central to this cultural heritage are the Geetkudias folk narrators, poets, singers, and composers—who serve as the custodians of tribal wisdom, community memory, and artistic expression. Through song, dance, and storytelling, they reflect the philosophy, lifestyle, ecological awareness, and collective consciousness of their people. These multi-talented individuals, transcending tribe and caste, celebrate life's joys and sorrows, invoke nature, and voice concerns about the erosion of traditions and environmental degradation. Their performances, often during festivals and marriages, become communal events that bind the community together. However, the advent of modern entertainment and changing socio-cultural dynamics threaten their relevance and existence. This article underscores the critical role Geetkudias play in preserving tribal oral traditions and calls for urgent recognition and revitalization efforts to ensure their survival for future generations.

Key Words: Gitakudia, Hilltop, Tune, Environmental Consciousness, Chhatkan.

The undivided koraput and Kalahandi District of Odisha signifies a marked place in the Tribal Culture, folklore, myth and legends of Orissa. The inhabitants of Undivided Koraput and Kalahandi District live in the beauty of nature and take with equanimity the wrath of nature as well. Living with close proximity of nature they are a part of it and live and breathe nature. The land of Koraput, Kalahandi reverberates with melodies of Tribal song and dance when night falls resulting in everybody metamorphosed into a poet. Thus creativity is the second nature of the people of this locality.

The Tribal oral tradition of this region is rich indeed and offers the fullest possible range of life and its surroundings in its arena. Burdened with the bare realities of life, the folk-mind has never hesitated to express its creative ability and imagination through the oral tradition and performing arts. As community life is basic social character of the people of this arena, they always enjoy their creative arts with the participation of the whole community. The Geetkudias of this locality not only form an integral part of the oral tradition but also become the medium to preserve and continue the flow of folk songs. The exact meaning of Geetkudia in English is Folk Narrator. In Oriya it means a hut of songs which suits the very essence of them, but in Desia language they mean a person in particular who is an expert poet/lyricist, composer, singer and dancer on any given situation i.e. festivals or occasion like marriage etc. Again, they are an abundant treasure of folk tales, riddles, songs and sometimes hymns. What amazes one is their spontaneity that flows like fountain singing the melodies of jungle life. The speciality of Geetkudias of the locality lies in the fact that they are never from any specific tribe or clan or caste. They can be any one who understands the very essence of the soil and its people to the fullest sense. They are called Geetkudia because they help spreading the folk songs from one place to` other and by that help the Tribal oral tradition not only continue but also remain in the heart of the people of the said region. Interestingly Geetkudien is not the wife of Geetkudia but the female counterpart of him.

A close glimpse in to the life of Geetkudias reveals the truth that, even though they are not educated or little educated they have a deep knowledge of the geography, history, festivals, traditions, life style, beliefs, culture, food habit, cultivation system, herbal medicines used and almost all the activity of the locality. By presenting all these knowledge through songs is the only pleasure and motto of their life. Even though they have the expertise of presenting songs at any given place and situation, usually festival and marriage are the occasions when we see them in full throated ease. The event gets pre-planned and the evening that day comes to the place with all colours and hue. They perform amidst the stepping of both young male and female dancers known as *Dhangda* and *Dhangdi*. Musical instruments such as *Dhumsa/Nissan, Dhol, Mahuri, Tasa, Dhap* and *Jhanj* add a mesmerizing setting to the atmosphere. The dancers form group either male and female and the singing of each group lies with a Geetkudia or Geetkudien of their choice. Thus a competitive scenario prevails among the Geetkudias and the performance continues the whole night. Instances are there that to defeat the rival Geetkudia/geetkudien the opponents continue singing for even seven nights. By singing they not only set a perfect dancing platform but also instill energy to the dancers. Their songs are basically inspirational and love expressing. The Geetkudias go on asking and answering for which they have to be much attentive during the performance.

The songs of Geetkudias are usually love songs reflecting the local and tribal touch. They begin with devotional songs invoking their deities. Their songs often reflect their understanding of life philosophy and can range to any aspect of life. Although they have typical style of lyric and tune they enjoy using all types of South-Western Orissa folk tunes. *Chhatkan* a special style of additional song dialogues follow each song as male follows the female in life. In the olden days since such performance was the only source of entertainment the role of Geetkudias was highly appreciated. As such folk people live in a world of dream and reality and for them nature is the only and sole source for living. Thus the folk songs reflect the activities of life having a close affinity with day to day life. Usually they invoke nature in the first couplet and there after go on comparing activities of nature with human life. For them without nature life is meaningless. Thus Tribal life lives with nature. The fullest enjoyment and expression is inherent in their singing and dancing and playing music by them. But the Geetkudias are different- they not only hand over the Tribal oral tradition from one generation to other with the non-appearance of authorship but play the vital role to let the flow of folk songs continue.

Being in the 21st century is a time not only to cherish the world of science and technology but a time to fear for the loss of many a tribal world. But the tribals know their time ahead and the Geetkudias sing the future songs of gains and loss. They know what the reality future will offer. Thus the Geetkudia sings –

> Duma Dumi, Chere Chura,
> > Sabu gale sari,
> Asbe sabu bhatar luka,
> > Sabu debe sari,
> Jhar jiba, jiba jungle aur,
> > Munush maker jete,
> Dekhu thibu dug dug,
> > Kahake kahebu sate,

> *E jiban thibar tak,*
>> *Tui mor mui tor,*
> *Dekhu dekhu sarijiba,*
>> *Kahake kahebu mor,*
> *Munush marba munush k,*
>> *Jantu k kie pachare,*
> *Geet jiba, katha latha,*
>> *Khaid pindhan jibare,*
> *Ghar jiba ghar bhedi lagi,*
>> *Suin heba e sansara,*
> *Amra juga sari jiba,*
>> *Sabu heba asara………*

(Spirits, birds all are gone, the outsiders will finish things, grasslands, jungles, men and monkeys all will vanish, you will only be a helpless spectator my dear. Till life is there you are mine and I am yours. Soon bad time would come- man will kill man and who cares for animals. Our songs, culture, food and living style everything will be finished. My dear, we'll be homeless and our days & civilization will be over, the world will be all meaningless.)

Tribals understand what nature mean to their life and thus much serious of its protection and well being. Well, they might not be as serious as we are in regards of environment consciousness, but for them nature and Dharni i.e. Mother Earth means life. Geetkudis reflect the need of environment protection in their songs-

> *Jal jaungle jami hela jeebara adhar,*
>> *Jal jungle jami gale gala sansar,*
> *Etar lagi pete dana, dehike kapda,*
>> *Samhal etake Dada,hoi harabara.*

(Water, jungle and land are source of life, without them nothing is left, you get food and clothes because of them, be careful to save them and be worried)

or

> *Kati kati kati delu banar jete gachha,*
>> *Kati jibu hetir lagi eta mane rakha,*
> *Akal heba, sukhba jharan jiban,*
>> *Ebe b samiha kahuche sikha puta sikha.*

(You have recklessly cut down trees, you will be cut off for this, there will be droughts, streams and life would be dried up, My son, you still have time to consider.)

Geetkudias are aware of the happenings around and therefore sing events to create awareness among their people. Environment consciousness is always there in the core of the Tribal songs since jungle and its surroundings mean life to tribal people. Geetkudias thus celebrate nature and sing the saga of Tribal life and more importantly play the key role of that of a messenger of the whole region. The strong sense of belongingness is always there with them. But with the advent of modernity things have changed like anything. The new world of television and other sources of entertainment have snatched away their demand and smile. Their number is getting fewer day by day. Thus unlike the tribal civilizations, the threat of their extinction is always there. Again since the Geetkudias are part of Tribal oral tradition, their absence will result the missing of not only the creative impulse of their life and living, also bring a dark future to the Tribal oral tradition which is the life-pulse of the people of undivided Koraput and Kalahandi who share their love and affection, joys and sorrows, pains and pleasures in the community with a great sense of belongingness. Thus they say:-

Man thiba pate gauthimu geeta,

ame tame mita makara,

pasri gale pasri jimu geeta nacha,

jebe Sukhijiba rudera.

(Till you love us, we'll sing, you are our friends for ever, you forget us and our tunes and songs cease, we die.)

The Tribal oral traditions are handed down from generation to generation. The Geetkudias still living in the land seem to be the last of their kinds, as in the coming days and the future generation may not either appreciate or provide apt platform to them to sing the jungle life and tunes. Is it not concerning?

Reference:

- Padhi, Dr rajendra, koraputara Adibasi loka sanskruti, subarnashree prakashani, Baleswar.2009
- Bidika, Simon, Nabarangapura Aadibasi Lokasahitya o sanskrutika parampara, Pakhyighara prakashani, bhubaneswar, 2022.
- Pradhan, Ranjan, Adibasi Nacha o Geeta, Creative Odisha, kendrapada, 2015
- Mund, Parameswar, kalahandira Loka sahitya, Mahavir Sanskrutik Anusthan, Bhawanipatna, 2003
- Mishra, Mahendra Kumar, Folksong of Kalahandi, Mayur Publications Bhubaneswar, 1989
- Mishra, Mahendra Kumar, Visionig Folklore, Lark Books, Bhubaneswar, 2002

Black Eagle Books

www.blackeaglebooks.org
info@blackeaglebooks.org

Black Eagle Books, an independent publisher, was founded
as a nonprofit organization in April, 2019. It is our mission
to connect and engage the Indian diaspora and the world at
large with the best of works of world literature published
on a collaborative platform, with special emphasis on
foregrounding Contemporary Classics and New Writing.

www.ingramcontent.com/pod-product-compliance
Lightning Source LLC
Chambersburg PA
CBHW081144020426
42333CB00021B/2661